Motorbooks International Illustrated Buyer's Guide Series

Illustrated

Mercedes-Benz

BUYER'S ★ GUIDE℠

Frank Barrett
with Alex Dearborn

Motorbooks International
Publishers & Wholesalers ®

This book is dedicated to the
23,000 members of the Mercedes-Benz Club
of America, who are involved enough with their
cars to understand why it needed to be written.

Acknowledgments

Without the help of dozens of experts, this book would not exist. Alex Dearborn contributed mightily on the postwar 170 and 220 models and wrote most of the material on the 1950s 300s and the 300SL. Henry Magno wrote on prewar cars plus the 170 and the 220, while hearse-owner Bob Gunthorp and SL expert Will Samples sent useful information. Through previous contributions to *The Star*, the magazine of the Mercedes-Benz Club of America, others who contributed include Dennis Adler, Scott Grundfor, Frank King, Peter Lesler, Frank Mallory, George Murphy, Robert Nitske, Bob Platz, and the many readers who wrote in with questions and comments.

Thanks to Lee Gohlike for his first edition. Much gratitude to Tim Parker and Michael Dregni at Motorbooks International for offering the opportunity to write this new edition, and thanks to the Mercedes-Benz Club of America for the chance to gather much of this experience and knowledge. Not least, thanks to Mercedes-Benz AG and Mercedes-Benz of North America, especially Mercedes-Benz Museum Director Max von Pein, MBNA Public Relations Director A. B. Shuman, and Public Relations Manager Fred Heiler for photographs, information, and other valuable assistance.

First published in 1994 by Motorbooks International Publishers & Wholesalers, PO Box 2, 729 Prospect Avenue, Osceola, WI 54020 USA

© Frank Barrett 1994

Motorbooks International books are also available at discounts in bulk quantity for industrial or sales-promotional use. For details write to Special Sales Manager at the Publisher's address

Library of Congress Cataloging-in-Publication Data

Barrett, Frank.
Illustrated Mercedes-Benz buyer's guide / Frank Barrett. --2nd ed.
    p.   cm. -- (Motorbooks International illustrated buyer's guide series)
    Rev. ed. of: Illustrated Mercedes-Benz buyer's guide / Lee Gohlike. 1986
    Includes bibliographical references and index.
    ISBN 0-87938-902-8
    1. Mercedes automobile--Purchasing. 2. Mercedes automobile--History. 3. Mercedes automobile--Collectors and collecting.
I. Gohlike, Lee, 1945- Illustrated Mercedes-Benz buyer's guide.
II. Title. III. Series.
TL215.M4B37 1994
629.222'2--dc20   94-1462

On the front cover: The Mercedes-Benz 300SL "Gullwing" Coupe owned by Gary Gallup. *David Gooley*

Printed and bound in the United States of America

Contents

Preface

Whether you're looking for a Mercedes-Benz to show or to drive to work, this book can help you to find one that will fit your needs, give you excellent value for your money, and be a joy to drive and own. This is a *buyer's* guide, not just a collector's guide.

Almost any Mercedes-Benz can be reliably enjoyed for both utilitarian and enthusiast pursuits. You can drive a postwar production Mercedes-Benz to work or on trips, then clean it up for a car show. The older the car, the less practical it is to drive daily, but every morning thousands of people climb into twenty-five-year-old Mercedes-Benz cars and head for the office or the store. For that, you can thank the engineers and builders who endowed these cars with durability and reliability.

You can also thank Mercedes-Benz for keeping a strong parts inventory for older models. No other foreign maker remanufactures and stocks more mechanical parts for older cars than does Daimler-Benz. They keep technical literature available longer, too. You can still buy owners manuals, parts books, and workshop manuals for most postwar models from any Mercedes-Benz dealer.

How you'll use the car affects your choice of models. A diesel sedan and a 280SL are both reliable and practical, but most people find the sedan more suitable as a daily driver, the Convertible more enjoyable as a Sunday afternoon automobile. Surprisingly, both can make good show cars. Speaking of shows, don't let nit-pickers keep you away from them; most people appreciate an old Mercedes-Benz whether or not it has the "correct" taillight lens gaskets.

Is a Mercedes-Benz a good investment? See your accountant. This is an automotive guide, not an investment guide. Price guides are often out of touch with reality even before they're printed. Worse, they do not just report the market, they influence it. This book is written for enthusiasts, not investors. It will help you find a car that you'll enjoy, which is the whole point, isn't it?

Rather than recite history best covered elsewhere, this book is designed to help you find the best car. For similar reasons, detailed technical specifications are not listed, and rather than splitting hairs, only the most significant options and production changes are mentioned. Although we concentrate on US models, significant non-US versions are mentioned where necessary.

We've concentrated on the most attainable cars, mainly postwar models of both the collectible and daily driver persuasions. In many, cases these are one and the same, as today's Mercedes-Benz is often tomorrow's collector car.

Unless noted otherwise, years listed are model years, not calendar years. Production for the next model year typically began in September and ran through the following August. Thus, a car built in September 1965 could be considered a 1966 model. Then, because of varying laws, the year on a title may differ from the model year indicated by a chassis number. In the question of model year, the chassis number governs.

We can't turn you loose in the used Mercedes-Benz market without a few words about safety, a subtle yet significant reason to invest in these fine but not inexpensive cars. Mercedes-Benz has led the world in automotive safety. That's one reason the cars cost what they do. When choosing a car that you or your family will drive, remember that ABS brakes, air bags, and computer-designed body structures offer tremendous advantages in avoiding and surviving accidents. If you or your family will log a lot of miles in this "new to you" Mercedes-Benz, pick one with the latest safety features.

Mercedes-Benz first installed ABS anti-lock brakes on a production car (the 450SEL 6.9 liter) in 1978. By June 1983, ABS was available on all European models. Beginning with the 1985 model year in the United States, ABS was standard equipment on the 500SEC, 500SEL, 380SL, 380SE, and 300SD, and an option on the 190E 2.3 and 190D 2.2.

Other than to cleverly hand you the belt in a Coupe, Mercedes-Benz has never used motorized seatbelts, preferring air bags and self-tensioning seatbelts, which appeared in the 1984 model year. By 1985 the Supplemental Restraint System was standard on the 500SEL and 500SEC and optional on the 380SL, 300SD, 380SE, and the 190s. By 1986 a driver's side air bag was standard on all models, and right-side air bags appeared in 1989. By 1990, all US models had dual air bags.

Finally, a word to the wise. When shopping for your first Mercedes-Benz, avoid the trap of expecting too much and then being disappointed when reality intrudes. No car, not even a Mercedes-Benz, is perfect. Gottlieb Daimler was wise enough to say, "The best or nothing," not "Perfection or nothing." If he'd held out for the latter, not a single car would have emerged from his factory.

Investment Ratings

While all Mercedes-Benz cars are good, various models have been designed and built to best satisfy different needs. Some models are faster or more economical or more sporting than others. Some are appreciating in value; others are depreciating. Some are more desirable or collectible than others.

Like other titles in this series, this buyer's guide uses a five-star rating system to help the newcomer to Mercedes-Benz to judge various models in general comparison with others:

★★★★★ High performance, elegant styling, museum-grade collector value, and/or very rare.

★★★★ Excellent performance, elegant styling, high collector interest, and/or low production.

★★★ Moderate performance and good styling, moderate collector interest, modest desirability, and/or not uncommon.

★★ Moderate performance, modest styling, depreciating, little collector interest, and/or readily found.

★ Modest performance, utilitarian styling, depressed value, almost no collector interest, and/or supply exceeds demand.

Like any other, this rating system is unable to represent the priorities of every buyer, but it will help you to spot those models generally thought to be most desirable. Of course feel free to establish your own ratings; ultimately your individual judgment will guide you to the car that best suits your needs.

Chapter 1

Choosing and Finding the Right Mercedes-Benz

Why Mercedes-Benz?

The best of anything—art, clothing, food, wine, even company—rewards you beyond the ability of its ordinary equivalent. As a company and as an automobile, Mercedes-Benz has enjoyed legendary durability. As other car builders drifted away, Mercedes-Benz not only survived but led the world in engineering and often on the racetrack. Old or new, their cars project a distinct character, a unique feel that defies imitators and thrills you every time you drive them.

Which Mercedes-Benz?

Which of the hundreds of models do you want? Are you interested in style, economy, performance, safety, comfort, rarity, or practicality? Will your car be old or new? Who will maintain or restore it? Which can you afford?

Start by considering how you will use your Mercedes-Benz. Will it be a show car or your everyday driver? A sedan or a sports car? Will family members drive it, too? Can you afford to maintain a complex model, or should you shop for something simple? Can you afford to license, insure, and garage the car properly? Do you prefer a collector car appreciating in value, or can you forego that for the practicality of a daily driver? If you plan to keep the car only a few years, how easy will it be to sell?

Antiques

Pre-World War II cars demand special financial commitments to buy and to maintain. Their usefulness is limited, and you'll need a tow vehicle and a trailer to move them. Your thrill from these cars will come in preserving and demonstrating automotive history to others.

Postwar Coupes, Convertibles, and Sedans

Postwar cars can be enjoyed more, and prices are generally lower. Your choice is between sedans, Convertibles (and Coupes), and sports cars. Invariably, the price rises when the top drops. For a bargain, buy the similar sedan version of a Convertible. If you want a rare Convertible with plenty of available spare parts, choose one with a sedan equivalent.

SLs

The 1950s and 1960s SL models will always be collectors' favorites. They are among the easiest to buy, restore, and sell. And nothing compares with a top-down cruise on a warm summer afternoon. Avoid paying too much for a recent SL or buying one too soon. After initial depreciation, they begin appreciating. The trick is to buy just before the value rises.

Daily Drivers

For a daily driver you'll have plenty of choices, but your big decision will be gasoline or diesel power. A Mercedes-Benz "driver" is not only safe, reliable, and comfortable, but it can be a great long-term buy. Because recent models are so durable, you can keep them longer, use them more, and enjoy lower depreciation. You're better off buying a used Mercedes-Benz than a new Anything Else.

Find a good example of the model that you're considering, and drive it to see if it fits your needs and lives up to your expectations. Using it as you intend to use the car you'll buy provides a benchmark for judging similar cars later.

Sources and Signs

Finding a good Mercedes-Benz is no different from finding a good Ford. Actually, it's easier. Because Mercedes-Benz cars are higher quality and generally better cared for, many good cars await you. Most models are numerous enough so that you can find what you want nearby.

Private Parties

Private owners are a knowledgeable buyer's best source for good older cars. One advantage in buying from an owner is that you can get an idea of what kind of use and care it had. If he's a slob, look out. If he's meticulous, so much the better. How long has he owned the car? How did he use it, and where? Does he have service or restoration records? Why is he selling? If he can't or won't answer these questions clearly, beware. The drawback is that you normally get no guarantee.

To find private owners, check newspapers first; they offer the most current lists of cars for sale. A good car can justify an out-of-town trip. Before you travel, hire an appraiser or a good mechanic or persuade a friend nearby to check it out for you.

Dealers

If you're looking for a car less than ten years old, Mercedes-Benz dealers tend to handle cars in the best condition, albeit at a price. They offer warranties on used cars and are usually convenient to deal with. Some dealers advertise collector models in national magazines such as *AutoWeek* and in newspapers in larger cities.

Some independent used car dealers specialize in Mercedes-Benz. Visit those that have been around for a while. They can usually find cars not in stock, even out of town. Beware of ordinary used car lots, whose cars may come from unusual sources, including auctions, and may even be salvaged cars.

Check *Hemmings Motor News*, *AutoWeek*, and club publications for specialist dealer ads. Ask own-

---

Future Classics

Some say that any Mercedes-Benz may eventually become at least a loosely defined classic, but some are far more likely to grow into that much abused term than others. Here are our picks for the ten best future collectible models of the 1980s and 1990s:

1968–1971 300SEL 6.3 Liter: This king-of-the-road sedan is the hands-down winner of the bang-for-the-buck category, but its 1960s engineering is reflected in its handling and shifting. Expensive to fix, but once done, any repair should last a lifetime. A sleeper in appearance and price. Get yours now.

1973 350SL: The most widely overlooked SL, it has pure early design without the later battering-ram bumpers and luxury gewgaws. You could even get it with a manual transmission.

1973 450SE: Relatively light and simple compared to later S-Class sedans, its only drawback being its fuel thirst. Advantages include low price, space, and nimble handling.

1975–1979 450SEL 6.9 Liter: More civilized, less raw than the 300SEL 6.3. European versions may have ABS and slightly more power but are more likely to have been abused. Find a good 6.9, keep it that way, and you can enjoy driving an investment that draws interest for years.

1992–on 500E: A bahnstormer. Low volume, ultra-high performance, subtle styling, and a capacity to carry four in leather luxury made this an instant classic. Drive one, and you'll sell your soul to own one. For those on a budget, the 400E costs far less yet does 90 percent of the job.

1986–1987 190E 2.3-16: Get yours while they're affordable. Mostly because their wings and spoilers broke the conservative image of US models, this sixteen-valve four was imported for only two years. Go for the five-speed manual transmission. The car just feels right, and it's so much fun to drive. In Europe, try for a 2.5 Evolution version.

1991–on 300CE Coupe and Cabriolet: The subtle little Coupe out-accelerates a new 300SL (it's lighter). Pass on the 1988–1989 models; 1990 and later have the four-valve head with variable intake valve timing, giving almost 40 more horses (221 instead of 177). The top drops, so the 1993 Cabriolet is the 280SE 3.5 Convertible of the 1990s.

1993 600SEC: The first production V-12-engined Mercedes-Benz Coupe. Apart from its 6.0 liter displacement and nearly 400hp, this large personal luxury car merits the old 600's name. It combines the best in safety, comfort, engineering, style (well, the headlights give it character), and panache.

ers and restorers which collector car dealers are best. Brokers can be difficult to deal with because many take money from both buyer and seller.

Welcome to the Club

Joining a club gives you an edge. The Mercedes-Benz Club of America is the largest such club in the world. Its more than 23,000 members have owned examples of practically every model built. MBCA has 80 local sections, each publishing a newsletter (listing cars for sale). Its national magazine, *The Star*, carries ads for hundreds of cars in every issue. Smaller clubs exist for the 190SL and 300SL, but many of their members belong to MBCA, too, so it's the place to start.

A club's national experts can answer technical and restoration questions. Local members can point you to good cars before they even enter the market. You can examine good examples at car shows and chat with owners about what to look for when buying, what the cars are like to live with, and so on.

Auctions

The *worst* place to buy a Mercedes-Benz is at a typical collector car auction. The fast-paced, circus-like atmosphere may be exciting, and the cars may shine, but it's all show-biz designed to exchange cars for money, strictly one way.

Auction scams are legendary, too many to repeat here. There's never enough time to check a car thoroughly. Can you drive the car before buying it? Do you know who actually owns it? Do you know who you're really bidding against? Is there a warranty? Will paperwork be properly processed?

Reported auction prices must be taken with a shovelful of salt. These numbers often bear no relation to a car's value. They may be run up artificially by a pair of wealthy egotists determined to beat the other guy. Cars are "bought-in" by auctioneers, their shills, or an owner who can't stand to sell for a low bid. This circus is no place for the novice.

Computerized Sales

Various computerized collector car sales services have appeared. Most have short lives, and some seem more interested in charging the owner for listing his or her car than in finding buyers. The most avid users of these services are likely to be computer hobbyists, not car hobbyists. Proceed with caution.

Buying by Remote Control

Some say you should never buy a car without seeing it, but with care you can do so successfully. But the opportunity to get nailed rises significantly when dealing by remote control.

Buying a car based on photos is a huge gamble. The owner isn't going to photograph the bad side, and he wiped off all the leaking coolant before he photographed the engine. Did he send photos of the entire interior? And the trunk? Did he shoot the car on a lift from underneath? You can't hear, feel, or drive the car in a photo. Cars always look better to a camera than they look through human eyes.

If you can't go to see, feel, listen to, and drive the car yourself, find someone knowledgeable to do it for you. The best at this are professional (*not* amateur) automotive appraisers. The next best are experienced mechanics or restorers, especially if they work on similar cars. For pay, they may be able to take the car to their shop and run a leak-down test. Brokers can also help, as long as they are working only for you, not the seller. If you belong to a nationwide car club, ask a nearby fellow member to look at the car or recommend someone who can do so.

The best course is to go and see for yourself. Even several expensive trips can be justified by finding the right car.

Gray-Market Cars

Mercedes-Benz builds cars for many different markets. Until the 1970s, it didn't matter much whether a car was a US version or a European model, but as emission and safety laws grew tougher, that became more important. US-legal cars were equipped to meet these laws, and the government made it difficult to import nonconforming cars. An industry grew, converting European models to meet Environmental Protection Agency (EPA) and Department of Transportation (DOT) requirements. In the early 1980s the so-called gray market brought thousands of European Mercedes-Benz cars to the United States. Supposedly, all were made US-legal. In fact, many were not, and many more were doctored in ways that make them poor risks.

The gray market offered some models before they became US models. Others never came over otherwise. The 500SL, with more performance and more options than the contemporary US 380SL, for less money, was probably the most popular gray-market car.

Still, gray-market cars invariably are worth far less than the equivalent US models. They were often incorrectly converted or not converted at all. Many conversion companies were fly-by-night; few survive. Uncle Sam can still seize cars not meeting the law. Gray-market cars are cheaper to buy, but when you sell one, it will not be worth as much as a US model. Most dealers don't want them as trade-ins.

Some insurance companies will not insure a gray-market car. Mechanics may refuse to work on them, and some parts are difficult to get. Owners manuals and workshop manuals are tough to find. An improper conversion may leave you with a car that at best has some quirks and at worst is useless. If an equivalent US model exists, a gray-market car isn't worth the risk.

Converting a European model to US specs varies in difficulty. Obvious items such as instruments and lights are easily changed. (Climate controls used Celsius markings even on some US cars. European cars of the 1970s and 1980s were more likely to have velour interiors than leather or MB-tex.) Not so easy are substitutions of proper safety-related equipment. The smaller European bumpers on W116 sedans and SLs (the same as 1973 US models) were often left in place, and side door beams were often a joke. Ignition and mechanical systems are even more difficult to convert. Some states now require all original emissions equipment to be present (whether the car passes their smog tests or not).

By 1986, Uncle Sam had cracked down on conversion shops, and European models had begun using catalytic converters. When European and US versions began using the same engines, there was no power incentive to import German versions.

US cars have a perforated sticker on the doorpost and the vehicle identification number (VIN) tag on the left windshield post. Gray-market cars should have EPA and DOT papers documenting conversion, but don't assume that they will pass current emission tests. Velour upholstery, metric instruments, and European bumpers often betray partially converted gray-market cars. Mercedes-Benz of North America's (MBNA) region offices have been known to check the VIN of a car and determine its origin.

For some, a factory-built Mercedes-Benz is just a place to start. This is a Koenig-modified special.

Modified Cars

Mercedes-Benz owners tend to keep their cars in original configuration. Many frown on modified cars, perhaps because performance and appearance modifications are often done poorly. Appearance updates are a matter of taste. About the only tuner consistently able to provide well-integrated modifications has been the German firm, AMG. Their power, handling, and aerodynamic modifications are widely seen in Europe, where cosmetic "improvements" are more common. In 1993, Mercedes-Benz dealers began selling AMG wheels and spoilers for current models.

Beauty is in the eye of the beholder, so if you want spoilers and air dams, that's your business. Be aware that most Americans think them silly on a dignified sedan, so the market value of such a car may be lowered. It's fun to customize your car to suit your own tastes, but it's a lousy investment. Wheels, body parts, and mechanical pieces cost more than for other makes, yet at sale time they subtract more from the price.

Avoid irreversible modifications. When looking at a modified car as a potential buyer, consider which changes you'll revert to original and how you'll do so. The tougher that process will be, the more useful it is as a bargaining point.

Suspension modifications generally come as its from German tuners. Typical kits include shorter and stiffer coil springs, stiffer shock absorbers, larger sway bars, and new bushings. Recent models with the excellent five-link rear suspension can shift from luxury toward performance. The factory's Sportline performance option, first appearing on 1992 models, is highly recommended for the enthusiast.

For ride comfort and less aquaplaning, original wheels tend to be narrower on US models. Tires are relatively high-profile and slender. Since they are easy to switch, wider and larger-diameter wheels are common. Modestly broader wheels and tires capitalize on the potential of the excellent suspensions of recent models.

When considering a car with wider wheels and low-profile tires, check for unusual tire wear, vibration, harsh ride, and increased steering effort. Wheels differing much from stock offset cause wheel bearing wear or front-end misalignment. If tire diameter has been altered without recalibrating the speedometer, it will read incorrectly. Fuel mileage may suffer. Does the car have a suitable spare wheel and tire? Wide, low-profile tires grip better on dry pavement but ride more harshly and aquaplane more easily. Still, it's usually simple to return to stock configuration.

Mechanical modifications are more difficult and expensive to reverse. AMG and a few other tuners have done excellent engine work on 1980s and 1990s models, but there's real schlock out there, too. Avoid add-on turbochargers. Factory turbocharged models are designed to withstand the additional loads on engine, drivetrain, and cooling systems. Performance cams and exhaust headers are more durable. Count on zero warranty on any engine modification. With this stuff, it's once around the block or midnight, whichever comes first.

Even the best tuners have difficulties with driveability, reliability, and safety. Do the wheels, tires, brakes, and suspension of the modified car match its horsepower? Since DBAG now builds factory hot rods, you're better off with a 190E 2.3-16 or a 500E than with a locally modified car.

Be sure that the modified car is legal in your state, even in your own community. Many states now require that all original emission equipment be in place. Original smog gear is hard to find, and catalytic converters are expensive. If you're hoping to register an out-of-state car in California or another state with strict laws, be cautious. You can have a car tested elsewhere, but it still may not pass your local tests.

Agreeing on a Price

Although this book is not intended to be a price guide (real-world numbers change far too quickly for that), we can offer you some suggestions on negotiation.

Be prepared. Know how much you can spend, including possible restoration costs. Arrange a loan in advance. Some banks specialize in loans for collector cars.

Do your homework on typical prices. Price guides may reflect differences in condition, accessories, and other factors, but they usually don't cover geographic price differences. For example, Convertibles are worth more in warmer climes;

likewise, where the local economy is poor, Mercedes-Benz prices are likely to be low.

Refuse to be rushed. Don't be pressured by an owner telling you that another potential buyer is in the wings. If you lose the deal, you're no worse off than before you started, but if you let yourself be rushed, you may get a bad deal or a bad car.

Is the car's value rising or falling? The best time to buy a car is just as its depreciation stops and appreciation begins. If you'll keep it, it's alright to pay a little too much for a car that will eventually be worth much more. Why lose a good car for $500 if you know that it's appreciating and that you'll keep it for ten years?

Any car is worth what seller and buyer agree upon. Make an offer lower than what you would actually pay, then negotiate upward but only up to your limit. If this doesn't work, walk away and tell the seller to call you if he changes his mind.

All of that said, it must be admitted that many lucky folks have successfully violated every rule. Sometimes the car speaks to you, sometimes there's no time for even a compression test, and sometimes the price is too low to wait when you know another serious buyer is half an hour behind you and approaching at flank speed.

For novices, though, caution is best. If you're reading this in a lather, dreaming about that gorgeous red 280SL that you're rushing off to look at, slow down. Enthusiasm is no substitute for experience and knowledge, and too much desire can get you into a bind. Don't plunge into anything until you know enough to judge a car properly. Buy what you can comfortably live with for years. You may have to do just that.

Practice by looking at as many cars as possible. Each one that you examine will teach you restraint and some useful facts that will prove valuable later on...when you find and check out a car that you *really* want.

Chapter 2

Checking the Car

Having found a candidate car, you're vulnerable. Desire can overcome reason. Be careful. Some of my most enjoyable days have been spent rushing off with trailer in tow, certified check in pocket,

Model identification plates fitted to the radiator top cross-member carry data regarding the individual car and its accessories. *DBAG*

and hopes high. Some of the most tragic hours have been spent on arrival, when the object of lust finally appears in the flesh, a rust-holed shadow of its owner's glowing description.

This description of checking a car applies to most models; specific tips can be found in the appropriate chapters.

First, decide how particular you're going to be. If you're looking at a rare antique to restore completely, you'll be less critical about condition than if you're checking a two-year-old car. If you're looking for a daily driver, you'll be less critical in some areas than you would be with a show car (and maybe more critical in other areas).

Line up the references you'll need to check chassis numbers, production numbers, current values, options, etc. Make sure the person you're dealing with has the right to sell the car. If a private party, does he or she actually own the car? It could be leased, or it could have an existing loan against it for more than his price. It could even be stolen. Look at the title, and check with anyone else listed as the owner. Make sure that the chassis or VIN number matches the title and registration documents.

Prewar cars usually have a stamped identification plate on the firewall. On post 1970 cars, the VIN is on the windshield post and elsewhere. A chassis identification plate is on the cross-member above the radiator of most recent models. Obviously, if the plate is missing or the numbers don't match the papers, steer clear. Plates have been known to be switched or inexplicably "lost," and replacement plates have been available.

Check the service records. Mileages on recent invoices should conform to the odometer mileage. Don't rely totally on service records, though. An

11

owner can conveniently misplace certain disastrous invoices. Look for mechanics' comments, particularly such telling phrases as "Customer declines..."

Too often, potential Mercedes-Benz buyers are put off by high mileage. Some even make a fetish out of finding and preserving extremely low mileage cars at crazy prices. That's dumb. Lack of use kills a car; regular use and maintenance will best preserve one. Use this mileage phobia to your advantage. If the basic car is sound, almost any fault can be repaired to new or better condition.

Bodywork, Paint, and Trim

Daylight, preferably bright sunlight, best reveals bodywork and paint flaws. Look at the car (doors and lids closed) from the front, rear, and sides. Look at the tops of the fenders for dents caused by mechanics leaning on them. A dent in the hood will drive you crazy if you keep seeing it from behind the wheel. Dark-colored cars show body irregularities easily, but be careful when looking at light-colored cars, which can hide uneven bodywork.

Condition of trim is important because of the expense of replacing or restoring it properly. *FDB*

Does the car stand level? Do its panels line up? Are door, hood, and trunk gaps even? Is any trim missing? Do both bumpers fit properly? Is the paint consistent in color and gloss? Sight down the body sides, using reflections to show ripples, unnatural breaks in contour, and dull paint. In the paint, look for orange peel, grinder marks, overspray, shrinkage cracks, scratches, pinholes, chips, and rust spots. A good repaint is almost undetectable. New paint should be the same color throughout, including the underside of the engine and trunk lids, inside the engine compartment, the doorjambs, and other tough-to-paint areas.

Open the doors, hood, and trunk lid. How is the plating on the handles? Do the locks, latches, and hinges operate smoothly and quietly? Do the doors close smoothly with a proper thunk? Postwar engine hoods should close properly if simply dropped from a couple of feet. Are panel edges around doors and lids properly painted? How are the seals? Are the undersides of the lids properly finished, and are the door drain holes open? Nooks and crannies in the doorjambs tell you a lot. Tough to reach, they're the last area of a car to be cleaned well. If they are clean, that's a good sign.

Look at the inner and outer glass surfaces. Most postwar models have the trademark Sigla (or other German brand) etched into the glass. Is the windshield chipped, or has it been scratched by the wipers? Is the glass fogged at the edges? Is there overspray on the glass?

Exterior trim may be bent, scratched, loose, or even rusty. Replacement trim may not fit as well as the original or may show grinder marks or uneven plating. Thin, fragile trim is often bent or dented. Bumpers are expensive to straighten and replate. If rust has eaten into trim, replating may be infeasible, so it must be replaced.

Put the car on a lift—or at least a floor jack (with jackstands). Get underneath with a cloth, a screwdriver, and a flashlight. Check for rust in the panels behind each wheel where water, gravel, and rocks are thrown upward. Is the rocker panel paint the right pebbled texture? Are the floor panels dented? Do they have the factory-made indentations, or are they dead flat, indicating replacement? Check the footwells for rust. If new panels have been welded in, they should be butt-welded—joined edge to edge, not overlapped. Fresh paint or undercoating often hides rust or badly repaired sheet metal. As old factory undercoating lifts off the metal, rust forms beneath it.

Accident damage is usually easy to spot. At each corner of the underside, look for sheet metal that isn't shaped right (compare the shapes from side to side). If one side looks odd, it may have been straightened. Look for overspray and "too new" body parts. Newer cars have original spot-weld shapes that bodyshop welders don't duplicate. Run your hands around the inner lip of each wheel opening to detect rust or body filler.

Some expensive late models have another potential snag. Someone may have made one car out of two. With one car hit in the front, another hit in the back, it doesn't take a genius to figure out that the good ends can be joined, making one "good" car out of two wrecks. This was popular with S-class sedans. Pay attention to the body near the rear doors. If the doors don't fit well, that's a clue. Pull up the carpets. Fresh undercoating (or even a weld—some guys are more brazen than others) is an even bigger clue. Look for unusual wiring connections and paint that doesn't match in color or texture.

Mercedes-Benz exhaust systems are rust-prone, expensive, and hard to replace. Make sure pipes and mufflers are sound, properly shaped, and secured with factory brackets and fasteners. Most postwar systems are welded together, strapped in position by flexible rubber rings unlike US replacement straps and hangers. Exhausts often corrode on rarely used cars from condensation. Aftermarket stainless-steel systems are available for most postwar models, usually at prices similar to those for original equipment exhaust parts. With the engine running, block the exhaust outlet for a few seconds and listen for exhaust leaks.

Look for bent suspension members, loose or leaky shock absorbers, old brake hoses, rusty fuel lines, and worn control cables. Check the insides of bumpers; dirt and salt eat them from the inside out. Look for body filler that has oozed through trim mounting holes.

Look for fluid leaks from the cooling system, engine, fuel lines, transmission, power steering, and differential. A leak is almost always above and forward of the stain. Coolant is usually blue-green; it's poisonous, so don't taste it. Automatic transmission fluid is reddish, going to brown if it's old. Obviously, motor oil is black and slippery. Brake fluid is less viscous, clear to black, with a pungent smell. Ask a mechanic to demonstrate.

Look for leaks from front and rear oil seals on the engine and from the transmission. Look for brake fluid leaks at the master cylinder, slave cylinders, or calipers. Brake fluid should be clear. Check for fuel leaks around the carburetors or injection pump and the fuel pump, fuel lines, and filters.

All 1950s, 1960s, and 1970s Mercedes-Benz manual transmissions use automatic transmission fluid. Regular gear oil can allow damage to the needle bearings in these transmissions.

Seats, Upholstery, and Interior Trim

Good interior repair is expensive, so look for flaws. Usually the interior will be the best part of a Mercedes-Benz. The materials seem to last forever, and people take better care of what they can easily see and reach.

Look up at the headliner or Convertible top. Does it fit, is it clean, will it need replacing? Check the wood, leather, or fabric trim. Is it dirty, scratched, or worn? Any signs of water leaks around the windows? Does the sunroof work?

Look at the panel between the rear seat and rear window. Check the window moldings for dirt and broken glass. Check door panels for dirt and wear, and try every window mechanism and door lock, especially on cars with power windows and locks. Vacuum locking systems are often weak, especially on older cars where the rubber diaphragms and hoses have perished.

Check the seats for wear at the edges and seams. Mercedes-Benz interiors can be cloth (velour), vinyl (called MB-tex), or leather. On 1970s and 1980s models, cloth interiors are common on European models. Is the leather brittle and cracked? Is the seat stitching dry and strong, or is it rotted? If the seats have been reupholstered, was factory material used, or are they done in hide of the nauga? Sunlight and pets can ruin upholstery.

If the wood trim was damaged by sun fading or window leaks, it will be expensive and time consuming to restore correctly. Most Mercedes-Benz wood uses a veneer over a solid core. Any sanding almost immediately ruins the thin veneer, so amateur wood "refinishing" is usually to be avoided.

In recent models, look for holes and wires as evidence of poorly mounted telephones, sound systems, and alarms. Installed incorrectly, these can cause electrical problems as well as appearance flaws. If the ashtray's clean, you'll know the driver didn't smoke in the car—or else he replaced the ashtray.

Carpets should be reasonably clean. Diesel models invite tracking fuel inside the car, leaving the tell-tale smell. You'll probably cover the original carpet with floor mats anyway, so don't worry much about worn carpets on a daily driver. If the battery is above the passenger footwell, as on 1950s models, be sure that acid hasn't eaten through the battery box, allowing water (and acid) to drip into the footwell.

Accessories

Is the mirror glass clear? Does the radio antenna work? (Mercedes-Benz power antennae often fail.) Headlight, turn signal, driving/fog light, and taillight lenses should be clear and uncracked; one inconsistently faded lens indicates a replacement, possibly because of an accident. Do interior, exteri-

This 500SEC's clean engine compartment is the sign of a caring owner. *FDB*

or, instrument, courtesy, indicator, and other lights work? This may sound trivial, but a current model may have as many as 100 light bulbs!

Original Mercedes-Benz Convertible tops were usually made of tightly knit canvas fabric. If the fabric is stained, it will likely remain so. Does the Convertible have a tonneau cover?

Does the car have an owners manual? It can help you to check the function of options, especially on older cars with unlabeled controls. Many older models also came with a parts picture catalog showing exploded views of all assemblies, including the engine, transmission, brakes, body, and trim.

Does the car have a spare wheel, an original jack, a lug wrench, and a tool kit? If the car has a central lubrication system, does it work? If not, suspension parts may be worn.

Engine

Because it's the most impressive, most expensive, and noisiest part of a car, most buyers spend too much time looking at the engine as if they expect it to say, "Hi, I'm fine." or, "Damn, I feel like throwing a rod today." With the hood up, they stand there sagely listening to the engine idle, rev up a bit, then idle again. They'd be better off driving the car and listening for strange sounds. Better yet, they should drive it to a mechanic and let him do a leakdown test.

Unlike a compression test, a leakdown test determines not just whether or not the engine is worn, but where. The mechanic hooks up an air line to each spark plug hole, pumps air into the cylinder, and listens for it to exit the crankcase (worn rings), the valve cover (worn valve guides), or the intake and exhaust system (worn valves and valve seats). If you can't do this, pay someone to do it for you. It's worth it.

OK, if you must do a compression test, it's bet-

ter than nothing. If you're looking at an ancient, frozen engine, don't waste time trying to free it enough to see if it will run. You're going to overhaul it anyway, so be patient, and try to avoid damaging it.

Don't put much stock in clean oil on the dipstick. Dirty oil is easy to change. Check the oil change records. Water droplets on the dipstick indicate coolant in the oil; overhaul time. Some white sludge on an oil filler cap is normal, especially in humid climes.

When the engine is cool, unscrew the radiator cap and look inside. (With a warm engine, the system will be under pressure, so unscrew the cap slowly with a rag on your hand.) Fresh coolant is blue-green; a gray mixture means that exhaust gas is getting into the coolant, possibly through a blown head gasket. An oily film means that oil is leaking into it, even more serious. Look for coolant leaks around the water pump, radiator (get underneath), hose joints, sensors, and heater fittings. On cars with automatic climate control, check for coolant leaks at the servo, located in the engine compartment.

Electric fans in front of the radiator should come on automatically as the engine idles and warms up; as the engine cools, the fan should stop automatically (exact temperatures vary). The viscous fan drive on the fan behind the radiator should turn freely with the engine off. As the engine idles, the fan should turn normally; as rpm increase, the viscous clutch releases, and the fan coasts.

Has the engine fan hit the radiator? Is the water pump squealing due to a worn bearing? Are the drive belts cracked or frayed? Most are easy to replace. If you hear a squeal when you punch the throttle, a slipping accessory drive belt needs adjustment.

Does the engine smoke from the exhaust pipe? A little white fog of condensation is normal from a cold engine on a cold day, but persistent white smoke usually means a blown head gasket. If the smoke is blue, the valve guides or piston rings and cylinder walls may be worn. If smoke persists, a leakdown test can determine its cause. Black smoke is caused by a rich mixture on gasoline cars, indicating a need for carburetor or injection system work. Black smoke from a diesel engine is usually caused by a maladjusted or worn injection pump. Only prewar engines, with their looser clearances and more primitive carburetion, should smoke under normal operation.

How does the engine smell? If you smell raw gasoline, it may be running too rich, or it may have a fuel leak. If you smell burning oil, an aged valve cover gasket may be allowing oil to leak onto the exhaust manifold; look for blue smoke. If you smell burning plastic, wiring may be overheating.

Electrical

Mainly you must rely on whether or not a given mechanism works to determine the state of the electrical system. Try out everything electrical: heater blower, radio, wipers and washers (windshield and headlight), power seats, power windows, sunroof, horn, power mirrors, station wagon tailgate closer, and so on. Older cars have fewer lights: headlights, parking lights, brake light(s), instrument lights, maybe turn signals, and interior lights.

Newer cars have dozens of lights. You can find over 100 in a current (pun intended) Mercedes-Benz. Most bulbs and switches are simple to replace, but a circuit that won't deliver power may indicate a major problem such as improper accident damage repair or rust.

Do all instruments work properly, especially the tachometer? All 1981–1982 US models had 85mph speedometers. Zero the trip odometer, then check it and the normal odometer after your test drive.

If you don't know how to operate the climate control, read the owners manual. Then try all heating and air conditioning modes and all fan modes. Air conditioning compressor noises indicate problems with belts, bearings, or seals. If it's the compressor, the noise will stop when the compressor stops. A foul smell in the car may be caused by algae in the condenser drain, which can be flushed by spraying disinfectant through the heater blower. Make sure the blower motor works; on some 1960s and 1970s models these are tough to replace.

Check the battery, including electrolyte level, cables, connectors, clamps, and tray. The tray area should be clean, with no evidence of acid corrosion. Check the chassis end of the ground wire. Are all fuses intact?

Is all wiring stock and original, or did someone fit an alarm with wires strung across the exhaust manifold? Are the plug wires in good shape (old ones can cause an engine miss). Have wires been burned or patched? Are all original wire clamps in place?

Whines or rattles near the front of the engine can mean a stretched timing chain and/or worn chain tensioners or belt tensioners.

Road Test

Road-testing a car reveals its condition and gives you an idea of what that model is like to drive. If the car is a nonrunner, or if you are unfamiliar with the model, try to find a good, running example that you can drive to see if this model is for you.

A car represented to be a runner should start and idle reasonably well, allowing for its age and technology. As a cold Mercedes-Benz engine starts, the oil pressure gauge should peg itself at the high end of the scale. As the oil warms, pressure will fall, but even at idle it shouldn't go below about 15psi, about one atmosphere of pressure. Low oil pressure indicates worn bearings or a worn oil pump.

While driving, listen for knocks and whines. A knock on acceleration means worn main bearings. A knock on deceleration usually means worn rod bearings. A ping under heavy engine load is detonation, possibly due to poor fuel or incorrect ignition timing. A tapping sound can be due to loose valve lifters. A whine from the rear of the car can indicate worn differential gears, not an uncommon problem. A differential whine varies directly with the speed of the car and is usually most evident under power.

Check the cooling system while driving. Older models may overheat when idling in traffic on a hot day. Let the car idle for five minutes or so, and watch the temperature gauge. It may rise above boiling with no problem, but if it hits the red zone, a cooling problem exists. Overheating can indicate a worn water pump or more serious problems such as a blown head gasket or an engine rebuilt with insufficient clearances. Once overheated, any engine loses part of its useful life. Aluminum heads on Mercedes-Benz engines warp relatively easily.

Checking a manual transmission is mostly a matter of listening closely under acceleration and deceleration. If each gear works without whining, it's fine; noisy bearings need replacement. If shifts can be made without grinding, the synchromesh is in good shape. Bad synchros show up earliest in the lower gears. If the transmission jumps out of gear, usually high gear, either the internal parts or the linkage may need rebuilding.

The clutch should engage and release smoothly. Clutch chatter can be caused by oil leaking onto the clutch, wear, loose engine or transmission mounts, or driveline misalignment. A slipping clutch is easiest to detect in higher gears under heavy throttle. Punch the throttle going uphill in top gear. Some slip may be adjusted away, but the clutch is more likely to need replacement, which may even include the flywheel. A dragging clutch grinds as you shift, especially going into reverse or first with the car stationary.

Until the 1980s, Mercedes-Benz automatic transmissions were less smooth than their US counterparts. No matter how healthy any automatic seems, it can fail tomorrow. Likewise, it can feel bad but last a decade. Thoroughly testing a Mercedes-Benz automatic transmission requires connecting a set of special gauges, and then driving the car through a prescribed routine. You're probably unable to do that, but you can make sure that the transmission functions reasonably well and doesn't leak. Open the hood, pull the automatic transmission dipstick, and smell the fluid. If it smells burned, you have a problem.

Drive off in each gear of an automatic. Slip or a significant delay in engagement means problems. Shift up and down manually; each gear should engage quickly, smoothly. Automatic shifts should be firm but not harsh, with no over-revving. Older Mercedes-Benz automatics with fluid couplings instead of torque converters are known for hard shifting. Harsh shifting in diesels is commonly caused by loss of vacuum pressure. The modulator pressure valve of most automatics can be checked and adjusted to reduce hard shifting.

When you floor the accelerator at a reasonable speed, the transmission should shift down. Most pre-1980s transmissions are slow to do so. Early examples (1960s models) can be downright clunky. If the model was available with a manual gearbox, try one before making a buying decision.

Feel a vibration in the drivetrain? Many models have two-piece driveshafts with a center bearing. Wear here or at the universal joints or flex disks causes vibration. If vibration persists when the car is coasting, out of gear, the problem may be in the driveshaft, bearing, or joints. If vibration ceases when coasting out of gear, the problem is more likely in the engine or clutch.

If the car has cruise control, try it for more than just a few seconds. Mercedes-Benz cruise control systems are not exactly synonymous with total reliability, especially on diesels, and fixing them can be expensive. But then, real drivers like you don't use cruise control, do they?

Suspension, Steering, and Brakes

Other than looking for obvious problems under the car, or feeling for loose wheel bearings with the wheels off the ground, your judgment of the suspension system will come mainly from driving the car.

Check the tires. Make sure they carry the recommended pressures (modern models list pressures on the fuel filler door and in the owners manual). If the tread is worn in unusual patterns, wheel alignment may be incorrect, a matter of adjustment or possibly due to worn suspension bushings. Make sure the speed rating of the tires suits the top speed of the car. Some owners try to save money by replacing VR or even ZR tires with cheaper ones. The owners manual lists the original speed rating.

Wider wheels and tires must clear the bodywork throughout the entire steering range and suspension travel. Driving the car into a steep driveway with the front wheels turned sharply usually reveals clearance problems. Look for tire chafe marks on inner fender panels, brake lines, and suspension parts.

On the road, does the car maintain a straight line without constant steering corrections? If the steering wheel pulls to one side on rutted asphalt, front camber may be excessive. (If the car pulls to one side under braking, chances are the cause is a brake problem.) If the steering shimmies, especially on bumps, then steering and front suspension joints may be worn. A mild steering wheel vibration is usually due to wheel/tire imbalance, and is easier to fix.

Testing shock absorbers via the old "bounce up and down on the bumper" method isn't valid. You're better off checking the service records to see when shocks were last renewed. Drive on a bumpy road and see if the shocks work. A frozen shock absorber can cause a jarring ride. Shock absorbers are relatively easy and inexpensive to replace.

Most large 1950s to 1970s models with coil-spring suspension (not air suspension) used a rear compensating spring above the differential to supplement the springs at each rear wheel. If the rear sags, this spring either needs replacement or has been improperly replaced. Air suspension is covered in detail in chapter 12.

Many 1950s and 1960s Mercedes-Benz cars have vacuum-assisted brakes fed by a large, circular brake booster, usually on the firewall. If the brakes need high pedal pressure, the booster may need to be rebuilt. To test it, find a long hill (trust us) where you can safely coast the car, with the engine off. As you glide downward, apply the brakes maybe a dozen times, to use up any available vacuum. Note how much force the pedal requires. Now, start the engine, go back to the top of the hill, and do the whole thing again but with the engine running and the transmission in neutral. If less pedal pressure is needed this time, the booster works.

With your hands just off the steering wheel, and the front tire pressures equal, brake to see whether the car pulls to one side. If the brakes drag and don't release properly, the usual cause (in older cars) is clogged brake hoses. Flexible rubber brake hoses deteriorate internally. Broken-up lining material clogs them, preventing brake fluid pressure from releasing, and causing brake drag. If enough drag occurs, the fluid will boil, rendering that brake unit temporarily ineffective. Feeling each wheel hub to see if one is hotter than the others can pinpoint the trouble, but if this happens at one wheel, all flexible brake hoses should probably be replaced.

After your test drive, look under the hood and under the car for leaks. See if brake backing plates or the back of the tires are wet with brake fluid.

This isn't the end of your job. Specific items to check on various models are included in the appropriate chapters.

Chapter 3

Antique Mercedes and Benz 1886–1926

Building the best cars in the world is not new for Mercedes-Benz. They have been doing so since the company's pioneering cars of 1886.

Joint credit is given to Carl Benz and Gottlieb Daimler for inventing practical automobiles in 1886, but Benz deserves the most. Daimler adapt-

This 1893 Benz Victoria with a one-cylinder engine of 4.5hp could do about 20mph.

ed his engine to an existing carriage, but Benz designed and built an entire car. By 1900, Daimler had caught up, as evidenced by his new Mercedes, which set the pattern for future automobiles.

The early years involved minuscule production numbers. Not until 1934 did Daimler-Benz annual production exceed 10,000 cars. Some prewar cars thus come onto the market rarely; the rarest may appear only once in a lifetime. You're more likely to find an early Benz than a Daimler or a Mercedes. For instance, in 1900, as the world's largest auto maker, Benz built 603 cars, Daimler 96. Total 1908 to 1926 production of Benz cars was just over 27,000. In this time Daimler built fewer than 20,000, but more of his Mercedes cars have survived.

Benz Veterans 1886–1914 ★★★★★

Benz started it all with his three-wheeled Patent Motorwagen of 1886. Its one-cylinder, 954cc, water-cooled, horizontal engine ran on the equivalent of cleaning fluid. His first car was the sole Model 1, but starting in 1888 about twenty-five of the similar Models 2 and 3 left the workshop. Benz's wife, Berta, drove the car on its first long trip, in 1888. Having driven a replica, we can report that the sensation involves a lack of power and stability. Hills cause major concern, and in sharp turns you worry about the high three-wheeler tipping. Visibility and ventilation are unbeatable!

For the company's 1986 centennial, Daimler-Benz built eleven 1886/1986 replicas, and an English company made several more, so despite the rarity of the real thing (only one is known to exist), the Patent Motorwagen is the earliest collectible model, albeit in replica form.

In 1892 the Benz Victoria and Vis-a-Vis models appeared, and in 1893 the first Benz came to the United States. The world's first production car was the Benz Velo; about 1,200 were built between 1894 and 1899, so these are the most common today. Its one-cylinder, 1.5hp engine gave it a 12mph top speed. The car was somewhat practical for the real world, but most were sold to wealthy folks as toys. The Velo was developed into the 1896–1901 Benz Comfortable. The Benz Dos-A-Dos seated four back to back, hence its name, using a horizontally-opposed twin-cylinder engine.

After 1900, Benz cars had front engines, and the 1903–1904 Parsifal model used some new design principles demonstrated by Mercedes. The best Benz was the 40hp 1906 Double-Phaeton for Prince Henry of Prussia. (Even then Benz had sales outlets in foreign countries, so cars turn up in unexpected places.)

Daimler Veterans 1886–1914 ★★★★★

Daimler was more adventurous than the traditional Benz. He and his associates went on to develop such features as the vee-twin engine, mechanical inlet valves, the use of ball bearings, and low-tension magneto ignition.

Daimler's first car was a horse-drawn carriage with his air-cooled 1.5hp single-cylinder engine driving the rear wheels through a two-speed transmission. Water cooling, a four-speed transmission, and an all-metal car were early improvements; the 1889 car's twin-cylinder engine, metal frame, and wire wheels abandoned the carriage chassis.

Daimler powerplants powered boats, rail vehicles, buses, trucks, and even early lighter-than-air craft. Daimler licensed others to build engines and cars in France and Britain. (The resulting Daimler cars from England eventually developed separately and bore no real connection to their forefather.)

By 1896, Daimler had built the world's first front-engined vehicle, epitomized in the Phoenix. He is credited with the world's first truck and bus plus many marine engines, electrical generators, an early fire pumper, and the first rail car.

Daimler's landmark model—for the entire automotive world—came just after the turn of the century. His 1901 Mercedes was the first car to look like what we now think a car should look like: low-slung, with a honeycomb radiator up front and an inline, upright, four-cylinder engine behind it, all on two steel channel frame rails. From 5.9 liters the engine made 35hp, giving the light car good performance. Instead of relying on suction to draw in the fuel, it had the first mechanically operated intake valves, controlled by an external camshaft.

A flywheel fan drew cooling air through the radiator and engine compartment, and a water pump

Benz's first car was a tube-framed three-wheeler. *DBAG*

circulated coolant. The H-pattern shift lever operated the coil-spring clutch and the gearbox shafts. The weak spot was probably the underdeveloped four-speed transmission, which drove the rear wheels via chains. Leaf springs supported each corner of the tapered channel steel frame, and internally expanding drum brakes were fitted at the rear.

For 1902 an improved 6.5 liter engine made 40hp, and a 60hp version appeared for 1903. When the 90hp factory racers were demolished in a fire, this 60hp car became legendary by winning the 1903 Gordon Bennett race in production form against all-out racers. Today, the three 60hp cars known to exist are among the most desirable Daimler antique models.

Daimler Motoren Gesellschaft then led the automotive design world, and its inventions were widely copied. By 1906, Mercedes cars grew larger, more powerful, and faster, mainly thanks to a new six-cylinder engine generating up to 95hp. Even this smoother power unit continued to use total-loss lubrication; adjustable sight-glasses on the dashboard meant that driving required mechanical knowledge. Four-cylinder models, from the 2.6 liter 10/20 on up, continued with smaller bodies. All engines had huge one-piece cylinders and heads cast in pairs, slid down over the pistons, and bolted to a cast crankcase.

By 1908, buyers could choose either chain (*Kettenantreib*) or the new shaft (*Kardanantrieb*) drive, the latter with a differential featuring two ring gears, set at an angle to allow proper positive camber at each rear wheel. This choice continued

The 1901 Mercedes set new standards for future cars. *DBAG*

Daimler's first car, built in 1886, was carriage-like, mid-engined, and leaf-sprung. *DBAG*

19

until at least 1914. Mercedes abandoned the cone clutch for a metal-to-metal plated unit, allowing smoother starts and shifts.

Windshields began to appear in 1910, and the cars became heavier and faster. The last big chain-drive Mercedes was the 90hp model introduced in 1910. Its advanced engine had three overhead valves per cylinder. Most of these cars were fitted with limousine or touring car bodies. Four-cylinder models were named for their horsepowers—15/20, 25/30, 35/40, 45/50, and 65/70—capped by the six-cylinder 75/80.

In 1914 came the luxurious Mercedes 28/95, but only 25 were built before World War I; 574 more were built by 1924. The 28/95 used an aircraft-derived six-cylinder, 7.2 liter motor and shaft drive as well as a vee-shaped radiator and outside exhaust pipes. Front-wheel brakes were fitted.

In 1915, Daimler Motoren-Gesellschaft (DMG) celebrated its twenty-fifth anniversary, but just a year afterward car production was halted by war, not to resume until 1920.

Between 1910 and 1924, DMG also built Mercedes-Knight cars with sleeve-valve engines. Their advantages were quiet operation and low-end power, but they were followed by clouds of oil smoke. Despite a racing version finishing fifth in

This 1902 Mercedes Simplex used a four-cylinder, 5.0 liter engine to make 37mph; racing versions were faster. *DBAG*

the 1913 Indianapolis 500, the production cars were a financial failure. The best Mercedes-Knights were probably the 16/40, 16/45, and 16/50 models.

American Mercedes ★★★★★

In 1905, American Mercedes cars were built by piano makers Steinway in Long Island City, New York. Financial complications and a fire wiped out the whole plot, or things might be different today. The American Mercedes was built to the design and standards of its German equivalent. Its 6785cc, T-head, four-cylinder engine made 45hp at 1100rpm.

Various castings and forgings came from Germany; many gears and shafts were machined in America of German steel. A metal spiral spring clutch ran in oil, final drive was by chain, and 60mph was guaranteed. Seven-passenger bodies, sheet aluminum over a wooden frame, were built and trimmed by Brewster. Two wheelbases—3225 and 3279mm—were offered.

The number of American Mercedes produced is unlikely to have exceeded 100. Today the only known survivor, restored in 1985, graces the lobby of Mercedes-Benz of North America's headquarters in Montvale, New Jersey.

Racing Versions ★★★★★

Mercedes racers came to America to compete for the Vanderbilt Cup. Ironically, these hard-used cars survived in greater proportion to production models, perhaps because they were more treasured. The 1908 racers that gave Daimler its first

Cross-section of the Knight sleeve-valve engine revealed the complicated system of sliding sleeves that served as valves. Poor lubrication and wear caused problems. *DBAG*

The 1910 Mercedes-Knight used a sleeve-valve
engine, which emitted plenty of smoke but not
much power.

This Mercedes 90hp touring car was sold by the
American importers in 1912.

Grand Prix win are the most desirable early race cars. Several survive, along with the other famous Mercedes racers, the 1914 Grand Prix cars.

Meanwhile, the Blitzen Benz made Americans aware of the skills of German auto engineers. Under Barney Oldfield and Bob Burman, it raced all over the country. Today the car is preserved in the Mercedes-Benz Museum. In 1915, after a disappointing failure the previous year, a Mercedes driven by Ralph DePalma won the Indianapolis 500.

The Early 1920s ★★★★

After Germany emerged from World War I, only the clever could build cars, and only the wealthy could afford them. Daimler and Benz engineers had learned from their aircraft engine work, but the scarcity of good raw materials and the need to keep prices low meant that the first post World War I cars were small and simple.

Not until 1921 did racing resume, led by Max Sailer's Targa Florio success in the 28/95. A production Roadster was built, and three are known to survive. Derived from the DF80 aircraft engine, their six-cylinder, 7.3 liter powerplant must have influenced W. O. Bentley, whose de-

signs bore a similar gear-driven overhead cam.

The 1923 Mercedes 10/40/65 boasted the first supercharger on a production car; this 2.6 liter four-cylinder sports model soon gained front-wheel brakes. The Roots supercharger, driven from the crankshaft via a clutch, was activated only when the driver floored the accelerator. It forced air into the carburetor, designed to handle the pressure.

The 4.0 liter 15/70/100 and 6.0 liter 24/100/140 Mercedes were the most sophisticated DMG cars before the 1926 merger with Benz. Not only did these six-cylinder models make great touring cars, but they did well in competition, too.

What to Look For

If the car you are looking at has been restored, as most have, your main concern is authenticity. An antique car is mostly gauged by its historic value, so it had better be the real thing. Provenance is important. Ask for documentation on owners, restoration, or shows. A car may be a "confection" of new and old parts. If another example exists that is known to be genuine, compare the two. If you will drive the car occasionally, try it. Rather than adapting these cars to your driving

This is the only known surviving American Mercedes, built by Steinway in 1905.

needs, you must adapt to their abilities.

When looking at an unrestored original, authenticity remains important, but the difficulty of restoration becomes paramount. The restorer should examine the car before purchase to estimate the task's cost and complexity.

Restoration

Owners and restorers of these early antiques are responsible for preserving automotive history. Winning an award takes a back seat. Few restorers are qualified to take this approach, so finding one with a good record is critical.

Be prepared to fabricate your own parts. Sometimes it's possible to find others who need parts to jointly fund a production run. An informal international network of veteran Mercedes-Benz owners enjoys Daimler-Benz assistance, but prepare for great expense and effort in restoration.

Summary

Apart from the racing models, the 1902–1903 Mercedes is the most significant pre-1926 model. It inspired other car designers and set the standard by which their products were judged. If you plan to drive an early car, try a 1920s model; the bigger the engine, the better. Performance and driveability are secondary. These historic artifacts should be preserved for future generations. Their owners are more caretakers than users.

Supercharged 1923 Mercedes Targa Florio Roadster helped to get DMG back into international competition after World War I.

Chapter 4

Vintage to Classic 1926–1940

By 1926, Daimler and Benz could not survive in competition with each other, so they merged, effective June 1926, into Daimler-Benz. Afterward, differing philosophies and old rivalries stifled creativity. During the 1930s, though, engineering and styling bloomed, yielding some cherished classics.

Luxury and Sport Models: Type K ★★★★★
    The Type K replaced the 28/95. Based on the 630 (24/100/140), the K (for *Kurz*, or short) had a shorter wheelbase but more power—110hp unblown, 160hp blown—from its 6.24 liter, overhead-cam, inline six. The four-speed transmission could

be coupled with several optional rear-end ratios. Type Ks were heavy; a bare chassis weighed about 3400lb, and complete cars usually exceeded 5000lb. Top speed was said to be 90mph, but brakes were marginal. A typical touring version sold for $16,000 in the United States in 1927, ensuring that the cars would always be rare. Before production ended in 1929, only about 150 Ks had been built.

Type S, SS, SSK, and SSKL 1928–1934 ★★★★★
    Strong-willed Ferdinand Porsche shook up the design department. His talent and effort created the classic 1927–1928 Type S sports car. Thanks to

Type K used either spoke or wooden wheels; inline six was supercharged, but the blower cannot be used continuously. *FDB*

MERCEDES-BENZ Kompressor-Sechszylinder
Polizigen Tourenwagen mit aufgestelltem Verdeck

Most Type Ks carried mundane but spacious bodies. *DBAG*

its supercharger, dual carburetors, and dual ignition, the Type S 6.7 liter engine made 120hp unblown, 180 blown. A four-speed transmission was used, and the huge drum brakes were vacuum-assisted on some cars. Underslung rear springs and a lighter frame arched over the axles to lower the car and improve handling. Production models could touch 100mph, and race versions pushed 120.

Besides the factory-built Sindelfingen bodies, the production Type S was dressed by Saoutchik, Van Den Plas, Zeitz, D'Ieteren, Freestone, and Webb—even Murphy. The 7.1 liter SS, which followed, has a higher engine hood and 225hp. The shorter-chassis, 170–225hp SSK followed in 1928 and the extremely rare, lightened SSKL in 1929.

Only 146 Type S cars were built, followed by 111 SS and 33 SSK models. Production ceased about 1934. Pseudo-SSKs and SSKLs were confected during the 1950s and 1960s, so insist on documented provenance. Because the replicas are known, owners of genuine cars are prepared to prove their history.

380, 500K, and 540K 1933–1943 ★★★★★

The scream of the supercharger made these cars legendary, but their excellence goes beyond that. This luxurious line commenced in 1933 with the 380, with four-wheel, coil-spring independent suspension. Its new overhead-valve straight-eight displaced 3820cc and was supercharged, but the 380 never had the "K" appended to its name. In a year only 154 were built; the car was underpowered, especially with a large formal body.

Next came the 1934 500K, the "K" denoting *Kompressor*, or supercharger. Boring and stroking the engine to 5019cc boosted output to 160hp with supercharger engaged. Wheelbase stretched to 129.5in, and gleaming exhaust pipes cascaded from the right side of the hood. In 1935 and early 1936 a handful of 500Ks were fitted with early 5.4 liter eights, but the 180hp 540K was officially introduced for 1936.

The 380, 500K, and 540K used wood-framed bodies, making them labor-intensive to build (and to restore). Other features included a twelve-volt electrical system, central lubrication, vacuum-assisted hydraulic brakes, and electric windshield wipers. The four-speed transmission had synchromesh on second through fourth gears. A typical 540K demanded a gallon of fuel every ten miles, making good use of its 29-gallon tank.

The 540K was then the fastest production automobile, and 406 were built with bodies ranging from four-door sedans to Special Roadsters and a few Special Coupes. Most are Cabriolets—the A (two-seater), B (four-seater, two side windows on each side), and the C (four-seater, one side window). The factory's Sindelfingen bodyworks built eight models: a sedan, an open tourer, Cabriolets A, B, and C, a Coupe, a Convertible Coupe, and a sensational Special Roadster, the most sought after prewar Mercedes-Benz. Most were on a 3290mm (129.5in) wheelbase, but a few sportier versions used a 2980mm (117.3in) chassis. Apart from Sindelfingen's selections, some were bodied by Erdmann & Rossi, but other coachbuilders were engaged. Only twenty-five Special Roadsters were built, and only three Special Coupes. A series of *Aktion P* armored 540Ks was built during World War II.

Most 540Ks had a single wide rubber strip in the bumper, and most 500Ks had two narrow strips, but exceptions exist. Custom features were common, and the cars could be right-hand drive or the more usual left-hand drive. Four-wheel independent suspension used coil springs. Fuel consumption was roughly 8mpg, 0–60mph required about sixteen seconds, and top speed might be 105mph, all depending upon the body.

380, 500K, and 540K Production Figures

Model	1933	1934	1935	1936	1937	1938	1939	Total
380	93	61	—	—	—	—	—	154
500K	—	105	190	59	—	—	—	354
540K	—	—	—	97	145	95	69	406

Grosser Mercedes: The 770 1930–1943 ★★★★

Even more imposing than a 500 or 540K is the 770, built in two series of long-wheelbase models bodied as limousines or open cars for parade use.

The first series, with the W07 chassis and 7.7 liter M07 inline eight-cylinder motor, was built from 1930 through 1938 and included 117 cars. These had a box-section frame, leaf springs, beam axles, and a 150hp engine; an optional supercharger raised power to 200hp. The tall, upright bodies were clearly styled in the late 1920s, with wooden artillery wheels or wire-spoked wheels.

The later series, on the W150 chassis with the M150 inline eight, ran from 1938 to 1943, with eighty-eight built. This lower, sleeker 700 was redesigned on a tubular frame with coil-spring in-

Sindelfingen-bodied S tourer has classic sports car lines; engine hood was lower than that of the SS, SSK, and SSKL that followed it. *DBAG*

This restored Type S is no doubt much fancier than it was in 1927. *Dennis Adler*

About to be delivered, this 500K Cabriolet A has twin flagstaffs, possibly indicating that it was intended for a prominent owner. *DBAG*

The Special Roadster is the most desirable 500K or 540K body style. *FDB*

The six-cylinder, 3.7 liter flathead engine of the 370S
makes 75hp; brakes are vacuum-assisted. *FDB*

This 1932 370S Mannheim Cabriolet Sport has a
two-seater factory body and was capable of up to
about 80mph. *DBAG*

dependent suspension, disc wheels, and a five-speed transmission. Built only with a supercharger, the engine made 155–230hp. Many of these cars were armored.

More myths have developed around the 770 than any other Mercedes-Benz. Almost every one is said to have been used or owned by one potentate or another. Be skeptical.

This short-wheelbase 1936 290 Cabriolet A's Sindelfingen body is almost a reduced-scale version of the 540K. Its six-cylinder engine produced 60–68hp. *FDB*

Mannheim-bodied 1936 290 Cabriolet A is quite different from Sindelfingen version. *Dennis Adler*

Apart from military vehicles, Mercedes-Benz wartime automobile production was almost zero. The last 770 was built in 1943, and although a V-12 version was being developed, none apparently survive.

Mid-Range Models 1926–1940 ★★★

The medium-price, late 1920s 2.0 liter, six-cylinder Stuttgart and early 1930s 3.7 liter, six-cylinder Mannheim were named for German cities, but the bigger 4.6 liter, straight-eight Nürburg (1928–1933) was named for the Nürburgring race circuit. Except in sports-bodied form, these cars were fairly mundane. Their normally aspirated, side-valve engines provided utility, not performance, and most were bodied as heavy sedans. Many more were made than the luxury and sporting models, but fewer survive.

The Stuttgart 200 and 260; the 300, 320, 350, Mannheim 350, 370, and 370S; and the Nürburg 460 and 500 were mid-1920s designs with beam front axles and mechanical brakes. (Before hydraulic brakes, Mercedes-Benz employed the Bosch-Dewandre system, using engine vacuum to boost the mechanical brakes.) These models used conventional chassis and side-valve (flathead) engines. Typical sedans were tall and boxy. The Nürburgs were impressive; the Nürburg 500 was actually built until

1939 in small numbers, but it was a utilitarian car, less advanced than the 500K, 540K, and 770.

Open models, especially with custom coachwork, are attractive restoration candidates. The 370S Mannheim Roadster and Sports Cabriolet are quite desirable. The Stuttgarts were modest, but a Sports Roadster would be a find. Total production of these series was only about 23,000 units.

290 and 320 1933–1942 ★★★

Independent front suspension spread to the mid-range 290, 320, 370, and 380. The 290 could be bodied in myriad short- or long-wheelbase variations—sedans, touring cars, Cabriolets (A, B, C, D, or F), plus at least one Roadster and by 1938 even military vehicles. Bodies emulated the bigger cars, with a broad choice of options.

The 290's 2.8 liter, side-valve six made either 60 or 68hp. Its chassis used three front springs: one transverse leaf and two inboard coils, the latter acted upon by rocker arms. DBAG quoted top speed as 70mph; 0-60mph required 44 seconds.

An unusual model was the streamlined 1934 150 Sports Roadster. With its 55hp, four-cylinder engine mounted amidships and driving via an automatic overdrive, it was ahead of its time. Few survive.

The 290 and 320 are substantial-appearing clas-

Designed to sell as a moderately priced model, the late 1920s Stuttgart used six-cylinder engines in sober bodywork. *DBAG*

sics with styling flair at less cost than a 540K. Short-wheelbase, five-passenger 290s seem short for their bulk, and the massive Cabriolet F and Pullman Limousine are ponderous. Look for excellent originals with sound bodies needing minimal work. The streamlined and special-bodied sedans are rare.

Late 320s have a 3.4 liter engine and overdrive—*schnellgang*, which lowers engine rpm. The 320 Cabriolet A and Roadster, long and short, are rare. The long-wheelbase 320 Cabriolet B and Cabriolet D are handsome, with dual side-mounted tires and split windshields.

200, 230, and 260D 1933–1943 ★★★

Numerous bodies were built on the 200 and 230, on long (3,050mm) and short (2,700mm) wheelbases. There were as many as four Cabriolet A models, three long and one short-chassis. Two-seat models are most desired. Short-chassis models have a shorter wheelbase than the 170V and stand higher at the beltline, making them tall for their length. The Cabriolet A and Roadster look good. The late 1939–1943 230 (W153) got a lighter X-plan frame. Five-passenger W153 cars had all-steel bodies, a first for Mercedes-Benz.

Daimler-Benz marketed the first diesel passenger car, the four-cylinder 260D, in 1935. Its body was derived from the gasoline-powered 230. Using Bosch mechanical fuel injection, its overhead valve (cam-in-block) 45hp engine got the car to 55–60mph and averaged over twenty miles per gallon. Most 260Ds became taxis and limousines, but some were sold as family cars. Most collectors consider the 260D the only diesel car of serious historic interest.

Mercedes for the Masses: 170 and 170V 1931–1942 ★★★

In 1931, the unpretentious 170 economy model brought four-wheel independent suspension to Mercedes-Benz production cars. Despite the Depression, this 1.7 liter, six-cylinder car boasted central lubrication, four-wheel hydraulic brakes, pressed steel wheels, and (maybe *because* of the Depression) an anti-theft steering lock. The 170 began as a sedan, a Cabriolet A, and a Cabriolet B.

In 1936 the 170 was superseded by the 170V. Despite replacing the six with a four, this is the best prewar 170. The ladder frame was replaced by an oval cross-section, tubular frame. Power rose, and a four-speed transmission appeared. Bodystyles blossomed into ten varieties including the Roadster, the rarest and most desirable. A coal-burning 170VG made its debut in 1939.

Between 1931 and 1939, about 39,000 170s were built. Early six-cylinders are scarce, so the 170V is the most available. The Roadster and Cabriolet A are beautifully styled and well worth restoring. When considering a prewar 170 sedan, remember that a postwar 170V looks the same but has improvements which make it easier to restore, maintain, and use. Many prewar 170Vs were retrofitted with postwar engines. An original en-

The world's first diesel-powered passenger car, the 260D was designed as a commercial vehicle but appealed to private owners as well. *DBAG*

31

gine is a mixed blessing because replacement of its Babbitt bearings requires an expert. Thin-wall bearing inserts in postwar engines provide better fit, heat dissipation, and life.

Rear-Engined 130H, 150H, and 170H 1934–1938 ★★★

The most unusual production Mercedes-Benz models ever, the 1934–1938 130H, 150H, and 170H, were rear-engined on a central-tube frame. Volkswagen-like in appearance, these small four-place cars used inline four-cylinder engines hung out behind the rear axle. The alloy, air-cooled, VW engine was light enough for this, but the H's tall, cast-iron, water-cooled unit unbalanced the car. Rear swing-axles used coil springs, and the front suspension had a transverse leaf spring; four-wheel hydraulic brakes were fitted.

In five years only 5,816 were sold, as a sedan or as a semi-Cabriolet with a roll-back fabric roof. A 26hp 130H or a 38hp 170H is interesting—and usually modestly priced—but these cars are best appreciated as historic artifacts.

What to Look For

As prices of the glamorous cars rose, collectors with modest budgets turned to unsupercharged models. Today, even some owners know little about these cars, so they are often mis-described. Check identification plates carefully.

Parts can be difficult to find—and expensive—so finding a complete car is important. Even in poor condition, an assembled car provides a reference point. Photographs and organized disassembly make reassembly easier than puzzling over boxes of parts.

The wooden structure supporting the sheet-metal requires skill to repair properly, so its condition is critical. Is there evidence of botched repairs or rotted wood? Do the doors sag or twist? Do engine hood and top fit well? A tired original body can provide patterns, but a botched repair can destroy evidence of what the original wood looked like.

Restoration

It's unusual to find an unrestored 1930s Mercedes-Benz; you're more likely to find one that needs re-restoring. Because of the high standards of classic restoration, your most important decision will be choosing a restorer. Two factors make a pre-war restoration project more difficult than a post-war restoration.

First, original parts are scarce. Except for the 170V, no prewar model was produced again after the war, so postwar parts interchangeability is nonexistent.

Second, most prewar cars have wood-framed bodies which will need repair. An advanced amateur with woodworking skills and equipment can tackle the job, but this exacting work requires patience. Even good restorers encounter few wood-framed bodies; some may send you elsewhere or let your car gather dust.

Get involved in the restoration. Research authenticity, find parts and materials, and oversee the job. Restorers charge for research and parts locating, so you gain more than knowledge by being an expert on your own car.

Summary

The late 1920s and 1930s offer many cars, but not all measure up to the top models. The latter have skewed most people's judgment of the desirability of the mid-range and economy models. Not every 1930s Mercedes-Benz is comparable to a 540K.

Power, style, and engineering count. Open cars are preferred, especially those with independent suspension, hydraulic brakes, and overhead valve engines—the more cylinders, the better. To spend less, move into the sedans. If you're a contrarian, find a 260D diesel or a 170H.

Consider postwar models with similar vintage styling but all-steel bodies and better parts availability. It is usually less expensive to buy a properly restored car than to restore an original.

An early 770 makes an impressive concours d'elegance entry. *FDB*

The sportiest 170V was this 2+2 Roadster, with its second seat covered by the folding lid. *DBAG*

Production Figures

Model	Years	Chassis Type	Engine Type	Engine Specs	Production (Approx.)
400 (15/70/100hp)	1926–1929	—	—	6-cyl/3920cc	911
630 (24/100/140hp)	1926–1929	—	—	6-cyl/6240cc	508
Model K	1926–1929	—	—	6-cyl/6240cc	150
630 with K engine	1928–1932	—	—	6-cyl/6240cc	117
8/38hp	1926–1929	—	—	6-cyl/1988cc	9105
300 (12/55hp)	1926–1927	W03	—	6-cyl/2968cc	834
300 (12/55hp)	1927–1928	W04	M03	6-cyl/3030cc	2485
320 (12/55hp)	1928	W04	M04	6-cyl/3131cc	202
350 (14/60hp)	1928	W05	M09	6-cyl/3444cc	355
350 (14/60hp)	1928–1929	W09	M09	6-cyl/3444cc	358
460, Nürburg	1928–1929	W08	M08	8-cyl/4622cc	1385
Type S	1927–1928	W06	M06	6-cyl/6800cc	146
Type SS	1928–1933	W06	M06	6-cyl/7065cc	111
Type SSK	1928–1932	WS06	MS06	6-cyl/7065cc	33
200, Stuttgart	1929–1933	W02	M02	6-cyl/1988cc	6452
260, Stuttgart	1928–1934	W11	M11	6-cyl/2581cc	6757
260L, Stuttgart	1933	W11L	M11	6-cyl/2581cc	50
350 Mannheim	1929–1930	W10	M10	6-cyl/3444cc	65
370 Mannheim	1929–1934	W10	M10II	6-cyl/3689cc	1162
370K Mannheim	1931–1933	W10	M10II	6-cyl/3689cc	213
370S Mannheim	1931–1933	WS10	MS10	6-cyl/3689cc	183
460 Nürburg	1929–1933	W08	M08	8-cyl/4622cc	1508
500 Nürburg	1931–1939	W08	M08II	8-cyl/4918cc	931
380	1933–1934	W22	M22	8-cyl/3820cc	154
500K	1934–1936	W29	M24I	8-cyl/5018cc	354
540K	1936–1939	W29	M24II	8-cyl/5401cc	406
770	1930–1938	W07 (K)	M07 (K)	8-cyl/7655cc	117
770	1934–1939	W150	M150	8-cyl/7655cc	88
170	1931–1936	W15	M15	6-cyl/1692cc	13775
200	1932–1936	W21	M21	6-cyl/1961cc	9281
200 Long	1934–1936	W21	M21	6-cyl/1961cc	6341
290	1933–1936	W18	M18	6-cyl/2867cc	3476
290 Long	1934–1937	W18II	M18II	6-cyl/2867cc	3929
260D	1935–1940	W38	OM138	4-cyl/2545cc	1967
130H	1933–1936	W23	M23	4-cyl/1308cc	4298
150H Roadster	1934–1935	W30	M30	4-cyl/1598cc	5
150H Sport	1934	W130	M30	4-cyl/1598cc	6
150V Sport	1934–1935	W130II	M30	4-cyl/1598cc	11
170H	1935–1939	W28	M28II	4-cyl/1697cc	1507
170V	1935–1942	W136	M136	4-cyl/1697cc	71973
200V	1938–1939	W149II	M149II	4-cyl/2007cc	31
230	1936–1937	W143	M143	6-cyl/2229cc	966
230L	1936–1941	W143	M143	6-cyl/2229cc	19324
230	1938–1943	W153	M153	6-cyl/2229cc	4210
230SV sports Roadster	1938	W153	M134S	6-cyl/2229cc	33
230 sports sedan	1939	W153	M153S	6-cyl/2289cc	19
320	1937–1942	W142	M142	6-cyl/3208-3405cc	5097

Chapter 5

Beginning Again: 170 and 220 Sedan, Coupe, and Cabriolet 1946–1955

To satisfy a rebuilding nation needing basic transport, the first Mercedes-Benz back on the production line in 1946 was largely a prewar design.

170V, 170Va, and 170Vb 1946–1953 ★★

Had DBAG started from scratch in 1945 with an all new car, it couldn't have created anything more appropriate. The simple, inexpensive 170 models were descendants of the 170V that appeared in 1936. These postwar rebirths had flat-head four-cylinder gasoline or diesel engines, with a four-speed transmission. In 1946, bodystyles varied from a police car to ambulances *(krankenwagen)*, trucks, and vans. The charming little four-door sedans appeared in mid-1947.

The 1946 170V had several improvements on the prewar car: insert bearings; additional displacement; more power; an outside trunk lid; integral heating and ventilation; larger brakes, front spindles, and wheel bearings; and a hypoid rear axle.

Postwar 170Va four-cylinders were intended as basic, economical transportation. *DBAG*

35

Suspension was by twin transverse leaf springs up front, with the coil-sprung swing-axle in the rear.

In May 1950 the 170Va appeared with 1767cc, 45hp, and a 72mph top speed. Tires widened modestly from 5.25x16 to 5.50x16in. Updated to the 170Vb in 1952, the car now had horizontal instead of vertical engine hood louvers, softer springs, a different rear axle, a larger windshield, and front bumpers that began to curve around the fenders.

170S and 170Sb 1949–1953 ★★★

In 1949, Mercedes-Benz introduced its first new postwar models, the 52hp 170S sedan, Cabriolet A, and Cabriolet B. Refinements included a downdraft Solex carburetor; a larger fuel tank in the rear instead of under the hood; and coil-spring front suspension instead of the transverse leaf spring. The spare tire moved into the trunk, allowing the lid to hinge at the top instead of the bottom.

The 170S body was slightly larger than the 170V, but more important, it was all-steel on the sedan and Cabriolet B. The Cabriolet A still used structural wood. The sedan was also sold with a canvas sunroof.

In 1952, the 170Sb took over, with a shifter on the column instead of the floor. The 170S Cabriolet models were dropped in 1951.

170D, 170Da, 170Db, and 170DS 1949–1953 ★★

Postwar diesel 170s included the 170D, from May 1949, then the 170Da, 170Db, 170DS, and 170S-D. Diesels used the new OM636 engine. This 1.7 liter flathead, with 19:1 compression and Bosch fuel injection, pumped out 38 hp and 71lb-ft of torque. Maximum speed was 62mph, fuel consumption about 30mpg.

The 1950 170Da came with vent windows and 40hp, replaced by the 170Db in 1952; the latter was also sold as an ambulance, a taxi, and a station wagon, usually bodied by outside coachbuilders. In 1952–1953 a diesel version of the 170S, the 170DS, became available.

The most Spartan model, the 170D OTP (*Offen Tourenwagen, Polizei*, Open Touring, Police), was built mainly for German police departments from May 1950 to April 1952. This four-door, canvas-topped device had a 40hp OM636 diesel engine (OM means *oel motor*), a folding windshield, painted trim, and bench seats.

Technical Specifications			
Model	**170Va**	**170D**	**170S**
Engine			
Type	Inline side-valve four (all)		
Engine # prefix	M136VI	OM636VI	M136III
Displacement	1767cc	1767cc	1767cc
Bore x stroke	75x100mm	75x100mm	75x100mm
Compression ratio	6.5:1	19:1	6.5:1
DIN horsepower	45hp @ 3600rpm	40hp @ 3200rpm	52hp @ 4000rpm
Torque	11mkg @ 1800rpm	10.3mkg @ 2000rpm	11.4mkg @ 1800rpm
Fuel system	Solex 30 BFLVS	Fuel injection	Solex 32 PICB
Fuel required	Regular	Diesel	Regular
Coolant capacity	9.5qt	9.5qt	11.1qt
Chassis			
Type	Tube (all)		
Body	Steel, wood-framed	All-steel	All-steel
Chassis # prefix	W136 (all)		
Transmission	4-speed manual (all)		
Rear-axle ratio	4.125:1		4.375:1
Rear suspension	Swing-axle, coil springs		
Front suspension	Transverse leaf springs	A-arms, coil springs	
Wheels	3.50x16in		4.5x15in
Tires	5.50x16in		6.40x15in
Brakes	Drum (all)		
Fuel capacity	11.1gal	9.8gal	12.4gal
Weight	2,612lb (sedan)	2,756lb	2,690lb (sedan)
Performance			
0-60mph	32sec	45sec	30sec
Top speed	72mph	65mph	76mph
Fuel consumption	20–24mpg	24–32mpg	20–26mpg

This 1952 170DS interior is fitted with a steering-column-mounted four-speed gearshift and cloth upholstery. *DBAG*

170S-V and 170S-D 1953–1955 ★

Except for these stripped-down versions, the 170's final model year was 1953. The 170S-V and the 170S-D, mating the all-steel 170S body with the V (gas) or D (diesel) engine, were priced below the new unibody 180 and the earlier 170S and DS. Built on the older chassis, the S-V and S-D were strictly economy cars. Collectors prefer the better-appointed S and DS.

What to Look For

Since the postwar 170V's steel body is built on a wooden frame, age and the elements can cause the suicide doors (the front doors are hinged at the rear) to sag. Proper wooden frame rebuilding is difficult and expensive. Look for leaks and wood damage along the drip rail and the molding between rear deck and roof. Look for poor-fitting doors, loose striker plates and door hinges. Be wary of new paint over a patched-up, weak body structure.

On the 170S, watch for rusted box channels in the lower body, rust in the trunk floor, and, on Cabriolets, in the lower quarter panels. The front suspension may be worn due to clogged central lubrication lines; front-end parts are rare. Try for a complete car including the correct lights, bumpers, bumper guards, interior hardware, and instruments—especially sun visors and rearview mirrors on Cabriolets. An original radio is a bonus.

Restoration

Few of the 150,000 170s were exported. Today they aren't exactly considered classics, but they are rare and inexpensive. Touches like flip-up orange turn-signal trafficators give them an endearing personality. Some folks have sunk money into fancy restorations on Cabriolets, even the lowly

Early 1950s 220 sedans look old fashioned but were technically advanced with a six-cylinder overhead-cam engine and four-wheel independent suspension. *Dennis Frick*

170 Chassis and Engine Prefix Numbers

Years	Model	Chassis prefix	Engine prefix
1946–1953	170V, 170Va, 170Vb sedan, commercial	W136	M136
1949–1955	170S, 170Sv sedan	W136	M136
1949–1955	170D, 170Da/b, 170DS, 170S-D sedan, OTP	W136	OM636

170 Production

Years	Model	Production
1947–1953	170V sedan	45,741
1949–1953	170D sedan	26,758
1949–1952	170S sedan	28,708
1949–1951	170S Cabriolet A	1,603
1949–1951	170S Cabriolet B	830
1952–1953	170Sb sedan	8,080
1952–1953	170DS sedan	12,857
1953–1955	170S-V sedan	3,122
1953–1955	170S-D sedan	11,800

170D OTP, gilding the lily with fancy color combinations and whitewall tires. These cars were never plush, colorful, fast, or luxurious. Their modest colors and low power fit their quiet personalities, and they appear best that way.

Parts for the 170Vs are only moderately difficult to obtain. An OTP is Spartan; consider a more attractive prewar 170V Cabriolet B (wood-framed body) or an all-steel 170S Cabriolet B. They cost more to restore but are more comfortable and better finished, with bucket seats, roll-up windows, and padded tops.

A 170S is a good choice for a vintage look (free-standing headlights, running boards) with better parts supply than prewar cars. Reproduction wood parts are available. Its wood-framed body makes a Cabriolet A tough to restore, but its value can justify the cost.

The 170S Cabriolet B, overshadowed by the more stylish Cabriolet A, should not be overlooked. It has an all-steel body and a roomy back seat. If a Cabriolet B can be bought for little more than a sedan, only the leather versus cloth upholstery and the Convertible top will cost more to restore, yet a finished Cabriolet B could be worth two sedans.

220 Sedan 1951–1955 ★★

By 1951, DBAG had designed the 220, with a new, six-cylinder overhead-cam 2.2 liter engine, smoother and providing more useable performance. The 220 was sold as a sedan, Cabriolet A, Cabriolet B, Coupe, and as the Open Touring Police car.

The oval tube chassis was retained with a new hypoid rear axle and improved brakes. The grille moved forward to accommodate the longer engine, resulting in a longer hood, improving the body's proportions. Instead of being free-standing, the headlights were finally built into the fenders, an easy way to tell a 220 from a 170. All window glass was flat, and the 220s were the last Mercedes-Benz with rear-hinged front doors.

Swing-axle rear suspension continued, as did the central lubrication and the column-shifted, all-synchromesh four-speed transmission. With a 6.5:1 compression ratio, the new single-carburetor six gave 80hp DIN at 4850rpm, a major improvement. This power may seem meager, but the cars were relatively light. Drum brakes were hydraulic but unboosted, and the electrical system still ran on six volts.

The 220 sedans were trimmed sparsely, the usual upholstery being broadcloth with a floor mat of molded rubber. Square-weave carpet like that of early VWs (and 300SLs) was used on the rear floors and seat risers. The trunk had rubber mats on the floor and the luggage shelf, with black cardboard side walls.

Solid ash forms the dashboard top, but the fascia is stamped sheet metal. Regardless of trim color, both wood and metal were dark brown. The wood was not stained but colored with a tinted varnish for a near opaque finish. Headliners were felt-like cotton cloth. Knotted tassels on the pillars between the doors served as hand grips in fast corners. Often seen but never confirmed as a factory part were cut-glass bud vases—companions to the tassels. Rounding out the Victorian decor were the fine-looking but low-fi Telefunken radio and the trafficators.

Trafficators were outside-mounted signal arms. Rotating the horn ring left or right caused one to spring upward from its recess, light up, and sit there until canceled. Trafficators in good condition are rare. The dash includes an ignition timing control.

Sedans came without fog lights, trim rings on the wheels, or luggage. Leather was an option, but other embellishments were few. The small, nippled hubcaps are different from the domed style on 300SLs and later sedans. The hood star was rigid, part of the radiator cap that screws into the grille shell, and scaled to the 220. Some 220s had a vestigial crank handle hole in the lower grille shell, with a chromed cover. A full-length fabric sunroof was optional. Other options included a passenger-side hand grip and headrest, a radiator roller blind, fitted luggage, various radios, an underhood light, a heater blower, a spare parts kit, and a fold-down rear seat.

220 Cabriolet A 1951–1955 ★★★

The 220 was also built as a Cabriolet A and a Cabriolet B. Following tradition, the Cabriolet A was a two-passenger Convertible with a jump seat in the rear, distinguished from the four-passenger Cabriolet B by having only one side window. The padded top had chromed landau bars.

Technical Specifications

Model	220
Years	1951–1955

Engine

Type	Inline ohc six
Engine # prefix	M180
Displacement	2195cc
Bore x stroke	80x72.8mm
Compression ratio	6.5:1
DIN horsepower	80hp @ 4850rpm
Torque	14.5mkg @ 2500rpm
Fuel system	One two-barrel Solex 30 PAAJ
Fuel required	Premium
Coolant capacity	16qt

Chassis

Type	Unibody; steel
Chassis # prefix	W187
Transmission	4-speed manual
Rear-axle ratio	4.44:1
Rear suspension	Swing-axle, coil springs
Front suspension	A-arms, coil springs
Wheels	4.5x15in
Tires	6.40x15in
Brakes	Drum
Fuel capacity	17.2gal
Weight	2,975lb (sedan)
	3,175lb (Cabriolet)

Performance

0-60mph	20sec
Top speed	87-90mph
Fuel consumption	15-20mpg

Note: Performance figures, based upon original factory information and new car test reports, are approximate and depend upon the individual car, options, driving conditions, and other factors.

Production

Years	Model	Production	Chassis prefix
1951–1954	220 sedan	16,066	187011
1951–1953	220 Cabriolet B	997	187013
1951–1953	220 Cabriolet A	978	187012
1954–1955	220 Cabriolet A	300	187024
1954–1955	220 Coupe	60	187023
1953–1954	220 4-door Convertible (OTP)	41	187015

Typical 220 chassis number: 18701202532/51 (early); 1870244500046 (late)
Typical 220 engine number: 18092001234/51 (early); 1809234501234 (late)

An optional external spare tire increased trunk space. Fog lights and wheel trim rings were standard on Cabriolets, and fitted luggage was offered. Windshield wipers are electrical. The interior rearview mirror is on a clever swivel so that it can be raised to allow a view over the bulky folded top.

Cabriolet A and Coupe interiors were trimmed differently from other 220s. The dash fascia was leather-covered in a color matching the seats. The

Controls of the 220 sedan were straightforward and no frill.

dash top had veneered wood trim matching the windowsills in burled elm, burled walnut, or rosewood, matching seat color. A short, cut-pile wool carpet, usually referred to as Wilton, covered the transmission tunnel, the risers and kick panels, and

---

Driving Impressions: 220 Sedan

The 220 can be driven comfortably at highway speeds for long distances. Alex Dearborn drove a 1954 220 sedan all through the 1970s and recalls no trouble cruising at 70mph. The rear swing-axles were not yet the low-pivot version, so surprise oversteer lurked. The 220 had seven-plus inches of ground clearance and had positive camber built into the rear alignment in anticipation of heavy loads, so an unladen one was a challenge in fast corners.

Unassisted drum brakes require fairly high pedal pressure. Top speeds of the Coupe and the Cabriolets are in the high 80s, with 0–60mph requiring about twenty seconds.

The 1954–1955 220 Cabriolet A has a curved windshield and was one of the last Mercedes-Benz models to use a wood-framed body. *DBAG*

the rear floor. The carpet was bound in scived leather matching seat color except in the case of off-white leather, used with gray or "salt and pepper" carpet. Rubber mats covered the front floor.

The trunk had carpet, the same as the interior but always tan, matching the optional fitted luggage. A horizontal spare tire and wheel, with jack and tools, dominated the trunk. A shelf above was for fitted suitcases.

A 220 Cabriolet A is pretty, a sort of scaled-down 300S but friendlier. The Cabriolet A is the most valuable 220 today. Economy and good cruising performance from the 80hp engine are reasons to choose this as an only collector car. If you want a collectible for tours and club outings, this is your 220.

220 Cabriolet B 1951–1955 ★★★

The 220 Cabriolet B subframe is all-metal, like the sedan's. The four-passenger B has a roomy bench back seat and rear side windows. Its rear window is a small chrome-framed glass unit, like the Cabriolet A's. Interior trim details are the same as the sedan. The soft top was the usual padded af-

fair, bulkier than the Cabriolet A, and lay atop the rear deck when folded. A top boot made from top fabric was trimmed in leather matching the seats. An outside spare tire was optional. Positive camber was evident in the rear suspension of an empty car.

220 Cabriolet and Coupe 1954–1955 ★★★

By early 1954 the 220 sedan and Cabriolet B were replaced by the completely new unibody 220a, but the old 220 Cabriolet A and a new Coupe were assembled through 1955. The 1954–1955 Cabriolet A and Coupe can be distinguished by their curved windshields.

These so-called "second series" 220 Cabriolet A models were given 187024 chassis numbers but were little changed from the 187012 chassis cars. The curved windshield is a nice distinction, but only if it's not cracked.

Records show 85 Coupes produced, 13 with a sunroof, making them rare. The 1951–1955 220 Cabriolet A cars numbered 1,278; perhaps 300 were second-series cars. Incidentally, the 220 Cabriolet A is not a 220A, as it is often misla-

The 220 Cabriolet A's engine is nestled between two large heater ducts. *FDB*

Rarest 220 is this elegant Coupe, here with the particularly desirable sunroof. The 220 was the last Mercedes-Benz with suicide doors. *DBAG*

beled. The Coupe was pretty, resembling the 300S Coupe, with the added cachet of being rarer.

220 OTP ★★

DBAG made a police variant called the 220 OTP (Open Touring, Police), following the lines of the 170D OTP. The car was sparsely trimmed; its top was not padded or even lined. This was a four-door utility vehicle for transporting personnel. Compared to its predecessor, the 170D OTP, the 220 was a less modest performer. With dual Solex carburetors as later fitted to the 220S, the 220 OTP must have worried the bad guys a little more than the 170 had.

Rare today, the 220 OTP was a military-style vehicle. It would be a crime to tart one up. This is a jeans-and-mud, dogs-in-the-back-seat kind of collectible.

What to Look For

Because the 220 was so similar in construction to the 170S, caveats listed for that model apply here.

Look for rust first. The 220's rugged backbone frame has stringers going out to the jacking points. We have never seen a seriously rusted frame, but the subframe is another story. A sheet-metal box section runs parallel to the doorsills, fore and aft. The body rests on these, which in turn rest on the frame. Examine this subframe for rust or rust cover-up. We have seen subframes made of cardboard with undercoating as camouflage.

The Cabriolet A and Coupe have wooden subframe parts—the door frames, the doorposts to the windshield base, the rear top compartment frame, and the door sills. To determine the condition of doorsill wood, open and close the driver's door. If the door has to be lifted into place, then there is deterioration in the door structure or in the wooden sub-frames. Many "restored" Cabriolets have sagging doors, usually because the wood is rotten or weak. Remove the chromed doorsill plates to expose the wood structure. Oak pieces are being replicated. The higher value of this model might justify the expense of replacing the wood framing, but it can only be done with the car totally apart.

The 220 Cabriolet A trunk could accommodate factory fitted luggage and even a spare parts kit in a wooden box. *Alex Dearborn*

Restoration

Which 220 do you choose? The sedans are the least expensive and the most practical. Made in large quantity, they will never be rare. Still, they're seldom seen. Sedans are cheaper to restore than the Cabriolet A, and parts are fairly obtainable, used or new. A 220 sedan is affordable. Look for a good complete unabused original. A sunroof is a lucky find.

Expect to replace or rebuild most mechanical parts. Many cars were the victims of indifferent care and limited parts availability. Now, specialists provide new-old-stock and reproduction parts. Used parts are available through restorers and collectors.

The 220 engine remained in production until the mid-1960s, so parts are easily available. The original cast-iron heads are prone to cracking.

Many have been replaced; if not, an aluminum head from the late 1950s is recommended.

Before an extensive restoration of a 220 sedan, consider moving up to a Cabriolet B. These are rarer than the A (997 versus 1,278 produced), and with no structural woodwork, are easier to restore than a Cabriolet A.

The handsome 220 Cabriolet A is one of the more desirable Mercedes-Benz 1950s collectibles. Structural woodwork is an obstacle, but replacement wood is available. Because of the engine, the 220 is preferred over the 170S by most collectors. If you plan to restore a Cabriolet A, the 220 is a safer investment than the 170S.

The 220's purchase price will be higher, but restoration costs will be the same as an equivalent 170. If you'll do the restoration yourself and can't afford a 220 Cabriolet A, a 170S Cabriolet A might be in your range. If performance isn't a concern, you will have a fine car when finished, the same quality as a 220.

Summary

These charming small cars are sound buys when they need little or no restoration. Otherwise you can invest more than they are worth, but if you're going to keep and enjoy the car, so what?

The 220 models can be enjoyed on today's roads. In styling they look prewar, but mechanically they incorporate many practical improvements. Best buys are the 220 sedans, with prices a fraction of the more glamorous, lower-production models. As usual, most collectors prefer the Cabriolets. The graceful and rarer 220 Coupe is probably the most sought after 220, especially with a sunroof.

Chapter 6

The Luxurious 300s of the 1950s

Because they had historically catered to luxury car buyers, DBAG introduced upscale models as soon as possible after World War II, not only to satisfy the reemerging need but to protect its position in that profitable market.

By 1952, using a new 3.0 liter, overhead-cam six, Mercedes-Benz was building newly designed four-door luxury sedans and Convertibles plus smaller numbers of 300S and 300Sc two-door Cabriolets, Roadsters, and Coupes on oval-tube chassis.

Larger and with more luxurious features, these 300 models were much heavier and more complex than the utilitarian 170s and 220s. Low volume and high quality mean that parts cost more, but these were the most elegant automobiles of the 1950s.

300, 300b, 300c, and 300d 1951–1962 ★★★

The 300 four-door sedan (practically a limousine) appeared in late 1951, followed by the elegant four-door Convertible (sometimes called a Cabriolet or a Cabriolet D) in April 1952. With a compression ratio of 6.4:1 (for poor postwar fuel) and two Solex 40 PBJC single-barrel carburetors, the overhead-cam six made 115hp DIN. The four-speed manual transmission had its shifter on the column or on the floor (rare). A self-leveling rear suspension was fitted, along with central lubrication operated by a plunger beside the accelerator pedal; both were operated by the 12volt electrical system. The taillights were tiny horizontal slots just above the bumper.

The 300s were miles ahead of other luxury cars in engineering and taste. Despite fresh memories of the Recent Unpleasantness, these German luxury models became popular around the world. Besides show business personalities and heads of state, they were owned by refined persons who preferred to avoid the ostentatiousness of a Rolls-Royce or a Cadillac. Because the 300 served German Chancellor Konrad Adenauer, it soon became known as the "Adenauer" model, a nickname that stuck to it almost as well as "Gullwing" has stuck to the 300SL.

The 300b, introduced in 1954, had front vent windows, a pair of Solex two-barrel carburetors, higher compression, more power, and larger brakes. The 300c, built from September 1955 through July 1957, brought more carburetor improvements and an automatic transmission option, a first for Mercedes-Benz.

The three-speed automatic, built by Borg-Warner, was also offered in the succeeding 300d. This ultimate 1950s luxury car was introduced in 1957 on a 4in longer wheelbase (124in) than the 300c, subtly restyled in more modern fashion. Besides a wider grille, larger windows, longer rear fenders, larger upright taillights, and a new roofline, the sedan abandoned the center pillar and became, in effect, a four-door hardtop. Removable rear quarter windows make the side view more dashing. The 300d's mechanical fuel injectors were in the intake ports rather than in the cylinders, like those of the 300SL. The engine made 160hp.

Between July 1957 and early 1962, 300d production included 3,100 sedans but only 65 Convertibles. Custom bodies included parade cars (often with raised rooflines in sedan and Convertibles), ambulances, even hearses. All 300s appear elegant and conservative, but the 300d is undoubtedly the most attractive.

Technical Specifications

Model	300	300b	300c	300d
Years	1951–1954	1954–1955	1955–1957	1957–1962
Engine				
Type	Inline ohc six (all)			
Engine # prefix	186	186II	186II	189
Displacement	2996cc (182.8ci) (all)			
Bore x stroke	85x88mm (all)			
Compression ratio	6.4:1	7.4 or 7.5:1	7.4 or 7.5:1	8.55:1
DIN horsepower	115hp @ 4600rpm	125hp @ 4500rpm	160hp @ 5300rpm	
Torque	20mkg @ 2500rpm	22.5mkg @ 2600rpm	24.2mkg @ 4200rpm	
Fuel system	2 Solex 40 PBJC carburetors	2 Solex 32 PAITA carburetors	Mechanical fuel injection	
Coolant capacity	21.1qt	22.2qt	22.2qt	22.2qt
Chassis				
Type	Oval tube, steel body (all)			
Chassis # prefix	186II	186III	186IV	189
Transmission	4-speed manual (all)			(3-speed auto optional)
Rear-axle ratio	4.44:1	4.67:1	4.67:1	4.67:1
Rear suspension	Swing-axle, coil springs (all)			
Front suspension	A-arms, coil springs (all)			
Wheels	5x15in	5x15in	5.5x15in	5.5x15in
Tires	7.00x15in	7.00x15in	7.60x15in	7.60x15in
Brakes	Drum	Vacuum-assisted after 1954		
Fuel capacity	19.0gal (all)			
Weight	3,924lb (sedan)	3,924lb (sedan)	4,100lb (sdn)	4,299lb (sedan)
	4,034lb (con)	4,034lb (con)	4,211lb (con)	4,409lb (con)
				Add 88lb for automatic
Performance				
0-60mph	18sec	17sec	17–18sec	17–18sec
Top speed	99mph	101mph	96–99mph	103–105mph
Fuel consumption	14mpg	15mpg	14–15mpg	13–15mpg

Driving Impressions: 300 Sedan

Despite feeling cumbersome, the big 300 sedans and Convertibles move along well once you get them rolling. Performance was adequate, but who cares? These cars exuded presence, not speed.

Braking requires planning ahead, especially without vacuum-boosted brakes. The automatic transmission is probably best avoided in favor of the more reliable and enjoyable four-speed manual gearbox.

If you plan to drive the car much, we recommend a 300d, which has more power, by far the best visibility, and is more refined and better developed.

Restoration

Since the 707 Convertibles built are valued far more highly than the 10,723 sedans, the latter can be a bargain if it doesn't need restoration. Many of these cars were maintained well, so finding one requiring minimal restoration is not difficult.

Avoid cars requiring total restoration. These big, rare, and complex cars are expensive to restore. Many people restoring a 300 find it best to buy a parts car. Engine and drivetrain overhaul are relatively simple, but the size and complexity of the body, trim, and interior are something else. The Convertible's top is another challenge.

300S 1951–1955 ★★★★

The 300S was a two-door, grand touring model based on the 300 sedan. All three bodystyles—Coupe, Cabriolet, and Roadster—shared the same chassis and basic shape, shorter yet more voluptuous than the sedan. Their 3.0 liter, single overhead-cam, six-cylinder engine was

The 1952 300 sedan's six-cylinder overhead-cam engine made 115hp and went on to greater things in the 300S, 300Sc, and 300SL. *DBAG*

uprated from the sedan's with higher compression and three Solex 40 PBJC carburetors instead of two. This gave 150hp and a top speed of 110mph. Central lubrication was also fitted.

The hand-assembled 300S was rare and expensive. Only 560 were made. Most chrome-plated trim parts were solid brass, test-fitted to each car then removed for final plating and reinstalled. Radio choices were Becker and Grundig, all tube-types. Until 1955, when the small face-plate of the 1960s and 1970s was first used, radios had large face-plates.

Early 300S cars cost about $6,500 in the United States, twice the price of a Cadillac. By 1955, all three bodystyles were priced at $12,457 FOB California, almost double the price of a 300SL. The lucky owners were surrounded by the best leathers and wood veneered panels. Their weekend clothes could be packed in custom suitcases fitting the curves of the trunk. Additional fitted suitcases were available for the folding rear occasional seats.

Two oval frame tubes ran the length of the car. Four-wheel, coil spring independent suspension (swing-axles at the rear) gave a supple ride with little roll. The four-speed manual gearbox was shifted via a column-mounted lever. Some cars were fitted or retrofitted with floorshifts. Rear-axle ratio was 4.125:1. Neither an automatic transmission nor power steering was offered. Finned aluminum brake drums, vent windows, different heater boxes, and vacuum-assisted brakes were fitted to 1954 and later cars, sometimes known as the 300Sb.

Options were few, but lighting changed de-pending upon country of destination. German bulb-type headlights had narrow rims and large, round, fluted glass covers. US headlights had wide chrome-plated rims to accommodate the smaller, 7in sealed-beam units.

300Sc 1955–1958 ★★★★★

In late 1955 the 300Sc brought a few trim embellishments over the previous 300S, but all three bodystyles continued with nearly unchanged sheet metal. The plain chrome bumpers no longer had a rubber strip set in chromed brass channel as on the 300S. The "300S" lettering remained on the trunk lid, but the new model was identified by the large chromed letters *"EINSPRITZMOTOR"* in the rear bumper. Underneath, the Sc's cowl was better supported, and the transmission cover is not removable. Central lubrication continued. Other differences involve the fuel tank and radiator.

The big news was Bosch direct port fuel injection. Similar to that on the 300SL, it boosted power from 150 to 175hp. The engine block continued as cast iron with an aluminum head. The 300SL production engine produced more power and was canted in the engine bay, but the upright 300S/Sc design was similar. Like the 300SL, 300Sc engines used a dry-sump lubrication system, providing an additional 2.5 quarts of capacity over the 300S' wet-sump system.

Exterior changes included two chrome horizontal spears on the sides of the engine hood; the 300S had none. Chromed steel wheels replaced the painted wheels on the 300S. Body-color hubcaps were in-

Technical Specifications

Model	300S	300Sc
Years	1951–1955	1955–1958
Engine		
Type	Inline ohc six (all)	
Engine # prefix	188	199
Displacement	2996cc (182.8ci) (all)	
Bore x stroke	85x88mm (all)	
Compression ratio	7.8:1	8.55:1
Horsepower	150hp @ 5000rpm	175hp @ 5300rpm
Torque	23.5mkg @ 3800rpm	26mkg @ 4300rpm
Fuel system	3 Solex 40 PBJC carburetors	Mechanical fuel injection
Fuel required	Premium (all)	
Coolant capacity	20.6qt	21.1qt
Chassis		
Type	Oval tube, steel body (all)	
Chassis # prefix	188I	188II
Transmission	4-speed manual (all)	
Rear-axle ratio	4.125:1	4.44:1
Rear suspension	Swing-axle, coil springs (all)	
Front suspension	A-arms, coil springs (all)	
Wheels	5x15in (all)	
Tires	6.70x15in (all)	
Brakes	Drum, vacuum-assisted after 1954 (all)	
Fuel capacity	22.5gal (all)	
Weight	3,880lb	3,924lb
Performance		
0-60mph	15sec	14sec
Top speed	109mph	112mpg
Fuel consumption	14–16mpg (all)	

300S Production 1951–1955

Years	Model	Production	Chassis prefix
1951–1955	Coupe	216	188011
1951–1955	Cabriolet	203	188010
1951–1955	Roadster	141	188012

W188 chassis, M188 engine
Typical chassis numbers: 18801000074/52 (early); 1880105500006 (late)
Typical engine numbers: 18892000162/52 (early); 1889205500098 (late)

300Sc Production 1955–1958

Years	Model	Production	Chassis prefix
1955–1958	Coupe	98	188014
1955–1958	Roadster	53	188015
1955–1958	Cabriolet	49	188013

W 188 chassis, M 199 engine
Typical chassis number: 1880137500009
Typical engine number: 1999807500023

A 300c Convertible, as it was called in America, was often known as a Cabriolet D to European buyers. *DBAG*

Top down, the 300c Convertible still makes a great parade car. This one has a pair of unusual spotlights; its folded top recalls 1930s designs. *DBAG*

The 300's final iteration was the 300d, modernized with a 180hp SAE fuel-injected engine, sleeker roofline, removable rear quarter windows, upright taillights, and more. *DBAG*

Interior of the 300d sedan allows generous legroom front and rear. Visibility was much improved over earlier 300s. *DBAG*

terchangeable with the 300SL. Chromed brass wheelwell moldings were used for the first time.

Interior trim and layout remained as per the 300S. Radios were almost all Becker, with the familiar small face-plate. The only notable body change was a larger plastic rear window for the Roadster. A sunroof was optional for the Coupe. Various other options involved lights, keys, and so forth, but since these cars were often built to order, establishing an options list is folly.

Low-pivot swing-axle rear suspension, replacing the older swing-axle of the 300S, improved cornering power and stability. Rear-axle ratios were 4.44:1 for US cars, 4.11:1 for European. Drum brakes were retained.

Before the 300Sc line stopped in April 1958, only 200 were built, fewer than half as many as the 300S.

Driving Impressions: 300S and 300 Sc

These cars were grand touring predecessors of the 600SEC of the 1990s. Sports car buffs would be better satisfied by the 300SL. Still, power of the 300S was on a par with the better American cars, and roadholding was remarkable for a car of 3700lb.

The 300Sc could run in the fast lane in 1955. It may be the best all-around car made in the 1950s. Driving one today tempts comparison with expensive modern cars. The power-to-weight ratio compares favorably with the 1969 280SE Coupe. Zero to 60 takes about fourteen seconds, and the car will do 112mph. The fuel injection is reliable, and collectors prefer it to the tri-carb 300S setup.

What to Look For

Look for undamaged, complete, original examples with their trim intact. Items such as headlight doors, fog lamps, and grille shells were special to these cars and are hard to find. Apart from certain chassis parts, only such minor parts as fasteners were shared with the 300 sedan.

Rust is usually minimal, as the bodies were separate from the frame. The subframe box sections under the doorsills were apt to rust but are fairly easy to repair with the car apart. Check for rust under the headlights and in the trunk floor.

Engine numbers begin with 188 (300S) or 199 (300Sc), but do not match chassis numbers. Neither car had self-leveling rear suspension.

All 300S models had dense wool cut-pile car-

This 300S Roadster has painted wheels and European headlights; when lowered, its top disappears completely. Later 300S and 300Sc Roadsters have vent windows. *DBAG*

The early (no vent windows) 300S Cabriolet uses Landau bars; when lowered, its bulkier top stands above the rear deck. US versions have sealed-beam headlights inset into plated spacer rings. *DBAG*

pet trimmed in leather the same color as the seats. Interiors were trimmed in 4.0 ounce leather supplied to DBAG by the German leather company Roser. Lightweight, more supple leathers don't match the original appearance or give the firmness of the original cushions. The trunk carpet was normally dark tan, anticipating the tan fitted luggage, secured by a single belt with a chrome-plated roller buckle. Replica fitted luggage has been made.

Interior wood was usually rosewood veneer on an ash core. In cars with black or red leather, the rosewood was apt to be dark; with blue leather, it was usually light-colored. Burled walnut veneer was used in cars with tan or brown leather. This color and wood matching continued, with minor changes, in Mercedes-Benz Cabriolets and Convertibles through 1971.

The underside and engine compartment were finished in near-glossy black paint, not body color. The body-color tag on the firewall, near the chassis number plate, listed a two- or three-digit number ending in G or H (for example, 40G was black paint made by Glasurit). The body number (different from the chassis number) on the driver's doorjamb began "A 188..."

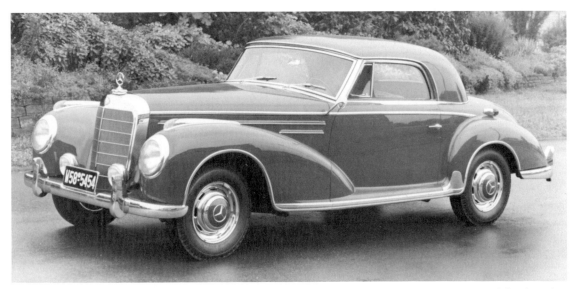

This handsome 1955 300Sc Coupe has a plain front bumper, horizontal trim on the sides of the engine compartment, chrome-plated fender trim, and chrome wheels. *DBAG*

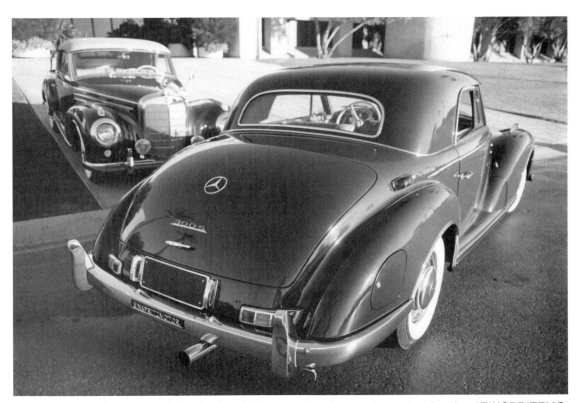

Matched 300Sc Coupe and Cabriolet (rear). The 300Sc used "300S" model designation on its trunk, supplemented by the *"EINSPRITZMOTOR"* set into the bumper. *FDB*

The 300S and 300SC Coupes were available with a factory-installed steel sunroof; some early ones had glass wind deflectors overlapping part of the side windows. Late cars (sometimes known as "b" models) had vent windows instead. Chromed brass plates cover the doorjambs.

The Cabriolet's padded top uses a horsehair mat over the top bows, under several layers of jute and the outer fabric. A loosely woven fabric headliner was light gray, light beige, or light tan. The top gave excellent sound insulation but is expensive to restore properly. A correctly restored top will be smoothly filled out, with the outline of the bows not easily visible. The top takes a little care to fold properly. Down, it rests in a stack on the rear deck and is covered by a large boot made from top fabric trimmed in leather to match the seats. A swing-up bracket allows the interior rearview mirror to be raised to allow rearward vision.

With the top up, rear vision is through a small, chrome-rimmed glass window. Chromed landau bars provide bracing and serve as an identification point for Cabriolet-spotters.

The 300S and 300Sc Roadsters used the Cabriolet body with minor changes. Its unpadded top has no headliner and stows in a well, covered by a leather boot color matched to the seats and attached by chromed Tenax fasteners.

On the 300Sc, look for the chassis number on the plate on the firewall. The body number plate in the driver's doorjamb should have a stamped number beginning with A 188. Body number will not match chassis number. Subtle differences exist between the fuel injection of the 300Sc and that of the 300d; for instance, the d's intake manifold has a clearance problem in the Sc. The 300Sc used the same trim and color combinations as the 300S.

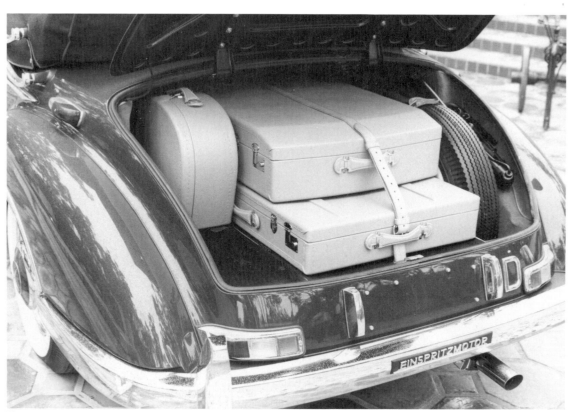

Fitted luggage for the 300S and 300Sc is now being reproduced to high quality. *Dennis Adler*

Lower the Roadster's top and it disappears into a well behind the seats; only fifty-three of these 300Sc Roadsters were built. *DBAG*

The 300S engine uses three Solex carburetors and has an unusual slanted head-block joint relating to the similar engine in the 300SL.

Chapter 7

The Pontons 1953–1960

These round-body 1950s four- and six-cylinder cars formed the first postwar armada of Mercedes-Benz exports and established the company's overseas markets. Today they remain easy to find and to own.

The German word *ponton* translates as "pontoon," describing the rounded shape of these unibody models. The four-cylinder 180 and 190 were strictly utilitarian four-door sedans (DBAG has never marketed a two-door sedan). The slightly more upscale sixes included the 219 (single-carburetor), 220S (dual-carburetor), and the 220SE (mechanical fuel injection).

The pontons were sensible cars with few unusual variants or options. Plentiful and simple, they are ideal for the beginning collector or restorer, yet they possess character. The earliest models that can be used everyday, the 220s are overlooked collector cars.

The 180-220 unit-body combined frame and body into one unit. Note the three rubber mounting points for the engine subframe. *DBAG*

180 and 190 1953–1960 ★★

In late 1953 the four-cylinder 180 began the ponton generation. The first low-priced Mercedes-Benz unibody, it went beyond the old-fashioned separate chassis and body, using sheet-metal body panels, resulting in a lighter yet stronger, simpler structure, now without running boards.

The 180's gasoline engine was the same sidevalve unit as in the previous 170S, with 52hp, but in 1957 this was swapped for an overhead-cam unit churning out 65hp. The 190 emerged for 1956, boasting an overhead-cam engine with a heady 80hp.

Mercedes-Benz built the workhorse 180 and 190 only as sedans, although they did supply chassis to coachbuilders for conversion to ambulances and station wagons. Economical and reliable, the 180 and 190 are appreciated far more as faithful servants than as collectibles.

Gasoline-fired examples included the 180, 180a, 180b, and 180c, but the 180 was more popular in diesel form as the 180D, 180Db, and 180Dc. The 190 was built in fewer models—the gasoline 190 and 190b and the diesel 190D and 190Db. For more on diesels, see chapter 18.

The 180's brightest claim to fame is that it set the official world's record for high mileage. In 1979, a 1957 180D owned and driven by Robert O'Reilly of Tacoma, Washington, was found to have reached 1,184,000 miles and thus entered the *Guinness Book of World Records*. The car still exists, although not with Mr. O'Reilly.

Updated with a new engine hood and grille in 1959, the ponton 190 continued into the 1960s, beyond the debut of the fin-back models. Most 180s and 190s are now extremely well worn. Few remain in daily use, and even fewer have been restored, but this is likely to change.

220a and 219 1954–1959 ★★

From 1954 through 1956, Mercedes-Benz built the 220a sedan which went on to become the 219, built through 1959. Both were powered by single-carburetor sixes making 85hp DIN (about 100hp SAE). Neither was offered in Convertible or Coupe form, and their entire demeanor was Spartan, with minimal wood trim, little exterior chrome, and few amenities. Still, their doors "chunk" closed with the best of them. The 220a is rare in the United States, but the 219 was more popular.

220S and 220SE Sedan, Coupe, and Convertible 1956–1960 ★★★

Bodystyles for the better known 220S and 220SE included an elegant sedan plus the more exclusive Convertible and the Coupe. Options included fitted luggage, two-tone paint, a front bench seat instead of two large buckets, reclining seats, whitewall tires, and more. Convertibles could have either a fold-down rear jump seat or an optional bench seat. Sedans occasionally can be found with a huge, folding fabric sunroof, and a few Coupes had a metal sunroof.

By now radios were common, usually Becker and Blaupunkt. Most were multi-band (AM, FM, and short wave) with some optional signal-seeking models. If the radio doesn't work, don't fret; these vacuum-tube units can still be repaired.

These were among the last Mercedes-Benz cars offering only a manual transmission, a four-speed with the lever on the steering column. The Hydrak option included a vacuum-operated clutch, electrically activated whenever the shift lever was touched. A fluid coupling allowed stopping and idling without disengaging the clutch. Available after August 1957, Hydrak found little favor, and conversions to a normal clutch were frequent. Factory air conditioning was unavailable, but a few cars had it as a dealer-installed option.

Most collectible are the Convertible and Coupe. Both were made in smaller numbers than the sedan, with more amenities. Built on a 4.7in

Technical Specifications			
Model	**190**	**220S**	**220SE**
Years	1956–1959	1956–1959	1958–1960
Engine			
Type	Inline ohc four	Inline ohc six	Inline ohc six
Engine # prefix	M121BI	M180III	M127I
Displacement	1897cc (115.8ci)	2195cc (133.9ci)	2195cc (133.9ci)
Bore x stroke	85x83.6mm	80x72.8mm	80x72.8mm
Compression ratio	7.5:1	8.7:1	8.7:1
DIN horsepower	75hp @ 4600rpm	106hp @ 5200rpm	115hp @ 4800rpm
Torque	13.9mkg @ 2800rpm	17.5mkg @ 3500rpm	19mkg @ 3800rpm
Fuel system	1 Solex 32 PAITA carburetor	2 Solex carburetors	Bosch mechanical fuel injection
Fuel required	Regular	Premium	Premium
Chassis			
Type	Unibody; steel (all)		
Chassis # prefix	121	180II	128
Transmissions	4-speed manual (all)		
Rear-axle ratio	4.10:1 (all)		
Rear suspension	Swing-axle, coil springs (all)		
Front suspension	Unequal-length A-arms, coil springs (all)		
Wheels	4.5x13in	5x13in	5x13in
Tires	6.40x13in	6.70x13in	6.70x13in
Brakes	Drum, vacuum-assisted (all)		
Fuel capacity	14.8gal	16.9gal	16.4gal
Weight	2,734lb	2,976lb (sedan) 3,108lb (Convertible)	3,020lb (sedan) 3,241lb (Convertible)
Performance			
0-60mph	20.5sec	17sec	15sec
Top speed	86mph	99mph	99mph
Fuel consumption	20-22mpg	17-20mpg	18-20mpg

Note: The 220S specifications cover cars built after August 1957; earlier cars had slightly lower power.

Chassis and Engine Prefix Numbers

Years	Model	Chassis prefix	Engine prefix
1953–1958	180 sedan	W120	M136
1958–1962	180 sedan	W120	M121
	180D sedan	W120	OM636
	180Dc	—	OM621
	190 sedan	W120	—
1951–1956	220 sedan	W187	M180
	220 Cabriolet A		
	220 Cabriolet B		
	220 Coupe		
1955–1956	220a sedan	W180	M180
1956–1959	219 sedan	W105	M180
1956–1959	220S sedan	W128	M180
	220S Coupe		
	220S Convertible		
1958–1960	220SE sedan	W128	M127
	220SE Coupe		
	220SE Convertible		

Engines and front suspension components are attached to the subframe and thus can be removed as a unit. *DBAG*

Production Years	Model	Production
1956–1959	219 sedan	27,845
1956–1959	220S sedan	55,000+
1956–1959	220S Convertible	2,178
1956–1959	220S Coupe	1,251
1959	220SE sedan	1,974
1959–1960	220SE Convertible	1,112
1959–1960	220SE Coupe	830

The 1959 update to the 180 introduced this padded steering wheel hub, widely used in other models into the 1970s. Gearshift lever is on the column. *DBAG*

shorter wheelbase than the sedan, the Convertible and Coupe looked similar to it at the front. At the rear, an extended trunk lid and near-finned rear fenders with larger taillights set off these two models. Inside, the two-door cars had much more elaborate woodwork and leather, plus chrome-plated covers on the doorjambs.

The 2195cc, single-overhead-cam M 180 III six of the 220S used two Solex 32 PAJTA carburetors and 8.7:1 compression to raise 106hp DIN (124hp SAE). Thanks to two-plunger Bosch mechanical fuel injection, the 1958-on 220SE made 115hp DIN (134hp SAE). These durable engines usually make 100,000 miles before blue smoke signals worn valve guides. Water pumps and engine mounts often need replacement. A clever device on the distributor permits easy timing adjustment to accommodate poor fuel, and the mechanical fuel pump's lever allows hand pumping. Fuel-injected cars

have an additional electric pump near the tank. Their characteristic cylindrical cast-alloy air intake plenum and long intake pipes are unmistakable. Compression of most cars (1958 and 1959 models) is 8.7:1, so they benefit from premium fuel.

Oil filters on these models, like other 1950s Mercedes-Benz cars, were crude. The wire-wound filter could be removed and cleaned, but it would only stop big chunks. Later replaceable paper fil-

This four-cylinder 180 is a 1959 model, with wider grille than earlier cars. *DBAG*

The 219 melded the front body and engine of the 220 with the rear body of the 180/190, creating the lowest-priced six-cylinder car. *DBAG*

ters don't fit. Air filtration is courtesy of an oil-bath air cleaner. Frequent oil changes are important.

The original 6.70x13in tires (on 5x13in wheels) are uncommon, but antique tire dealers handle equivalent sizes. Hubcaps are full wheel covers, and the star's background should be painted in body color. Brakes are vacuum-assisted drums with cast-in cooling fins. The 12volt electrical system powers bulb and reflector headlights on European cars; US versions got sealed beams. European cars used orange lenses in the fender-top turn signal lights; US cars used clear ones. Since clear lenses were unavailable for years, orange ones were fitted to many US cars. Home market cars had red re-

The 220S/SE sedan was dressed with chrome trim; this rare fuel-injected 1959 220SE is identical in appearance to the carbureted 220S. *FDB*

The 220S/SE Convertible (Cabriolet to Europeans) seats four in a more luxurious interior than the sedan; rear fenders and taillights are similar to those of the upscale 300d. *FDB*

flectors in their rear bumper guards; US cars got small body-mounted reflectors, too.

Performance wasn't the forte of these 3000–3200lb cars, but they can hold their own with contemporaries. Top speeds of the 220S and 220SE were around 100mph.

The 220SE sedan, Coupe, and Convertible began as 1959 models. The 220SE sedan was built only for that year, but the Coupe and the Convertible rolled on into late 1960 because the new finback cars offered no such variations. The Coupe and Convertible are four-seater cars; small rear seats fold to accommodate custom factory luggage.

What to Look For

Mechanically, the 1956–1960 220S and 220SE are predictable. All eventually need water pumps and engine mounts. As the result of improper repair or broken hangers, their exhaust systems often hang low. Door locks are frequently worn, and windshield wipers may be sluggish.

Body-wise, it's rust again. Look at the inner fender panels in the engine compartment near the headlights. Check beneath the battery (acid eats this panel and can eventually drip into the passenger-side footwell). Open the rear doors and look for rust in the rounded panel in front of the rear

Top down, the 220S/SE Convertible epitomizes growing German prosperity of the 1950s. *DBAG*

59

The steel top of the 220S/SE Coupe was fixed, not removable; few were fitted with a sunroof.

Chrome lower fender trim is similar to that of the Convertible. *DBAG*

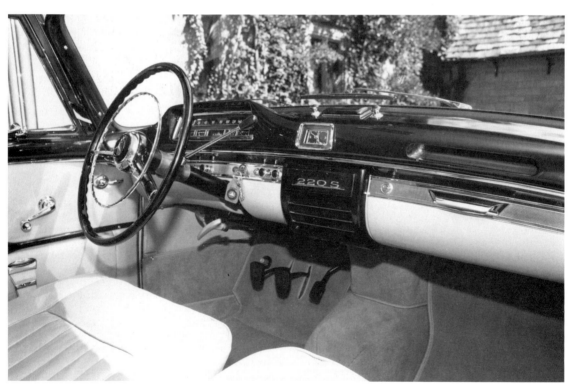

The 220S/SE Convertible interior is all leather, wool, wood, and chrome; veneered wood re-

quires skill to restore properly. Sedans had a much simpler dash and rubber floor mats. *FDB*

The 220SE engine is instantly recognizable by the huge intake manifold used with its mechanical fuel injection; power output was 130hp DIN.

Note the heater duct and windshield washer bag (left foreground). *DBAG*

wheel. Check the trunk floor, the spare wheel wells, and the front passenger compartment floor. If the car has a sunroof, its floor is more likely to be rusty. Make sure that the longitudinal arms from the rear suspension are securely attached to the body at their forward end; these mounts are vulnerable to rust.

Good bumpers (and bumper guards) are rare; bent ones can be restored, but rusty ones are tough to rescue. The chrome-plated grille surround is expensive to restore or replace. Trim strips along the rocker panel are hard to find in good shape. Convertibles with two-tone paint used a short, curved piece of chrome-plated trim behind and below the headlight that's extremely tough to find, and their lower body trim is likewise expensive to repair. The sedan's optional cloth sunroof has an intricate mechanism, so try it. Driving lights are expensive to replace. Because the hubcaps protrude beyond the tires, they have often been "curbed"; replacements should be painted.

The two-piece steering column is linked by a flexible fiber joint exposed to heat and oil in the engine compartment. As this joint ages, it can gradually separate. If you notice excessive steering play, the joint may be failing. Stop immediately and check it. The white steering wheel is a desirable option. Can't find the turn-signal lever? Turn the horn ring!

Brakes—drums on all these models—may pull to one side due to fluid or grease on the shoes or because of clogging of internally deteriorated rubber brake lines. If brake pedal pressure is unusually high, the vacuum booster may need to be rebuilt. See chapter 2 for a method of testing the booster.

The optional Hydrak automatic clutch depends upon a mixture of vacuum and electrical components to function; the potential for wear and other problems is high. Hydrak can be repaired or replaced by a standard clutch.

The six-cylinder 220 engines run about 100,000

The Hydrak automatic clutch uses a single-plate dry clutch mounted behind the flywheel and hydraulic coupler. The clutch releases and engages when the driver touches and releases the gearshift lever. This was as close as the 220S/SE got to an automatic transmission.

miles before needing attention beyond normal maintenance. Trouble usually begins in the cylinder head, with valve guide wear evidenced by smoking. If the coolant has not been changed regularly, the aluminum head can corrode internally, transforming it into expensive junk.

Check the condition of the heat exchanger ducts on each side of the engine compartment. These gather fresh air at the front and run it through a heat exchanger to warm it. The ducts were pressed cardboard, so they deteriorate. Fiberglass replacements don't look shabby enough to be original. Dash levers control coolant valves atop each heat exchanger. These tend to corrode and jam. The valves can be freed, but a stuck cable is more difficult to replace.

Look for a patched-together exhaust system, and check carefully for leaks.

Restoration

The ponton-bodied 220S and SE models are among the simplest to restore with few difficulties if the body is sound. Sedans form a good source of used parts for the rarer Coupes and Convertibles. Most mechanical parts remain available from Mercedes-Benz dealers and specialists, but external trim is another story.

The entire engine and front subframe can be wheeled out as a unit, making front suspension and engine compartment restoration easier. Replace the subframe mounts when you do this.

Proper tires can be hard to find, but later 14in steel (or even alloy) wheels fit. Taillights are easy to find for sedans. Replacements for the clear fender-top lenses were not made for years but are now being reproduced.

The 220 ponton sedans are fine, enjoyable cars, but they may be worth less than the cost of a thorough restoration. Rejuvenating a Coupe or Convertible is easier to justify economically but will cost much more because you're expected to restore it to show standards. Based on our own experience, we recommend the 220 sedans to anyone who wants an economical car with character to drive and enjoy.

Driving Impressions

The 180 and 190 sedans are decent drivers, but the 220S and 220SE are best for more extensive driving. The most usable is the fuel-injected 220SE, although vapor lock can be a snag. Fuel injection makes the 220SE more flexible and smoother to drive, with good torque over a wide rpm range.

Looking out through the shallow windshield, you see the clearly old-fashioned shape of the hood and front fenders. Most people will guess that this is a car of the 1940s rather than the 1950s.

Controls on the dash are unlabeled; read the owners manual. Some models used the horn ring to activate the turn signals. If the fuel and ignition systems are in good shape, poor starting and rough idling can indicate a burned valve, not uncommon.

The 220 models (and the 219) had their shifter on the steering column. The shift pattern is the usual H, with reverse outside it, up and toward you. The shifter isn't as precise as a floorshift, but compared to clunky automatics in other models, the manual transmission and clutch allow smooth shifts up and down. Be alert for vibrations; the two-piece driveshaft's center bearing can wear.

The front end must be in top shape for precise steering. Under the hood, on the left side, check the fabric joint between the upper and lower steering column; it can rot with age.

The drum brakes are effective and reasonably fade-resistant, but lack the bite of good discs. The front end dives under braking. Don't follow too closely; grilles and front bumpers are expensive. These cars handle well on dry roads, and a 220S or SE can keep pace with today's traffic on interstate highways or back roads. For years, a 1959 220SE sedan was our daily driver.

The rear swing-axle has no load-compensating spring, so if you overload the car, the rear sags and the wheels take on heavy negative camber. Ride should be quiet and smooth, without rattles, thumps, or squeaks. Interior comfort is good. Many of these cars lack seatbelts, but that's easily rectified. Heating, cooling, and ventilation are primitive by today's standards.

Summary

The 180 and 190 pontons are charming but will never be sought after, especially as diesels. Many dismiss the 1950s 220 sedans, but these are more elegant and more usable cars. We've enjoyed a 220SE for thousands of miles with few problems. These are some of the simplest, most durable, and economical collector cars for the beginning or low-budget enthusiast.

Chapter 8

300SL 1954–1963

After World War II the 300SL announced to the performance world that Daimler-Benz was back and a force to be reckoned with. Using expensive materials in a hand-assembled, low-volume, complicated car probably never made DBAG a pfennig, but the money could not have been invested in any more impressive or enduring form of publicity.

Early Competition Versions ★★★★★

The first 300SLs were race versions built in 1952, a year after the first 300 sedan on which the drivetrain was loosely based. Ten or eleven "W194" cars were raced by the factory then; records are unclear. The Coupes' doors opened only into the roof (later into the lower body), and some were open cars. Several were raced with dif-

This production 300SL has the sought-after Rudge knock-off wheel hubs. Wheels are painted body color. *DBAG*

The driver's side of the 300SL has "Mercedes-Benz"
trim. Compare side vent trim, headlights, and other
features with those of the 300SL Roadster. *DBAG*

The 300SL with its famous "Gullwing" doors
raised.

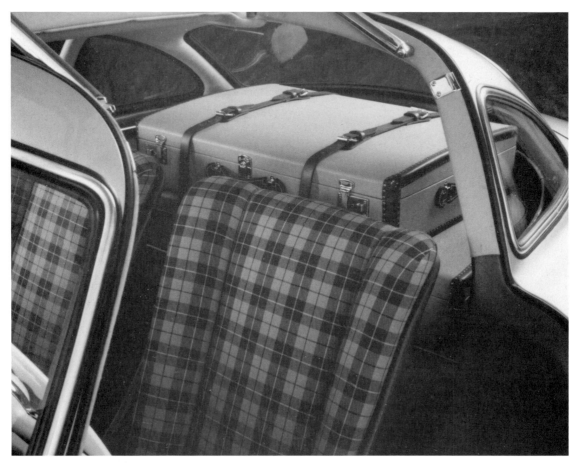

Early 300SL had plaid wool cloth seats. Fitted luggage is an attractive option resulting from lack of trunk space in the Coupe. *Paul Russell*

A 300SL leather interior. *Alex Dearborn*

ferent bodies, and at least two were later rebodied as semi-production cars. The originals had Rudge knock-off wheels and smooth, rounded bodywork, free of wind-catching details.

Innovations included a light but stiff multi-tube space frame and a three-liter engine based on the single-overhead-cam unit of the 300 sedan but tuned for 171hp DIN instead of 115. Using a dry-sump oiling system, the engine was canted leftward to reduce frontal area and fitted with three Solex downdraft carburetors. Wind-tunnel tests helped aerodynamics, and various induction systems were tried, including Weber carburetors and even, briefly, a supercharger.

The 300SL proved fast and reliable. Its successes, including Carrera Panamericana and Le Mans wins, are legendary. Several racing cars were later fitted with production bodies and sold

Driving Impressions: 300SL

A 300SL is like a 1950s Ferrari—fast, yet luxurious and attractive—but since it was built by Mercedes-Benz, it is also better engineered, higher quality, more reliable, even practical. The cars remain eminently usable, so they are popular for old car tours.

With the Coupe, entry and exit is tough only for skirted women who hope to remain dignified. The quick-release, hinged steering wheel eases driver entry and exit, and the seats are supportive for a 1950s sports car. Hot weather ventilation is mostly via pop-out side windows and wind wings. Some owners are reluctant to run at speed without the side windows—legend has it that under those conditions the rear window can blow out, although we've never seen it.

The 300SL is tractable at low speeds and even at low rpm, thanks mostly to the fuel injection. Low-speed steering may feel heavy, but on the open road at speed the car comes into its element.

Some 300SLs are still driven hard in vintage sports car races. The car is a great dual-purpose vehicle; you can drive it to the track and race. The engine is already in a state of tune suitable for racing, and further enhancements won't deliver much of a power increase. Racing prep might consist of detaching the hubcaps, lowering the front end a little, de-cambering the swing-axle rear suspension, hooking up the oil cooler, and driving to the event.

The suspension is supple, and there's little roll, which makes the car feel secure. Pushed too far, the rear swing-axle will deliver sudden oversteer, especially if the unsuspecting driver backs off in mid-corner. The best technique is to squeeze on a bit of power in corners. Other than this, the handling is well-suited to modern roads. The 4:11 rear end is a bit short for quiet high-speed touring; at 60mph the engine turns at about 3200rpm.

If you want a 300SL as a usable road car, drive one on a hot day for a long distance before deciding. A 300SL "roaster" probably won't overheat the engine, but it may overheat the passengers. Engine heat seems to enter either the Coupe or the Roadster everywhere. The cars didn't do this when new; the problem may be caused by heater valves that don't close completely or by missing or deteriorated insulation. A few owners had air conditioning fitted, by dealers or others, but it was not a factory option.

to the public; no W194 cars are known to exist in private hands with all-original bodywork, but at least two are unaccounted for.

Production 300SL ★★★★

The production 300SL Coupe introduced in 1954 was a street version of the W194 300SL racing cars. DBAG at first hesitated to build it, but in response to demand sensed by US importer Max Hoffman and others, the 300SL premiered at the International Motor Sports Show in New York in 1954. Fittingly, about three-quarters of all new 300SLs were sold in the United States.

This was one production car that made more power than its racing predecessor. With the newly developed Bosch direct-port, mechanical fuel injection, the W198 engine gave 215hp DIN at 5700rpm and 213lb-ft of torque at 4500rpm. The electrical system was 12volt, with its generator cleverly linked to drive the water pump, too.

Production bodies had eyebrows over the wheel openings, and larger doors eased entry and

300SL Production and Chassis Prefix Numbers

Years	Model	Production	Chassis prefix
1952–1953	300SL (racing)	10-11	194010
1954–1957	300SL (production Coupe)	1,374	198040
1955–1956	300SL (aluminum Coupe)	29	198043
1957–1964	300SL Roadster	1,858	198042

Chassis type: 198
Engine type: 198
Typical chassis numbers: 1980404500057 (Coupe); 1980427500694 (early Roadster); 19804210003168 (late Roadster)

Technical Specifications

Model	300SL	300SL Roadster
Years	1953–1957	1957–1963
Engine		
Type	Inline ohc six (all)	
Engine # prefix	M198 (all)	
Displacement	2996cc (all)	
Bore x stroke	85x88mm (all)	
Compression ratio	8.55:1 (all)	
DIN horsepower	215hp @ 5800rpm	235hp (approx.)
Torque	28mkg @ 4600rpm (all)	
Fuel system	Bosch six-plunger mechanical fuel injection (all)	
Fuel required	Premium (all)	
Coolant capacity	27qt	21qt
Chassis		
Type	Multi-tubular; steel body, aluminum doors, engine lid, trunk lid, rocker panels (all)	
Chassis # prefix	W198I	W198II
Transmission	4-speed manual (all)	
Rear-axle ratio	3.64:1 (options: 3.25, 3.42, 3.89, 4.11:1)	
Rear suspension	Swing-axle, coil springs	Low-pivot swing-axle, coil springs
Front suspension	A-arms, coil springs (all)	
Wheels	5x15in	5.5x15in
Tires	6.50x15in	6.70x15in
Brakes	Alfin drum	Alfin drum Dunlop disc (March 1961)
Fuel capacity	34.3gal	26.4gal
Weight	2,888lb	3,130lb; 3,219lb w/hardtop
Performance		
0-60mph	8–9sec (all)	
Top speed	146–161mph	137–155mph
Fuel consumption	15–20mpg hwy (all)	

To fit beneath the low hood and lower the 300SL's center of gravity, the engine was tilted 50degrees to the left. *Alex Dearborn*

exit. Because the doors opened upward, the Coupe was soon nicknamed the Gullwing. The factory called it neither a Coupe nor a Gullwing, just "300SL", but the nickname stuck. The main body was steel, with the large rocker panels, hood, trunk, and doors being aluminum. Exceptions were the twenty-nine all-aluminum-bodied cars produced in 1955 and 1956, about 175lb lighter than the steel-bodied Coupes.

The first production Coupes, built in early 1954, had a few features different from later cars. Their long, bent shift levers entered the floor ahead of the dashboard; later cars moved the lever back on the tunnel. Early cars also used Treadle-Vac brake boosters instead of the later ATE T-50 unit and had fender welting between eyebrows and fenders. Instead of the later Mercedes-Benz box, ZF steering went on the first 151 cars.

The 300SL was the first production car to use gasoline fuel injection, with a six-plunger mechanical pump forcing gasoline directly into its cylinders. Unusual even now, the dry-sump oil system used pumps to scavenge oil from the crankcase,

This 300SL Roadster has European headlights. From the Coupe, the gas filler was moved from inside the trunk to the left rear fender; windows now roll up; taillights are larger. Jack hole in rocker panel did not have a cover. *DBAG*

The optional removable hardtop made the 300SL Roadster into an all-weather car. *DBAG*

run it through a cooler, dump it into a tank, then pump it back into the engine. This ensured an oil supply uninterrupted by cornering forces.

The engine's 50degree tilt was necessary to fit the inline unit under the low hood. The block-head joint is angled to level it, so the combustion chamber extends beyond the head into round pockets in the block. Although the engine is related to that of the contemporary 300 models, it is not even close to being interchangeable.

A four-speed, fully synchronized transmission feeds power through a ZF limited-slip differential; rear-axle ratios were 4.11:1, 3.89:1 (standard on US cars), 3.64:1 (standard on European cars), 3.42:1, and 3.25:1. Depending upon gearing, a 300SL can reach 60mph in about 8 seconds and go on to 150mph or more. Much of the coil-spring suspension was adapted from the sedan. Brakes were specially developed finned drums with linings over 3.5in wide; the ATE T-50 vacuum booster is similar to that of the sedans. At 2849lb, the 300SL Coupe's power-to-weight ratio is almost the same as that of the heavier but more powerful 1994 600SL (11.85lb/hp vs. 11.45lb/hp).

The 300SL Roadster's US headlights, as shown here, differed from the glass-covered European units. *Dennis Adler*

Gullwing Spotter's Guide

Chassis numbers are on a plate riveted to the driver's side firewall, and, consistent with Mercedes-Benz practice, on the left front frame rail below the engine. Below the plate on the firewall is a smaller plate with the paint color code, a two- or three-digit number ending in "G" or "H." Standard colors were: 040 black; 050 white; 158 white gray; 166 blue gray; 180 silver gray; 190 graphite gray; 334 light blue; 534 fire engine red; 543 strawberry metallic; and 608 ivory.

Interiors were available in MB-tex combined with plaid wool. The plaid fabric was either blue (as in the factory racing cars), red, or green. This plaid appeared only on the seat facings, presumably for better grip while cornering and for better breathing. Full leather was optional, available in red, tan, beige, dark blue, gray-blue, light gray, black, green, or white. These colors were from the Mercedes-Benz family palette, but the hides were heavier than those in the sedans and quite smooth in texture.

Other Coupe options included fitted luggage (replicas are available), bumper guards, chrome wheels, windshield washers, Rudge knock-off wheels and hubs, the rear-axle ratio, a sport cam, stiffer springs and shock absorbers, a Becker Mexico radio, a Becker short-wave adapter, a cold weather radiator blind, and a spare parts travel kit. Not all were available in any one year, and some cars were built with custom touches for special customers, mostly involving exterior color and interior trim.

Headliners, gray or beige fuzzy cotton, extend down to the windowsills. A chrome luggage rail runs around the area behind the seats, where the luggage fit (the trunk was filled by the thirty-four-gallon fuel tank and a spare tire). In this luggage area was an access door for the battery. Floors got square-weave carpeting on the tunnel and trunk floor. The two footwells had ribbed rubber mats.

The outside door handles are unique; push in at the back, and a flush-mounted lever appears out of the slot. The lightweight doors are supported by spring cylinders. Originality buffs look for a concave star in the center of the grille instead of the later flat star. The concave original was phased out as a spare part; many restored cars have a flat one, which looks fine, so the difference is only for cocktail party discussions or a tie-breaker at concours events.

Bumper guards were standard, but many have been removed for a cleaner look. Certain European-delivery cars likely had no guards. The jacking hole in each rocker panel never had a plug.

Roadster interior and dash were developed from the Coupe. The radio mounts below the dash.
Dennis Adler

The 300SL's wheels were light-alloy 5x15in rims with either Rudge knock-off centers or bolt-on steel wheels. Rudge wheels, which add value, had either painted or chromed centers; with the latter, the rims were polished aluminum. Bolt-on wheels had a painted hubcaps and either painted or polished rims. Rudge wheels were unavailable with disc brakes. Putting knock-off wheels on a car that originally had bolt-on wheels is not simple, requiring changing front hubs and rear axles, but Rudge wheels were often retrofitted.

Alloy-Bodied Cars ★★★★★

The twenty-nine aluminum-bodied Coupes had Rudge wheels, plaid seat covers, plexiglass windows, and "NSL" engines. They were said to have been made as customer racers to help amateurs win production-car races and rallies.

The NSL engines were simply the best-running of a batch. They were dynamometer-tested then fitted with a sport cam, worth perhaps 20hp. The letters "NSL" appear on a small boss near the cam cover on engines so equipped. Since the standard engine can be blueprinted at rebuild time then fitted with the Roadster cam, the same as the sport cam, there is little value in an NSL engine.

Production 300SLs did well in competition, mostly on an amateur basis, but by the late 1950s they were outmoded by lighter, more purpose-built race cars. Production stopped in 1957 with about 1,400 made, and the Roadster took over.

300SL Roadster ★★★★

The 300SL Roadster that replaced the 300SL (Coupe) in 1957 was more refined, less of a racer. Doors opened conventionally, so access was easier, and since the side windows rolled down instead of popping out, ventilation improved.

Despite its snug-fitting soft top and roll-up windows, this car was known as the 300SL Road-

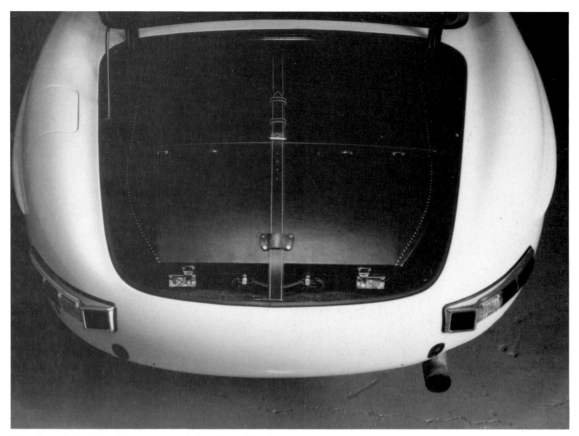

The Roadster trunk accommodates two fitted suitcases. *Paul Russell*

ster. First it was sold with only a Convertible top, but for 1958 and beyond, it was available with either a soft top, a hardtop, or both. The hardtop didn't fit over the soft top, so either the soft top's metal boot or the hardtop had to be left at home. Check that these parts are included with the car. Among the few other Roadster options were fitted luggage and a white or black steering wheel.

The Roadster's multi-tube space frame was similar to that of the Coupe but with lower doorsills. Its engine was basically that of the Coupe but with the sport cam. Wheelbase was the same, but rear overhang was longer; fuel capacity was reduced to 22 gallons, creating more trunk space. The fuel filler moved from inside the trunk to the left rear fender, and the Roadster's side trim was a bit more elaborate.

One could see which rear-axle ratio was fitted by looking down into the lower edge of the Roadster speedometer for the numbers. A 3.64:1 ratio was standard on US models.

The Roadster's low-pivot rear swing-axle reduced jacking and camber change, and therefore, oversteer. A horizontal compensating spring softened the ride, too. The transmission whine and the ratchety limited-slip differential action familiar in the Coupe were gone. Weight was up, offsetting the power improvement.

The Roadster offered more subtle improvements over the Coupe. Taillights, for instance, are larger, for better visibility. Headlight units incorporate turn signals and parking lights in one-piece housings. European Roadsters used a sleek glass headlight cover, but US cars simply had chrome trim around both lights. The revised instrument panel uses a vertical combination gauge instead of the Coupe's round dials.

Rudge knock-off wheels were optional on 1957–1958 Roadsters. The Alfin drum brakes were improved for 1960, and then replaced in March 1961 by four-wheel Dunlop-licensed discs, although the drums

The 300SL requires no unusual preparation to become a good vintage racer, and can easily be driven to and from the track. *FDB*

were always more than adequate for stopping the car.

For 1962, DBAG phased-in aluminum engine blocks, which looked identical to the iron blocks and had the same specifications. The aluminum engine is identified by an engine number beginning with 198 982. These engines were deemed "unrebuildable at the dealership level" by the factory, and factory bulletins suggested that worn engines be traded for new ones at dealerships.

This exchange system authorized new aluminum blocks to be re-marked with the original engine's number, although this wasn't always done. To further confound numbers fanatics, a customer could trade his worn iron-block Coupe or Roadster engine at a dealership. Since 300SLs chassis and engine numbers never matched, such an exchange is no deterrent to buying a car with any proper 300SL engine. A dealer's invoice for replacement gives a replacement engine the same value as an original.

Although official production ceased in 1963, the final 300SLs were three Roadsters built in 1964. By then the 300SL was twice the price of the Jaguar E-Type yet slower. The unibody sports car was about to appear. With 1,858 300SL Roadsters built, production ended, and the 230SL took over as the sporting Mercedes-Benz.

What to Look For

Look for the usual rust and bondo, especially in the headlight and grille area. The aluminum rocker panels unbolt and are still available, so if they are hopelessly full of filler or dents, they can be replaced. There is no exposed frame for a floor jack, so insert the factory jack through the rocker panel into the jacking hole. The Coupes removable, louvered, aluminum belly pans were often misplaced during mechanical work, but reproductions are available. Rust occurs in the headlight buckets, the sheet metal behind the rear wheels, and the rear roof posts of the Coupe.

The frame is unlikely to rust, but any corrosion will be hard to repair, requiring a proper frame jig. Coupe doors were built and fitted with quality. In spite of hinges in the roof, they should open and close precisely and fit snugly all around. Look for cracked paint in the roof around the hinges as a sign of prior damage.

Under the hood, check oil quality by smelling for gasoline. Oil diluted by gasoline won't lubricate well. The fuel injection system may leak gas into the oil, and the oil seldom gets hot enough to evaporate it. The oil tank is in the engine bay, behind the left wheel. The cap has the dipstick attached. Its bottom line indicates the twelve-quart level; the top mark is for eighteen. If the oil cooler is connected, this large quantity never gets hot, so savvy owners bypass the cooler for normal driving. Oil pressure should be 65–75psi at speed and at least 20psi at warm idle.

Although some have been polished, the intake manifold was originally a bare metal casting, and the valve cover was painted black.

The engine should run smoothly and strongly. Set up by a knowledgeable mechanic, these cars need minimum tuning. Only three reasons exist for poor running: (1) the car was tuned by someone unfamiliar with the specs; (2) the gasoline has gone stale and/or the fuel system is clogged; or (3) it's just plain worn out. The fuel injection system can deteriorate if the car has not been driven regularly. A separate, driver-controlled electric fuel pump helps to overcome vapor lock.

Restoration

Although you might think that by now few 300SLs exist in seedy enough condition to need restoration, forgotten examples continue to surface. Restoration standards rise, too, boosting cost. Excellent professional restorers of the 300SL can be counted on the fingers of two hands, so at least you have some choice. To reduce costs, mechanically inclined owners use the pros for high-skill jobs (bodywork, paint, interiors, engine overhauls) and do the disassembly and reassembly themselves.

Few parts are truly difficult to obtain. Most mechanical parts remain available from factory and aftermarket sources. Mercedes-Benz kept many parts in production and is reviving others in a vintage parts program. The Gull Wing Group has contracted for the manufacture of some crucial parts, and their technical literature is useful.

Summary

The 300SL is the most popular Mercedes-Benz collector car and will remain so. Professionals with the skills to restore and maintain the cars make ownership relatively easy, even for those not mechanically inclined. The big hurdle is the initial purchase, but handle that successfully, and you'll never look back.

No trailer queen, a 300SL can be a dependable, appealing driver, a car that you can enjoy using, even hard. The car's few quirks give it character. The 300SL will forever be seen as one of the finest products of Mercedes-Benz.

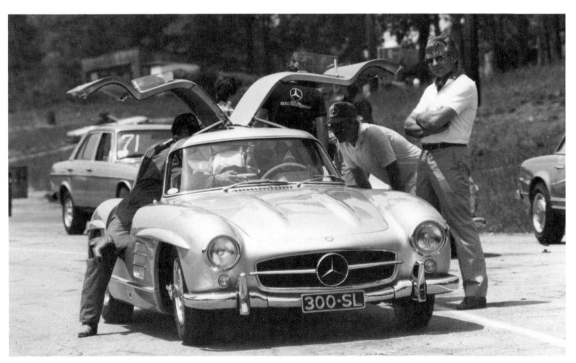

Easily the most recognized Mercedes-Benz collector car, the 300SL is supported by an active international owners group that even helps to supply rare parts. *FDB*

Chapter 9

190SL 1955–1963

The 300SL tempted only those able to afford it. The 190SL was a lower-priced sports car with broader allure. In styling the 190SL emulated the 300SL, but otherwise it was a shadow of its senior. Unlike the tube-frame 300SL Coupe and Roadster, the unit-body 190SL was solely a Roadster (more on that later). Its simpler, less energetic engine was DBAG's first overhead-cam four, similar to engines in the 180 and 190 sedans.

Origins

A prototype 190SL with "racing" accessories made its US debut alongside the 300SL at the New York Auto Show in February 1954, but the assembly line didn't roll until May 1955. The 190SL set the stage for future SL models, particularly in America, proving to DBAG that its future sports cars would be more successful if they were designed for the boulevard rather than for the racetrack. A total of 25,881 were built until February 1963, when the all-new, six-cylinder 230SL took over.

In comparison to its peers, the 190SL was a sophisticated sports car. Its top didn't leak, it was comfortable, quiet, dependable, warm in the winter, and everything worked all of the time. The 190SL could be serviced painlessly, and parts arrived with dispatch.

Some consider the 190SL fairly dull. It enjoyed only a minuscule competition career—it was heavy

The removable 190SL hardtop's rounded shape, reminiscent of earlier Mercedes-Benz Coupes, is well integrated with the rest of the car. Chrome trim on fender strakes and rocker panel indicates that this is a 1956 or later car. *DBAG*

Soft top folded, this 190SL clearly shows the vertical seams in the rocker panel. European headlights are non-sealed-beam. Unusually, hubcaps are unpainted; perhaps the DBAG press office was in a big hurry to shoot this picture. *DBAG*

Early 190SL lacks chrome trim on fenders and rocker panel but has small-window hardtop, sedanstyle hubcaps, and an unusual ski rack. *DBAG*

The four-cylinder 190SL engine is almost surrounded by an elaborate induction system; vacuum brake booster is at right. *FDB*

Prototype 190SL was first shown with cut-down doors, hood scoop, racing windshield, and other features. *DBAG*

This 1957 190SL has US headlights and bumper guards. *FDB*

and lacked tuning potential. The 1.9 liter, four-cylinder engine has only three main bearings, so souping it up was risky. Judson sold a supercharger for the 190SL, but most who installed them found cause to regret it. The only factory competition venture with the 190SL used a diesel engine, to set a standing-start, one-kilometer record of 61.3mph.

No 190SL history would be complete without the obligatory reference to one John Moore and his 190SL, winners of the Islander Race at the 1957 Nassau Speed Weeks. They beat a Jaguar, an Austin-Healey, and a Triumph TR-2, no less. Fame may be fleeting, but John lives on in the hearts of 190SL devotees.

The first unit-body SL from Mercedes-Benz, the 190SL used a steel chassis with aluminum doors, trunk lid, engine hood, dash, and a few other parts. It still weighed nearly 2600lb, light today, but leaden for a 1950s sports car. A Porsche Speedster weighed nearly 800lb less.

A subframe holds the front suspension and engine, and the entire assembly can be unbolted

and rolled out from under the car, but few actually do so. The subframe mounts, similar to engine mounts, must be in good condition. At the rear is a swing-axle, with coil springs fitted all around. The aluminum brake drums were cast with fins for cooling, and an ATE T-50 vacuum brake booster was fitted to all but a few early cars.

Nit-pickers will tell you that the 190SL was sold as a Roadster (with soft top only, chassis number 121.042...) or a Coupe (with hardtop only, chassis number 121.040...), but rarely are they described that way. Most were built as Roadsters and sold with the optional hardtop. Coupes are basically the same, with minor differences relating to the tops. Most people call the car a 190SL and leave it at that.

190SL ★★★

The 190SL experienced myriad running changes throughout its life. The most, over 100, occurred for the 1956 model year, at or near chassis number 01115. After that, chrome-plated trim was added on the fender moldings above the wheelwells, on the rocker panels, and as stone guards in front of each rear wheel, along with a glovebox door lock.

Hardtops came in two types. Early ones had a small rear window, late ones a much larger one, changing in September 1959 at chassis number 121.040.95.015061. For better visibility, most prefer the late version, which fits any 190SL. Most US-delivered cars had front bumper guards. Chrome-plated headlight rims should carry an engraved Bosch or Hella logo. The red rear reflectors, moved from below the bumper upward to the body for 1958 and later cars sold in the United States, are often missing.

Most 190SLs were powered by engine type 121.921, but in mid-1961 an improved 121.928 version appeared. Besides its 1mm larger diameter wrist pin, an 8.7:1 compression ratio, and a slightly different timing chain, the later engine changed camshaft lubrication from internal to external and had a slightly different valve adjustment arrangement. A variety of Bosch distributors used one-piece points until mid-1962, two-piece later. Early engines used knurled knobs to fasten the valve cover; late ones used hex-head bolts. To compensate for varying fuel quality, ignition timing was adjustable via a knurled knob on the distributor base; early cars had a cable leading to a knob on the dash. A three-point engine mounting system was used until 1956, when it was replaced with a four-point system.

Early seats were similar to the 300SL buckets, but in 1956 a wider, more padded style was installed, with pivoting backrests for package area access. Upholstery was usually vinyl (MB-tex), with leather and a transverse rear jump seat optional. Other options included skid plates, right-side sun visor, fog lights, heavy-duty springs, and a wind-up clock in the glovebox door (late 1956 onward). Also offered were an automatic antenna, a short-wave adapter, various horns, undercoating, radiator shutters, and heavy-duty cooling and suspension systems for "tropical" use.

Until mid-1957, a rotating horn ring operated the turn signals. During 1958 production a steering lock was first fitted. Original radios included Becker, Telefunken, and Grundig. Some post-1958 Becker Mexicos, the grandest, had a signal-seeking feature. Technically, dealer-installed air conditioning was an option, but we've never seen it.

One of the rarest options is the fitted luggage by Karl Baisch or Hepco (replica pieces are available). Three pieces fit the trunk, while two more rest behind the seats. Most of these suitcases had a vinyl fabric covering, but matching leather is not unknown. Even more rare would be a set of cut-down doors and a low windshield, factory-modified for racing. In thirty years, we've never seen these in original form, so maybe they exist only in the imagination of a few.

Floors were covered by rubber mats, with carpets in the rear. The first trunk handle combined a finger lift and the lock, but after chassis number 018346, handle and lock were separate. In 1956 the small taillight lenses were replaced by larger ones similar to those on the sedans. In 1957 the license plate lights moved from the body to the bumper guards. During 1958 the front parking lights switched to a three-prong, twist-in lens. If only one back-up light works, don't fret. That's how it was designed.

A floorshift controls the four-speed manual transmission; shift knobs were threaded on until sometime in 1958, when DBAG switched to a push-on type. Various windshield washing systems were fitted—hand pump, foot pump, and a few electric pumps—with various styles of washer bags. For 1957 production the nozzle was moved from the cowl to the hood.

The 190SL's bias-ply tires were small, 6.40x13 on 5in wheels; whitewalls were optional. Hubcap centers were painted body color and set off by a larger, separate trim ring. Early cars had a 3.70:1 rear axle; to aid acceleration, later ones used 3.90:1, and 4.10:1 was an option. With a redline of 6000rpm, top speed was about 105mph, and 0–60mph took about 13 seconds.

Driving Impressions: 190SL

The 190SL is an automotive sheep in wolf's clothing. Granted, a faithful and sturdy sheep in a sleek and elegant wolf suit, but its resemblance to the 300SL is strictly skin deep. Standing still, the 190SL was styled to look almost as fast as a 300SL. On the move, reality is less exciting. If you're buying an SL to drive, remember that about the same amount of money buys you a better road car in the later 230, 250, or 280SL—or even in a 350 or 450SL from the 1970s.

Despite its tendency to be used as a show car and a conversation piece rather than a long-distance driver or an autocrosser, a 190SL can be driven comfortably on interstates. The independent suspension works admirably, and the seats offer good support for a car of the era. The 190SL has no major vices; it just suffers from being slow. In compensation, the top goes down, allowing the exhilaration of topless motoring.

The 190SL's drum brakes require proper maintenance to work optimally. The ATE vacuum booster reduces pedal pressure (and feel). It's also prone to vacuum leaks, which result in increased pedal pressure.

What to Look For

Rust.

Starting at the front, look carefully at the grille and front bumper. How do they fit against the surrounding sheet metal? Front sheet-metal damage is common on 190SLs. Is there evidence of accident repair? Does everything fit together neatly, without unusual gaps, either between panels or from bumper to

Technical Specifications

Model	190SL
Years	1955–1963
Engine	
Type	Inline ohc four; three main bearings
Engine # prefix	M121BII
Displacement	1897cc
Bore x stroke	85x83.6mm
Compression ratio	8.5:1; after September 1959 (engine #65.03804) 8.8:1; 8.7:1 with 121.928 engine (summer 1961 and later)
DIN horsepower	105hp @ 5700rpm (120hp SAE)
Torque	14.5mkg @ 3200rpm (105lb-ft)
Fuel system	Dual Solex 44 PHH carburetors
Fuel required	Premium
Coolant capacity	10.5qt
Chassis	
Type	Steel unibody, aluminum doors, engine lid, trunk lid, and so on
Chassis # prefix	W121
Transmission	4-speed manual
Rear-axle ratio	3.90:1 (3.70:1 early, 4.10:1 option)
Rear suspension	Low-pivot swing-axle, coil springs
Front suspension	A-arms, coil springs
Wheels	5x13in
Tires	6.40x13in
Brakes	Alfin drum, vacuum booster
Fuel capacity	17gal
Weight	2,557lb, plus 44lb hardtop
Performance	
0-60mph	13–14sec
Top speed	106mph
Fuel consumption	19–25mpg

ID Numbers
Chassis type: 121
Engine type: 121
Typical chassis numbers: Roadster (soft top only) 121.042; Coupe (hardtop only) 121.040

Production

Years	Model	Production
1955–1963	190SL	25,881

fender, or different contours on each side? Remove the headlights and look inside their buckets for rust or evidence of repair (overspray, primer, and so on).

How does the engine hood fit? Is the gap even all around? Does the hood contour match the surrounding panels? In the rocker panel, behind each door, a vertical seam should be visible. If not, someone has covered it with bondo. How do the doors fit? Are the gaps even, or do the doors sag?

As you jack up the car, be careful. Jackpoints at either side frequently rust so much that they crumble when the factory jack is used. More seriously, the rear suspension is located by trailing arms that run forward and mount to the floor pan. These mountings often rust, loosening the arms. You can buy re-production floor pans and weld them in and install new bushings for the trailing arm mounts, but it's no weekend job. Make sure the chassis is solid around the top mounting of the rear coil springs.

Look for leaky axle boots, transmission seals, brake cylinders, and shock absorbers. Does the car sag on collapsed springs? Are any shock absorbers seized? Has any of the floor pan been replaced, or will it need to be? The floor pan should have pressed-in stiffening indentations; if the metal is flat, it's probably a replacement. The 190SL uses wooden floorboards; water can collect under them and rust the floors.

The box sections at the outer edges of the floors are notable for internal rust. The wheelwell "eyebrows" are equally susceptible to rust and to poor repairs, usually with body filler instead of new metal. Look for rust in the lip under the trunk seal and around the trunk floor.

Bumpers on an unrestored car may be dented and bent. Bumper parts are expensive to repair and replate properly. It's not unusual for a complete bumper to run into the thousands of dollars.

Check the engine number carefully. It's easy to substitute a sedan engine. The number should begin with 121.921 or 121.928; the change fell in mid-1961. The compression ratio is cast into the head, either at the rear or on the left side, above the coolant outlet. In 1959 the compression ratio changed from 8.5:1 to 8.8:1. The 121.928 engine's ratio was 8.7:1. You probably won't find the trouble light that plugs into the socket near the fuse box.

What carburetors are fitted? The 190SL originally had two side-draft, dual-throat Solex 44 PHH carburetors that dwarfed the engine in size and complexity. These heavy carburetors had a large, cast metal air intake box hung way out to the right and braced from below. The metal brace is difficult to reinstall, so some people just left it off, which stressed the manifold and often led to air leaks at its gasketed block joint. Correctly adjusted, Solexes should allow a smooth, even idle and acceleration, even from low rpm, without hesitation.

Many owners gave up trying to keep the Solexes synchronized and in tune. These carburetors depend upon vacuum to open the second barrel, so vacuum leaks, age, and other variables (temperature, humidity, barometric pressure) can upset them. Throttle shafts wear into the carburetor body, making a smooth idle difficult to obtain. Thus, you may see the less fussy Weber 40 DCOE or others in their place. If you're planning to just drive the car, this is fine, but if you'll show it seriously, the original Solexes will improve your score. With time, patient effort, and an overhaul kit, they can work properly. On the other hand, Webers are easier to tune, hold a tune longer, and make the car perform a little better. Take your choice.

Pressed cardboard heater ducts along both sides of the engine compartment were easily damaged. Fiberglass reproductions are available, but they are an obvious replacement. Cable-controlled by dash levers, the brass valves atop these air ducts direct coolant through heat exchangers in the ducts. Unless exercised, these valves corrode and seize. Look for corrosion under the battery and the brake booster.

To test the brake booster, find a hill on a lightly traveled road. Starting from the top, push in the clutch and let the engine idle as you descend at a reasonable speed. Use the brakes several times.

They should work with the same effort for several applications. If the system is losing vacuum, pedal effort will increase as it leaks. Bringing the engine up to normal operating rpm should restore the vacuum and ease pedal pressure again. Leaky brake boosters can be rebuilt.

The 190SL interior should be either all-vinyl or all-leather. Replacement leather is often thinner and softer than the original surface-dyed material, usually supplied by the German firm of Roser. Doorsill and transmission tunnel rubber mats are tough to find, so check their condition. If hard, they can be softened with a vinyl treatment such as Armorall, but tears are tough to hide.

Is the car complete? Some trim parts such as bumpers are extremely expensive to replace. While driving, watch the temperature gauge for signs of overheating.

Restoration

The 190SL has proven popular to restore. A cottage industry has grown up around 190SL restoration, furnishing nearly all of the necessary parts and services.

The 190SL's worst enemy over the years has been rust. Its steel body was never well protected when new, and corrosion is time-consuming to repair properly on any unit-body car. Most steel panels remain available, either from the factory or as reproductions. Unfortunately, these must be properly fitted and welded rather than simply bolted on. Every part that rusts (floor pan, fenders, inner panels) requires extensive labor.

Do you want a nice street car or a show winner? To avoid wasted time and money, decide before work starts. Will you use the car as a driver or show it? Can you do the work yourself? Will you choose a local shop or a top-notch Mercedes-Benz restorer? These cars are not simple, so a proper restoration can easily exceed a finished car's value.

The mechanical aspects of restoration are relatively simple. Any restoration shop that does much Mercedes-Benz work has probably restored several 190SLs. Ask the shop for names of references with similar cars, then contact them.

Summary

The 190SL's appeal is based largely on its superficial resemblance to the more sophisticated 300SL. Judged on its own merits, it's actually prettier than a 300SL. The simpler 190SL is easily attainable and practical for the average owner.

The restoration industry supports the 190SL well, and you'll have plenty of fellow owners to chat with. The 190SL is tractable, dependable, even economical, and those who see it and own it love it.

As a show car or as an enjoyable driver, the 190SL's popularity is enduring. *FDB*

The 190SL dash is quite simple; optional clock is not easy to find. *FDB*

Chapter 10

230, 250, and 280SL 1963–1971

The 230, 250, and 280SL models are for enthusiasts who want to use their collector sports car for pleasure *and* for practical pursuits. These cars can be shown on Sunday, then driven to work on Monday. Straightforward to maintain, sufficient numbers were built so that parts as well as expert mechanics and restorers will remain in good supply well into the future.

Origins

The angular 230SL succeeded two traditional 1950s sports models, the 190SL and the 300SL. It constituted an unusually fortunate compromise which still works for those who want to drive their SL or those who wish to show the car. The 230, 250, and 280SL models are uniquely styled yet thoroughly practical two-seaters. They are more advanced, more powerful, better handling, more comfortable, safer, easier to maintain, and more fun to drive than the 190SL—for about the same price on today's market.

The three models, known collectively by the 113 chassis designation, are renowned for their totally fresh look. The crisp, pagoda-roof styling has endured well, and the cars look equally attractive with the soft top folded beneath their flush metal deck. The only postwar Mercedes-Benz produc-

The 230SL, 250SL, and 280SLs are nearly identical; this 280SL has the US-mandated side reflectors, no trim beneath the license plate (as per the 230SL and 250SL), and flat hubcaps. *FDB*

tion cars styled outside the company, by Paul Bracq, the cars made their debut at the March 1963 Geneva Auto Show and became instantly popular as grand touring sports cars.

The 230, 250, and 280SLs had no significant competition career, beyond Eugen Bohringer's win in the Liège-Sofia-Liège Rally, but competition was not the point. It proved far more significant that the cars were the first Mercedes-Benz sports cars to be available with factory-installed air conditioning and an automatic transmission. The purists fumed, but the cars sold well.

230SL, 250SL, and 280SL ★★★

The 230SL emerged as a 1963 model, and despite a plethora of mechanical improvements and interior updates, this SL's W113 unit-body chassis changed only slightly until the last 280SL left the factory in March 1971.

All three models used an inline overhead-cam six, similar to those in contemporary Mercedes-Benz sedans. The 230SL used the trusty M127 II, making 150hp DIN (170hp SAE)—midway between the 190SL's 105hp DIN and the 300SL's 215hp DIN. The 250SL used a new M129 engine with seven main bearings (up from four in the 230SL) and higher coolant capacity. Besides a 10 percent boost in torque, the 250SL made 10 more horsepower—160 DIN. The 250's oil cooler used coolant as a medium; the 280's used air. To improve cooling ability, the 280SL's improved M130 engine differed in cylinder spacing. Thanks to higher compression and a few other changes, and despite its new emission controls, the US-version 280SL made 170hp DIN (195hp SAE) and another 10 percent more torque. All engines had Bosch mechanical fuel injection.

All three SLs also used disc brakes at the front

Technical Specifications

Model	230SL	250SL	280SL
Years	1963–1966	1966–1968	1968–1971
Engine			
Type	Inline ohc six (all)		
Engine # prefix	127.981	129.982	130.983
Displacement	2281cc (139.2ci)	2496cc (152.3ci)	2778cc (169.5ci)
Bore x stroke	82x72.8mm	82x78.8mm	86.5x78.8mm
Compression ratio	9.3:1	9.5:1	9.5:1
DIN horsepower	150hp @ 5500rpm	160hp @ 5500rpm	170hp @ 5750rpm
Torque	20mkg @ 4200rpm	22mkg @ 4200rpm	24.5mkg @ 4250rpm
Fuel system	Bosch six-plunger mechanical fuel injection (all)		
Fuel required	Premium (all)		
Chassis			
Type	Unibody; steel with aluminum doors, engine lid, trunklid, tonneau		
Chassis # prefix	113.042	113.043	113.044
Transmission	4-speed manual or 4-speed automatic (280SL 5-speed manual rare)		
Rear-axle ratio	3.75:1	3.69:1	4.08:1 (Europe: 3.92:1, 3.69)
Rear suspension	Swing-axle, coil springs (all)		
Front suspension	Strut, coil springs (all)		
Wheels	Steel, 5.5x14in	6x14in	6x14in
Tires	185HR14 (all)		
Brakes	F disc, R drum	F&R disc	F&R disc
Fuel capacity	17.2gal	21.7gal	21.7gal
Weight	2,866lb	2,998lb	2,998lb
	(add 176lb for hardtop, 88lb for automatic transmission)		
Performance			
0-60mph	11sec (13 auto)	12sec (13auto)	11sec (12 auto)
Top speed	124mph (121 auto)	121mph (118 auto)	124mph (121 auto)
Fuel consumption	16mpg (15 auto)	15mpg (14 auto)	14mpg (13 auto)

Production

Years	Model	Production
1963–1967	230SL	19,831
1966–1968	250SL	5,196
1967–1971	280SL	23,885

(Girling on the 230, ATE on the 250 and 280), and when the 250SL appeared, discs replaced the 230SL's finned aluminum rear drums. Brakes are vacuum-assisted and operate on dual circuits for safety. The 230SL was the first SL to be introduced with radial tires, and much was made of its wide track, 8in wider than the Jaguar E-Type.

Visual clues to the 230SL in the engine compartment include the flat radiator expansion tank; the 250SL and 280SL have cylindrical tanks. Only 230SLs and early 250SLs had rubber covers over the subframe mounts.

All 230, 250, and 280SLs could be bought with a four-speed manual or a four-speed automatic transmission. In 1969, a ZF five-speed manual was first offered as an option, but is extremely rare. The 250 and 280SL have a 21.6 gallon fuel tank, up from 17.1 in the 230SL. The 280SL has a self-adjusting clutch and a hydraulic rear compensator above the rear swing-axle instead of the compensating spring used on the earlier cars.

In March 1966, the 250SL took over from the 230SL; 5,196 were built before January 1968, when 280SL production began. By then the car had evolved more toward luxurious touring than sport-

ing use. Sixty percent of 230SLs had manual transmissions, and air conditioning was then unavailable. A 280SL was far more likely to have an automatic transmission—and Frigiking air conditioning.

Because the SL's weight increased along with power, performance changed little throughout the series, although the added displacement made the 280SL more flexible. Today's performance depends more on the condition and tune of a given engine than on which model you're driving.

One subtle model designation deserves mention. The 230/250/280SL could be bought new with a soft top, a metal hardtop, or both. With the soft top only, the car was sometimes called a Roadster. With the hardtop only, a Coupe. With both, it was infrequently referred to as a Coupe-Roadster or even a Roadster-Coupe. Just call it an SL.

Major options included the soft top and hardtop, a transverse rear bench seat, manual or automatic transmission, power steering (optional on 230SLs, standard on late US 280SLs), air conditioning, leather interior, whitewall tires, bumper guards, various radios, and more. Rare options include fitted luggage, a hardtop with a sunroof (very rare), ski and luggage racks, different rear-

Upon its introduction as a 1963 model, the 230SL, here with European headlights and hard-top in place, was immediately recognized for its styling and handling abilities. *DBAG*

axle ratios, and the ZF five-speed transmission. Rubber mats covered the floors of the 230 and 250SL, but the 280SL had carpet. The 280SL lacked the horizontal trim strip below the 230 and 250SL license plate. New safety requirements for 1968 models meant changes in control knobs, logos, and exterior lights.

All three SLs originally had steel wheels and hubcaps, the 230 and 250 with a small center cap with a separate chrome-plated trim ring, the 280 with larger and flatter one-piece cap over the entire wheel. In 1968, wheels were widened from 5.5 to 6.0in. Hubcaps were painted in hardtop color. If the hubcaps are unpainted, they're probably replacements, which came that way. The early 230SL spare tire stands upright; others lie nearly flat and take up more trunk space.

Many owners have fitted Mercedes-Benz alloy wheels, usually 6x14in. Introduced in late 1969, these wheels are technically correct only for late 280SLs, which could have had them dealer-installed or as a special option. The car looks handsome with them, so many owners forego originality in favor of personal preference.

Minor changes were blended into production as they were needed and developed. To satisfy US safety regulations, the 1968 250SL had side reflectors, and 280SLs had lights in these units. From 1963 to 1971 nearly 100 running changes can be documented. For a list, see *Vintage Reprint # 1, The 230/250/280SL*, available through the Mercedes-Benz Club of America. For color and interior samples, see the Mercedes-Benz *Refinishing Manual*, circulated to dealers by Mercedes-Benz of North America. It goes back to 1963.

European versions often found their way across the Atlantic. Because the law didn't require it, few pre-1967 European cars were converted to US specifications. Apart from their chassis numbers, they are usually distinguished by metric instruments and their one-piece, glass headlight covers.

Which is best for you, the 230, 250 or 280SL? The last of a series usually seems more desirable to collectors, and the more numerous (23,885 produced) 280SLs are likely to have more options and updates. The 280SL is the newest, quietest, most comfortable, and most developed of the trio. The 250SL's lower production numbers make it neither more nor less desirable. If anything, the 230SL is undervalued. It's a good buy if you can live without the improved engine, and no evidence exists that these engines are any less reliable than the later ones. Rear disc brakes can be retrofitted to the 230SL, but unless you're driving hard in autocrosses and time trials, you'll never miss them.

Driving Impressions: 230SL, 250SL, and 280SL

Unusual in a sports car, these SLs have wide doors for easy entry and exit, a roomy interior, good outer vision, comfortable seats, and excellent weatherproofing. The exhaust note defines the entire car—nicely sporty, but tasteful. Performance and handling are excellent for their day, but the rear swing-axle suffers from camber change, especially under heavy braking. The nose dives, the rear end rises, and rear camber goes from negative to positive. Braking hard from high speeds into a sharp and/or slippery curve, this can lead to oversteer, but you'll rarely drive this grand tourer that hard. Under other conditions the car has excellent grip, and the steering can be accurate and light (tire choice and inflation pressures play a role).

There's not much difference in handling among the three. A 280SL can exceed 3,000lb in weight, so the lighter 230SL feels more nimble. The car's track is wide, so they feel quite stable. Zero to 60mph takes about ten seconds, and top speeds were almost 125mph for the 230SL; the 250 and 280SL were slightly but not significantly slower. Added displacement makes the 280SL torquier than a 230SL at lower rpm, and the smaller-engined car needs to be revved a bit more. Fuel mileage is reasonable, in the high teens or better, depending on mechanical condition. In top gear with stock tires a 280SL engine turns at about 19mph per 1000rpm.

The color of the painted dash should match the exterior color. The soft top operates easily, but you'll need a friend and/or a hardtop winch to remove or replace the hardtop. One false move, and you can scratch or dent the aluminum tonneau cover.

What to Look For

As usual, rust is the main enemy. When using a magnet to check for body filler, remember the aluminum panels: doors, engine hood, trunk lid, and tonneau cover. These parts may not rust, but they are easy to dent, expensive to replace, and more difficult than steel panels to repair properly.

Areas most susceptible to rust are the front fenders (around the headlights, along the inner engine compartment panels at the top of the fenders,

The 230SL, 250SL, and 280SLs seem to look cleaner without the optional front bumper guards. Note the US headlights. *FDB*

Hinged aluminum boot neatly hides soft top. *FDB*

Even the trunk lid model designations resemble each other (this is a 280SL). Top, with plastic window, is easy to operate. *Dennis Adler*

and at the seams of the closing panels behind the wheels) and the rear fenders (along the bottom edge and around the taillights). Check inside the engine compartment for rust along the inner fender panels and in the recesses above the subframe mounts.

Underneath the car and ahead of the rear wheels are a couple of traps for dirt and rust; lift the carpet behind the seats and look for holes. Check the chassis just outboard and forward of the rear springs. Look closely at all fender lips. Check the

Even without the optional child seat, an SL can seat three in a pinch. Factory alloy wheels update the car's style. *FDB*

The 280SL dash has rounded control knobs; original radios such as this Blaupunkt are a plus. *FDB*

front cross-member, which is exposed to road salt and often distorted when incorrectly used to jack up the car. Look under the trunk mat and in the spare wheelwell on early 230SLs; leaky trunk seals let in water. Poke at the rocker panels and floor pan, especially around the pedal and seat mounting areas.

Look closely at the grille and surrounding sheet metal, often improperly repaired after accidents. Does the grille fit evenly against the body? Condition of the grille and bumpers is important because they are particularly expensive to replace. Dents can be fixed, but rust is more difficult to stop and replate over. The sheet metal behind the grille should be painted black, not body color; looking into the grille, all you should see is black. Along the inner edge of the headlight's plated trim ring, where it has a small bump, you should see a matching short (one-half inch) horizontal crease in the steel fender. Replacement fenders don't have this crease. If the fender has no crease, a body man has either filled it on an original fender or failed to build it on a replacement.

The hardtop is time-consuming to restore, so make sure the headliner is in good shape and that there's no rust in the lower rear quarters; drain holes should be clear. Replacement soft tops are reasonably priced, especially if you're willing to accept something less than show-quality material. Check the plastic rear window for fogging and scratches, sometimes removable via plastic cleaner. Be sure that the hand levers to operate the top latches are with the car; replacements are available.

Under the hood, first see that the engine is the right type. Because the contemporary sedans used similar engines, it's easy to swap them into an SL. Engine numbers should include the M-codes 127.981 (230SL), 129.982 (250SL), or 130.983 (280SL). A 250SL should have a viscous fan drive. A 280SL should have a bayonet oil filler cap rather than the earlier threaded type. All valve covers had a fine sand-grained natural finish and were unpolished.

Main engine areas of concern are the cooling system, fuel injection, timing chain, and cylinder head; any may have been neglected. The aluminum head may corrode from incorrect or infrequently changed coolant, often causing blown

U370.

All engines were mechanically fuel-injected using exceptionally long ram intake ducts. Here is the M127 of the 230SL. *DBAG*

head gaskets (steam out of the tailpipe) and overheating. Valve guides are generally the first top-end part to wear out, with blue smoke when starting as evidence. Timing chains stretch, and chain tensioners should be replaced along with them. Cam lobe wear can result from infrequent oil changes. Water pumps and motor mounts don't last forever, either. Check the viscous fan drive on the 250 and 280SL. The mechanical fuel injection pump is expensive to rebuild, but done properly it's a once-in-a-lifetime job.

If the engine won't start and run smoothly, and nothing is wrong with the ignition, suspect the fuel injection. With today's higher-volatility fuels, hot weather can cause vapor lock, which can be cured by activating the cold-start switch so that it also works when the engine is hot (via a momentary switch or a factory relay). A mechanic without proper equipment, knowledge, and experience can cause more fuel injection problems than he solves, so repair is best left to experts. To keep the fuel injection system working properly, drive the car regularly rather than letting it stand.

If the engine oil smells like gasoline, the fuel injection pump is probably set far too rich and is thus pumping fuel through the cylinders and into the sump, diluting the engine oil. This problem may be indicated by a higher than normal oil level. Bearings won't last long in a gas-oil mixture. About the only place these engines leak oil is at

Cross-section views of the M129 engine of the 250SL. *DBAG*

the front crankshaft seal. Oil pressure at hot idle may seem low, but around 2000rpm or so, the oil pressure gauge needle should rise and become pegged at its top reading.

These engines have a normal life of about 100,000 miles, although a well-maintained unit may go much farther. Original and factory replacement exhaust systems tend to rust, but stainless-steel replacements are available.

Original tire size on the 280SL's 6in-wide steel wheels was 185HR14, an 80 series profile designed for a smooth ride, light steering, and minimal aquaplaning. Today's best equivalent size is 205/70HR14. Since the car's four gears are widely spaced, a too-small or too-tall tire can have a major effect. Some opine that the stock gearing is low, but this is a revving six, not a lumbering V-8. The

The M130 engine of the 280SL. *DBAG*

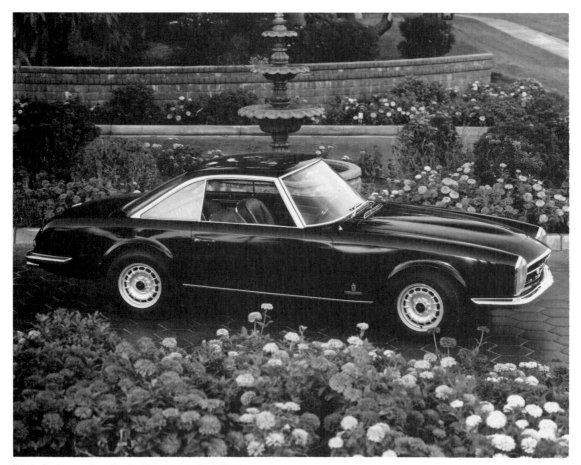

Pininfarina rebodied this 1965 230SL into a Coupe with a permanent top. *Dennis Adler*

automatic transmissions shift firmly; proper linkage adjustment may reduce hard thumps, but not to 1990s levels. The suspension requires lubrication, so look for clean grease nipples.

Newer radios are popular, but original 1960s Beckers are obtainable and can be repaired. The original air conditioners never iced anyone's nose, but with a top that drops, who cares? If hot air enters the interior with the heater off, the air control flaps need to be rebuilt and readjusted. Heater controls and the wiper works, entombed in the cowl, are difficult to reach. If the wipers don't work, you'll have a tough time repairing them.

The 1967 and earlier cars had unmarked heater controls with hard knobs; 1968 and later models had symbols on the rubber knobs. The interior rearview mirror finish changed from chrome to black plastic at about the same time. Interior wood

is usually sun-faded. To determine the true wood color, check the wood trim on the inside of the hardtop's rear window, where the sun rarely hits it.

Restoration

Any worn but sound example is a good restoration candidate, but so many good original cars survive that it pays to be patient. Find a good one, and avoid restoration altogether!

Because so many 230, 250, and 280SLs were built (48,912), and the cars have remained popular, an industry has developed around their restoration. For instance, sun visors used to be impossible to find, but now they're being made again. Specialty parts and services are easy to find, and more good reproduction parts appear regularly.

Most mechanical and major body parts remain available from Mercedes-Benz. Trim is more diffi-

One of the rarest options is this manually operated sunroof in the factory hardtop. *FDB*

cult to find and is expensive, particularly the front bumpers and grille. The aluminum panels are also not cheap, but fenders and other steel body parts are reasonably priced. Since the fenders are welded on, not bolted on, they require skilled labor to replace correctly. Mechanical parts shared with the sedans can be found new or used. Used hardtops are available but not cheap, so use the lack of a hardtop as a bargaining point. Try to get the soft top frame with the car; used ones are expensive.

Before restoration, decide whether you want the car to be a nice driver, a national show winner, or something in between. Changing goals in mid-restoration is expensive and frustrating. A 230, 250, or 280SL is moderately easy to restore, but being a Convertible, you have a soft top to replace and a hardtop to restore. Interior wood trim is minimal but vulnerable to sun damage. Most cars had MB-tex upholstery rather than leather.

Since these cars are so frequently restored, professional restorers have had a lot of experience with them. This also means that there are more good cars for you to pick from and avoid restoration altogether.

Summary

In numbers, style, usability, and affordability, the 230, 250, and 280SL models are the most collectible SLs. They drive well, they're appreciating in

Presence of this small crease in the headlight rim and fender is a clue to an original body—or good bodywork.

value, and they're reasonably simple to restore. What more can you ask? If you want a good car at a fair price, go for an early model. You'll pay a premium for the slight mechanical and psychological advantages of the last model year. Whichever you choose, you'll own one of the prettiest Mercedes-Benz models, and if you don't like it, you can always find someone else who does. But we can practically guarantee that you'll enjoy these cars—a lot.

Chapter 11

Fin-Backs, Coupes, and Convertibles 1960s

If one Mercedes-Benz model series has been unfairly reviled, it is surely the be-finned (and berated) sedans of the early 1960s. Underneath the skin, though, they are excellent cars. Alongside the finned sedans, these years also brought a subtle line of Coupes and Convertibles.

Suddenly, It's 1960

OK, let's get it over with and move on. Some think the finned 1960s sedans are ugly. Even if their tacked-on tailfins were designed to appeal to some German marketer's misperceived tastes of American buyers, these ugly ducklings only grow rarer and more collectible. Good "fin-backs" are tough to find.

The fin-back's body/chassis was completely new, with emphasis on safety, visibility, and space. Before regulations required it, these were the first Mercedes-Benz cars to be crash-tested. They used a variety of diesel and gasoline engines, from the 60hp, four-cylinder 190 diesels to the 195hp, six-cylinder gasoline 300s. These cars marked the first widespread use of gasoline fuel injection. One basic chassis served as everything from an economical taxi to a luxurious limousine.

Proudly presented to the world for the 1960 model year, the sleek new 220S was billed as "the elegant car with the 124 SAE hp engine." Nowadays it's mostly called the fin-back. DBAG

Chassis and Engine Prefix Numbers

Years	Model	Chassis Prefix	Engine Prefix	Description
1961–1965	190c	110	121	4-cyl. gas, 90hp
1961–1965	190Dc	110	OM621	4-cyl. diesel, 60hp
1965–1968	200	110	121	4-cyl. gas, 105hp
1965–1968	200D	110	OM621	4-cyl. diesel, 60hp
1957–1962	180a, b, & c	120 II–IV	121	4-cyl. gas, 65–68hp DIN
1959–1965	190b	121 III	121	4-cyl. gas, 80hp DIN

Driving Impressions: Fin-Backs

In a fin-back car, the first feature that may strike you is the large pad in the center of the steering wheel. Next, you'll spot the unique vertical ribbon speedometer. Exterior visibility is excellent thanks to the huge window area.

The sixes love to rev, and you'd better take advantage of that. These cars are slow off the mark, but once you get them rolling, they'll stay at high speeds. The 300s have more torque, so you need not downshift as much. These big cars are heavy, and their aging suspension and brakes may not live up to their power. Still, disc brakes are a big improvement over the 1950s drums.

The automatic transmissions are hard-shifting and sap power. A manual gearbox is smoother and more fun. Heating, cooling, and fresh air ventilation are generations behind 1990s cars.

190 and 200 Sedans 1961–1968 ★★

The four-cylinder fin-backs were plain and functional, built to provide inexpensive but reliable transportation. These are taxicabs, not collector cars. In relation to the tens of thousands built, few remain in daily use. Most are now well worn and no longer suitable for much but short drives. Their low power and pragmatic nature appeal to few.

The 190c, appearing in 1961, used a fin-back body, but was shorter than the 220Sb and SEb and had single instead of dual stacked headlights. The 200, another four-cylinder version, got two carburetors and higher compression, making 105hp SAE. Diesels are described in chapter 18.

220S and 220SE Sedans 1960–1965 ★★

The new-for-1960 111 chassis dual-carbureted 220, 220S, and fuel-injected 220SE used the six-cylinder engine of the 1950s cars. The 220 used dual Solex carburetors throughout its model run. The 220S had dual Solexes until mid-1963, when Zeniths appeared. The SE ("E" signifying *Einspritzer*) had mechanical, two-plunger, port injection. These models also brought automatic transmissions to the mid-range.

The fin-back even enjoyed a rally career. Factory 220SEs placed one-two-three in the 1960 Monte Carlo Rally and did well in other European, African, and South American events. Factory drivers won the 1960 and 1962 European Rally Championships.

One feature that gives grief are the Zenith 35/40 INAT downdraft carburetors on some models (220Sb, 230, and 230S from about 1963 to 1972). Even new, these were difficult to keep working properly. As they wear, and as the bodies warp, allowing air and vacuum leaks, they refuse to be tuned. Service experts are scarce, but after the leaks are patiently found and eradicated, the carburetors can work well. Some owners convert to Weber or Holley 32/36 DGEV downdrafts, but even these demand proper jetting and adjustment, especially with automatic transmissions (which

Little sisters of the six-cylinder 220 were the four-cylinder 190 and 190D. *Mercedes-Benz Sales*

Visibility was much improved, and the fin-back was the first Mercedes-Benz (and probably the first production car) to be thoroughly crash-tested. *DBAG*

use engine vacuum for shifting). Fuel injection is more reliable, but its pump is subject to wear and is not inexpensive to overhaul.

The 220S and 220SE fin-backs were the first mass-market models to provide factory or dealer-installed air conditioning. It's not very effective now, but you're not buying a 1960s car because it has a great air conditioner. Another first (apart from the 300SL) was the appearance of disc brakes in April 1962, albeit only at the front; the 190s switched from drums in August 1963. Dual-circuit brakes were first fitted in 1963.

230 and 230S Sedans 1965–1968 ★★

The final iteration of the fin-back came in the slightly larger engined 230 and 230S. If you must

have a fin-back, these (or a 220SE) are probably your best bet. The 230s are easy to find and economical. Except for the Zenith carburetors, they are dead simple. They exude an innocent charm, but even better, they are cheap. A few years ago a friend advertised his near-perfect 230S. After a few wary nibbles, the price eroded until it was shamefully low, $1,500.

Like the other small-displacement "finnies," both 230 models are slow, especially with the optional automatic transmission, a clunky affair. Try for a nice one with a floorshift manual transmission and a sunroof.

In February 1968, the factory gate finally closed behind the last fin-back. No matter what comments you hear about the styling of these cars, their charm grows on you, especially in these days of characterless cars.

Chassis and Engine Prefix Numbers

Years	Model	Chassis Prefix	Engine Prefix	Description
1965–1968	230	110	180	6-cyl. gas, 118hp
1965–1968	230S	111/1A	180	6-cyl. gas, 135hp

Chassis and Engine Prefix Numbers

Years	Model	Chassis Prefix	Engine Prefix	Description
1961–1965	300SE	112/3	189	6-cyl. gas, 185–195hp
1963–1965	300SEL	112/3	189	6-cyl., gas, 185–195hp

Technical Specifications

Model	220S	220SE	300SE/SEL
Years	1960–1965	1960–1965	1961–1965
Engine			
Type	Inline ohc six (all)		
Engine # prefix	180V	127III	189
Displacement	2195cc (133.9ci)	2195cc (133.9ci)	2996cc (182.8ci)
Bore x stroke	80x72.8mm	80x72.8mm	85x88mm
Compression ratio	8.7:1	8.7:1	8.8:1
DIN horsepower	110hp @ 5000rpm	120hp @ 4800rpm	170hp @ 5400rpm
Torque	17.5mkg @ 3500rpm	19.3mkg @ 3900rpm	25.4mkg @ 4000rpm
Fuel system	2 Solex 34 PAJTA (Zenith 35/40 INAT after July 1963)	Bosch mechanical fuel injection (all)	
Fuel required	Premium (all)		
Chassis			
Type	Unibody; steel (all)		
Chassis # prefix	111/2	111/3	112/3
Transmission	4-speed manual (all) (4-speed auto optional)		
Rear-axle ratio	4.10:1	4.10:1	3.92 or 3.69:1
Rear suspension	Swing-axle, coil springs (all)		
Front suspension			
Wheels	Steel, 5x13in	5x13in	6x14in
Tires	7.25x13in	7.25x13in	7.35x14in or 185H14
Brakes	F disc, R drum	F disc, R drum	4-wheel disc
Fuel capacity	17.2gal	17.2gal	21.7gal
Weight	2,976lb	3,042lb	3,649lb
Performance			
0-60mph	15sec	14sec	12sec
Top speed	103mph	107mph	115–120mph
Fuel consumption	16–18mpg	16–18mpg	14–17mpg

Note: Earlier 300SE Coupes and Convertibles had less power, 5x13in wheels, different rear-axle ratios, and so forth.

300SE and 300SEL Sedans 1961–1967 ★★★

The rarest and most desirable fin-back sedans are the top-of-the-line 300SE and 300SEL sedans, practically limousines. Their 3.0 liter, alloy, inline sixes pushed out up to 185hp SAE, but the chassis was lumbered with an early version of air suspension and automatic transmissions. The SEL rides on a 100mm (3.9in) longer wheelbase, with the extra space in the back seat area.

Both 300s had four disc brakes, with a dual-circuit system after 1963. Starting in January 1964, their two-plunger fuel injection pump was replaced by a six-plunger unit, boosting power by about 10hp. Compression ratio was nudged from 8.7:1 to 8.8:1 at the same time. Virtually all used four-speed automatic transmissions, although a four-speed manual was optional in Europe.

Underappreciated and rarely seen today, these fin-back flagships embody every styling concept of early 1960s Euro-chic. There is plenty of chrome, medium-wide whitewalls, a "300SE" logo cast into the C-pillar trim, even two-tone paint. They are eas-

ily spotted via the trim in the side body crease. A black 300SEL is *tres* elegant, but a two-tone blue or green example is nostalgia on wheels.

DBAG's first high-volume application of air suspension and power steering can leak via fittings, pump seals, and old hoses. The air suspension pump is coupled to the power steering pump, and air must be carefully bled out of the steering lines. Because the self-leveling air suspension is expensive to repair, some cars have been converted to coil springs. European fin-backs used a streamlined one-piece headlight housing; American cars use separate headlights and parking lights. Both 300 fin-back sedans were last built for the 1965 model year.

The 300s were among the world's fastest and strongest sedans. Led by driver Eugen Böhringer, factory 300SE sedans were successful in racing and rallying. A 300SE makes a fun vintage racer.

Compared to the 300SE Coupe and Convertible, the 300 sedans are bargains. In fact, nice four-doors are far more rare, though plenty of run-down examples are quietly rotting away out there.

Rear swing-axle is fixed to the chassis at the center; coil springs at each wheel are supplemented by a load-compensating coil spring at the center. *DBAG*

The 300SE Convertible is distinguished by the thin chrome trim in the side body crease, not present on 220, 250, 280, or 280SE 3.5 versions. Even on these luxury four-seaters, the top was still manually operated. *DBAG*

What to Look For

Condition is everything. No total restoration can be economically justified, so find the best original example. Rust likes to eat around the headlight buckets, along the edges of the wheelwells, and in the doors and rocker panels. Condition of trim is important because replacement pieces are hard to find. Bumpers seem especially vulnerable to dents; those can be fixed and replated, but you'll have to completely replace a rusty bumper.

Notice how a Zenith-equipped six starts and idles. Smooth driveability depends on the condi-

Last of the fin-backs was the 230S, seen here autocrossing. *FDB*

The 300SEL was the finest and the fanciest, with plenty of chrome trim and ample rear legroom backed up by a four-speed automatic transmission, air suspension, and power steering. A four-speed manual gearbox was an option, and even a few five-speeds were fitted. *DBAG*

Interior of the 300SEL could be swathed in leather or cloth, with select woods and wool carpets. With the demise of the 300d, this was the top Mercedes-Benz. *DBAG*

For 1970 the Coupe and Convertible grilles were lowered and widened; early version on left, 1970 and later version on right. Both of these cars have European headlights. Empty space between headlight and grille contained turn signals on US cars. *DBAG*

tion of the carburetors. The fuel-injected engines are smoother and more flexible. Since the automatic transmission is controlled by vacuum, shifts are subject to carburetor condition. Old motor mounts sag but aren't tough to replace. The preferred manual transmission's column shift should work smoothly and precisely; floorshifts were optional on some models.

If it has had any care at all, a 1960s interior should be excellent. MB-tex (vinyl) can't be killed, and most models had rubber floor mats. Sun-damaged wood is common; finding good replacement wood may cost less than professional refinishing. Amateur refinishing usually ends in a mess because the wood is just a thin veneer. As soon as sandpaper hits it, the thin veneer is gone, so a typical amateur just refinishes the base wood.

Restoration

Fin-backs were built in huge numbers, so used parts are plentiful. Sold as economy cars, they are uncomplicated and inexpensive to operate, maintain, and restore. Because few seek them, they can be stunning bargains.

If possible, stick to the fuel-injected models. The Solex and Zenith carburetors were poor in performance, durability, and fuel consumption, and they are expensive to replace or repair.

Professional wood restoration is expensive but best. A pro can match the existing color and grain (to see what it should be, see the inside of the glovebox lid) and make it last.

Good original fin-backs can be bought for less than the cost of a simple restoration. Resist an inexpensive project car. A truly cheap show car may be just around the corner. Even if you already own a fin-back, try to resist the urge to restore it. Unless it's rare—a 300SE or SEL or a Coupe or Convertible—better sell it and find another in better condition.

Summary

None of the 190s and 220s are widely considered to be collector cars, but they provide useful and economical transport. Because they are the newest and have the most powerful engines, the 230 and 230S are good for low-budget collectors. The best

fin-backs are beginning to be preserved, but restoration cost is far more than the cost of a better car.

The big 300SE and SEL sedans are rare; in fact, good sedans are rarer than Coupes and Convertibles. Most desirable are the ornate ones in full two-tone and whitewall plumage.

Driving Impressions: 220 and 280 Coupes and Convertibles

The 220 and 280 Coupes and Convertibles are more luxurious than the sedans, frequently including reclining bucket seats and, in later cars, power windows. A round speedometer and an equal-sized tachometer lie in an attractive wood binnacle. Air conditioning was not universal, but underdash Kuhlmeister units are found.

Performance is directly related to engine displacement. If performance is important, go for the 280SE, 300SE, or 280SE 3.5. Fuel injection means a much smoother, more responsive engine than the carbureted power units. The four-wheel disc brakes are powerful and easy to maintain. The automatic transmission usually doesn't match the sophistication of the rest of the car. Convertible tops on these models are manually operated, but simple to raise and lower.

Thanks to air suspension, the 300SE stays level in corners. Power steering can be vague. These cars sometimes suffer vapor lock in hot weather, partly because the high-pressure injection lines wrap around the front of the engine. Spraying cold water on the pump and lines gets you going, but switching gasoline brands and applying insulation can help.

Chassis and Engine Prefix Numbers

Years	Model	Chassis Prefix	Engine Prefix	Description
1960–1965	220b	111/1	180	6-cyl. gas, 105hp
1960–1965	220Sb	111/2	180	6-cyl. gas, 124hp
1960–1965	220SEb	111/3	127	6-cyl. gas, 134hp

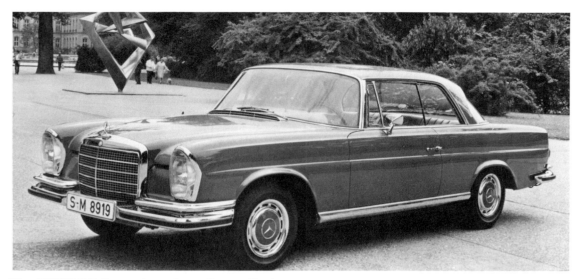

The 280SE 3.5 Coupe is perhaps the prettiest Mercedes-Benz of the era. Its high-compression V-8 made 230hp SAE.

220SE to 280SE 3.5 Coupes and Convertibles ★★

Early 1960s Coupes and Convertibles were mechanically similar to the contemporary sedans, but eschewed fins in favor of more subtly rounded rear fenders. A finely shaped roofline plus stylish C-pillars gave the Coupe an elegant look.

From the 220, the Coupes and Convertibles continued into the 250, 280, and 300 versions. As you can guess from those numbers, the biggest differences lie under the hood. The 220 Coupe and Convertible have the smallest engine; later models were somewhat better equipped and developed, too.

220SEb 1960–1965 ★★

Designed as a true 2+2, the 220SEb (the b sets it apart from the late 1950s round-body Coupe) was the first of a line of similar Coupes stretching into the early 1970s. The engine was the fuel-injected six, but its 134hp SAE has its work cut out shifting the 3200lb body.

Because they are outwardly similar to the more desirable 300SE Coupes and Convertibles, many 220SEs are overpriced. Lacking only air suspension and some luxury touches, they cost nearly the same to restore. Mechanically, they lack the 300's rear disc brakes, but as a bonus they were often equipped with manual transmissions. Wheels and tires were 13in, tough to find now, but later 14in wheels fit.

The M116 engine had a redline of 6050rpm. An automatic transmission was normally fitted, but a four-speed manual was offered. *DBAG*

300SE 1961–1967 ★★★

This model seems out of order because it came along right after the 220, in 1962. Set apart by a horizontal side trim strip and chrome-plated wheel-well moldings, a 300SE is the ultimate 1960s Coupe or Convertible. Its broad-shouldered M189 single-overhead-cam six shrugs off the 3500–3700lb weight. Performance is excellent, especially with the optional manual transmission (controlled by either a column-shifter or a floorshift). Top speed is 115–125mph, depending on final drive ratio (3.75 or 3.92:1 could be specified) and transmission. Tires were 13in through 1965, 14in thereafter.

A V-8 was a natural for the wide engine compartment of the 111 Coupe body; Bosch electronic injection was employed. *Dennis Adler*

These Coupes and Convertibles were built until 1967, so the later the better. Like the 300 sedans, they were air-suspended and had four-wheel disc brakes. Standard equipment included reclining seats and leather upholstery. Options varied annually but included cloth upholstery, power windows, bucket seats, and fitted luggage. These Coupes and Convertibles were rare when new, and today a good one is a keeper.

250SE 1966–1967 ★★

The 250SE Coupe and Convertible, built alongside the 300s as 1966 and 1967 models, enlivened the 220SE with a 300cc displacement increase and a boost in compression to 9.3:1, bumping power to 170hp. Wheel diameter went to 14in,

sprung via coil springs with a hydro-pneumatic compensating unit on the rear axle. Brakes were uprated to four-wheel discs.

280SE 1968–1972 ★★

For the 1968 model year, the 280SE replaced the previous 250SE and 300SE. Its 2778cc single-overhead-cam M130 six makes 180hp SAE and gets the big Coupe up to about 115mph. Other benefits of the new engine were improved cooling and seven main bearings. The 2.2 to 3.0 liter sixes can be expected to cover 100,000 miles without overhaul. Smoke usually appears first from worn valve guides; overheating indicates water pump, radiator, or head gasket problems.

In 1970, when the 3.5 liter V-8 was made available in this chassis, the hood and grille were

Chassis and Engine Prefix Numbers

Years	Model	Chassis Prefix	Engine Prefix	Description
1961–1965	220SEb	111/3	127	6-cyl. gas, 134hp
1962–1967	300SE	112/3	189	6-cyl. gas, 185–195hp
1966–1967	250SE	111	129	6-cyl. gas, 170hp
1968–1972	280SE	111	130	6-cyl. gas, 180hp
1970–1971	280SE 3.5	111	116	8-cyl. gas, 230hp

Technical Specifications

Model	250SE Coupe/Conv.	280SE Coupe/Conv.	280SE 3.5 Coupe/Conv.
Years	1965–1967	1968–1971	1970–1971
Engine			
Type	Inline sohc six	Inline sohc six	Sohc V-8
Engine # prefix	129.980	130.980	116.980
Displacement	2496cc (152.3ci)	2778cc (169.5ci)	3499cc (213.5ci)
Bore x stroke	82x78.8mm	86.5x78.8mm	92x65.8mm
Compression ratio	9.5:1	9.5:1	9.5:1
DIN horsepower	150hp @ 5500rpm	160hp @ 5500rpm	200hp @ 5800rpm
Torque	22.0mkg @ 4200rpm	24.5mkg @ 4250rpm	29.2mkg @ 4000rpm
Fuel system	Mechanical fuel injection	Mechanical fuel injection	Electronic fuel injection
Fuel required	Premium (all)		
Chassis			
Type	Unibody; steel (all)		
Chassis # prefix	111.	111.	111.
Transmission	4-speed auto or 4-speed manual	4-speed auto	4-speed auto
Rear-axle ratio	3.92:1	3.92:1	3.69:1
Rear suspension	Swing-axle, coil springs (all)		
Front suspension	Unequal-length A-arms (all)		
Wheels	6x14in (all)		
Tires	185HR14	185HR14	185VR14
Brakes	4-wheel disc (all)		
Fuel capacity	21.7gal (all)		
Weight	3,285lb	3,570lb	3,770lb
Performance			
0-60mph	12sec	11sec	10sec
Top speed	117–120mph	117–120mph	130mph
Fuel use	14–16mpg	14–16mpg	12–14mpg

lowered and reshaped to a more contemporary style. For 1970 and 1971, about 680 six-cylinder 280SE Coupes and Convertibles also used this low grille and hood.

The next best thing to a 300SE, the 280SE sixes are usually priced much lower, so bargains exist.

280SE 3.5 1969–1971 ★★★

The 280SE 3.5 Convertible is among the most collectible models of its era. When Mercedes-Benz developed its 3.5 liter V-8, the high-end Coupes and Convertibles were a natural home for it. The resulting five-passenger 280SE 3.5 Convertible is luxurious, powerful, and exclusive. Its folding top created an instant classic.

Introduced in 1969 as a 1970 model, the 280SE 3.5 was also available as a sedan and a Coupe (note that, bargain hunters). Its M116 V-8 power-plant used the new Bosch D-Jetronic electronic fuel injection, a transistorized ignition, and a 9.5:1 compression ratio to deliver 230hp SAE, more than 1hp per cubic inch. Most cars had four-speed automatic transmissions, but a few were built with a four-speed manual gearbox.

Rather than air suspension, the 280SE 3.5 used standard coil springs at each corner, so there's less concern about suspensions maintainance. Four-wheel disc brakes were standard, and a limited-slip differential was optional. The Convertible's top is easily lowered and raised by hand. The interior is clad in leather, wood, and chrome; amenities include power windows, air

This 280SE 3.5 Convertible is unusual in that it has no air conditioning (usually hung below the dash), no radio (note the blanking plate with the "280SE" designation), and a floorshift four-speed manual transmission. *DBAG*

conditioning, and reclining seats with center armrests. Fitted luggage was an option, of course.

The grille and hood of the 280SE 3.5 Coupe and Convertible were lowered, giving them an entirely new look from the more upright earlier models. As many as 1,232 280SE 3.5 Convertibles were manufactured for the 1970 and 1971 model years. Many more sedans (about 12,000) and Coupes (about 3,270) were built. The Convertible was the last four- or five-seat Mercedes-Benz Convertible until the 300CE Cabriolet of 1993.

What to Look For

Make sure the Convertible boot (top cover) is with the car. Check power window operation, too.

Because of the demand for Convertibles, some 1960s W111 Coupes have been made into Convertibles, sometimes to sell them at a higher price disguised as genuine Convertibles. If you're looking at a Convertible that had a Coupe equivalent, especially a 280SE 3.5, be sure that it is an original, factory-built Convertible. Verify the chassis number. The 1970 280SE Coupe numbers begin with 111.024, Convertible numbers with 111.025. The 1971 280SE Coupe numbers begin with 111.026, Convertibles with 111.027.

Check beyond the ID plate on the radiator support, which can be switched. If you buy a Convertible that turns out to be a phony, you could lose tens of thousands of dollars. An honest seller will tell you about a conversion; less scrupulous people may conveniently forget.

Safety is also a factor. To substitute for the steel top's rigidity, the original Convertible chassis was reinforced based on factory engineering and tests. Most conversions are done with little regard for structural integrity and safety. Since older cars are involved, often well-used examples, the basic structure can be lacking.

Restoration

These cars are young enough so that excellent original examples can still be found. Unless you plan to show the car, you are better off buying a clean original than obligating yourself to a huge restoration.

These are not small cars, so there's more to restore. Their low volume means that some parts are hard to find, but because of the cars' value, more parts can be expected to be reproduced. A Convertible is always more expensive to restore than an equivalent Coupe and often is in worse shape to begin with. Water and sun damage not only the top but often the leather. Mechanically there's no problem; the Coupe and Convertible use parts from the common sedans.

If you're farming out your restoration, find a shop that has done several then examine their work. If you want yours restored properly, experience counts. These cars are usually restored well, so if you plan to sell yours later, it will have to be restored properly to match the competition. Collectors expect these cars to be right, so short-cuts really show. Unless you already own a clean original example, buy a well-restored car rather than trying to rescue a poor one.

Summary

All 1960s Mercedes-Benz Coupes and Convertibles are elegant and interesting cars that can still be driven anywhere and maintained without fuss. The later and bigger-engined examples are preferred. If you can live without a folding top, the 280SE 3.5 Coupe is the best bargain. For perhaps a quarter of the price of the 280SE 3.5 Convertible, you get nearly the same car.

The 280SE 3.5 Convertible has great potential as a future collector car, but the Coupe version is much underrated. *DBAG*

Chapter 12

The 1960s V-8s

Mercedes-Benz engineers built their first production V-8 engine for a flagrantly luxurious limousine series, the 600. Then, using this and other V-8s, they created an upscale series headed by the amazing 300SEL 6.3, then the world's fastest production sedan.

600 1963–1981 ★★★

By 1962 the 1950s six-cylinder 300 luxury sedan and four-door Convertible had grown long in the tooth. As a replacement, DBAG planned a new luxury model that may remain forever unsurpassed in elegance, comfort, quality, engineering,

In five-passenger Sedan form, this is the shortest (or least lengthy?) 600 model. *MBNA*

and performance—the 600. For all of that, though, this car engenders a love-hate relationship among collectors: it's wonderful to own, painful to restore.

Introduced at the 1963 Frankfurt auto show, the 600 was built until 1981 as a four-door "short wheelbase" (ahem) Sedan, the most popular model; Pullmans (also known as Seven Passenger Limousines) with four or six doors; and—rarely—as a Pullman-Landaulet with a folding rear top section. The short Sedan version is often called the SWB, for short wheelbase. Pullmans and Landaulets stood on a 700mm (27.6in) longer wheelbase, allowing additional rear seats and, in some cases, three doors per side. At least one 600 Coupe was built, as chief engineer Fritz Nallinger's retirement gift.

Custom touches were the norm for 600s, so defining factory options is difficult, but apart from leather or velour upholstery, the most popular were a sunroof, a divider window, refrigerated bars, and, of course, flag mounts for the front fenders. All four seats plus windows, sunroof, trunk lid, and doors (on early models) were hydraulically power-assisted via a complicated system with pressures of up to 300psi. Even the cowl vent is power-operated.

Remote-control exterior rearview mirrors and vacuum-operated central locking were both firsts. Heating and cooling systems were mostly separate, each individually controlled for front and rear. Radio controls were duplicated for back seat passengers, who also had an intercom to speak with their driver (it simply wouldn't do to shout from way back there). The 600 was tantalizingly close to outrageous, a no-holds-barred example of luxury, power, and elegance taken almost—but not quite—to excess.

The 600 was the first production Mercedes-Benz car to be powered by a V-8 engine. The gigantic 6330cc mechanically fuel-injected motor looks as if it was winched out of a U-boat, with huge dual air intake tubes in the center and a cam atop each cylinder bank, splayed apart at a generous ninety degrees. This virtually bulletproof engine went on to power the 300SEL 6.3 and in different form, the 450SEL 6.9. Despite the weight of the 600s, which varied from about 5300lb to over 6000lb, and their huge frontal area, this motor's giant torque and power could push them to 125–130mph.

Hauling them down again required unusual dual-caliper front disc brakes plus normal discs at

The 600 Pullman was also available in six-door form. This car and the regular 600 have US headlights. *MBNA*

For occasions of state, may we present the ultimate 600, the Pullman-Landaulet, with folding rear top, perhaps for tossing flower petals to the peasants. DBAG

Driving Impressions: 600

Just opening and closing the door of a 600 is different. Its hydraulic door assists inspired those of the 1992–on 600SEL. The steering wheel can be adjusted in and out, and the parking brake releases automatically as you shift the column-mounted lever into gear.

A driver must become accustomed to the car's length and breadth, but once you do, driving a 600 is easy. You might expect such a luxury car to handle like the Queen Mary, but the 600 is surprisingly competent. Body roll is low, and once the car takes a set in a hard corner, it hangs on tenaciously. Great fun, even without a chandelier in the back.

Be aware of vibrations, possibly from the three-section driveshaft. The brakes should work evenly; if not, the calipers may have corroded, especially if the car has been driven rarely. A 600 deteriorates from lack of use. Test the suspension firmness adjustment. Fuel mileage? If you care, it's under 15mpg, depending on bodystyle and mechanical state.

Even thirty years later in a world jaded by stretched Lincolns, a 600 has more pure presence than any other luxury vehicle. You're going to be looked at in this car.

---

the rear. Brakes are boosted by compressed air from the suspension system, which uses air-bags and A-arms at the front and a self-leveling, low-pivot swing-axle at the rear. Shock absorbers are driver-adjustable, and the 9.00x15in radial tires (equivalent to today's 235/70R15) fit on steel wheels with painted and plated hubcaps rather than alloy wheels. Five vee-belts drive two alternators, the air conditioning compressor, the hydraulic pump, the cooling fan, and the air compressor.

Virtually every part was built solely for the 600 in small volume. All systems are complex, and interchangeability with other models is low except for the engine. Restoration is outrageously expensive. A 600 is even expensive to drive—highway fuel mileage hovered around 10mpg. Even undriven, the car consumes an inordinate amount of space.

We must add the obligatory mention that 600s were owned by such incomparables as King Hussein, Mao Tse-Tung, Queen Elizabeth II, the Shah of Iran, Hugh Hefner, Marshal Tito, Prince Rainier, the Beatles, and President Ceasescu of Rumania. Of course, the Pope had one, a special-bodied Landaulet with a raised roofline. What most people don't mention is that 600s were also owned by scallywags who thought they could use them to impress someone. It worked, too!

The 2,677th and final 600 was built in June 1981. The 600's eighteen-year life span remains the longest of any Mercedes-Benz model.

What to Look For

Apart from the normal points, be curious about the power-assisted systems, especially seats, windows, and air suspension. If they don't function properly, count on major expense and effort. The suspension is most likely to let you down, pun intended. (See the section on the 300SEL 6.3 in this chapter.) Neither end of the car should sag. Good air suspension should maintain the proper level even when parked for weeks.

Check the air conditioning and heating systems, and if the car has a divider window, make sure it works. The 6.3 liter V-8 is dependable, but some ancillary bits (water pump, alternators, fuel injection pump, exhaust system) bear watching.

Before you buy, make sure the 600 will fit your garage. The short-wheelbase Sedan is 18ft, 2in long, the Pullman covers 20ft, 6in, and the Landaulet simply requires a hangar.

Just because it's a great car, no 600 was immune to rust or accident damage. Everyone who sees your 600 will sight down those long, flat flanks and see every single door ding and ripple.

Restoration

With complicated engineering to match its imposing appearance, a 600 is full of hydraulics, sophisticated mechanisms, and expensive and rare trim. For instance, while a 1960s 220SE Coupe or Convertible has only twelve pieces of wood to restore, the average 600 has fifty.

A 600 can be restored, but any sane person will try to avoid the experience. Buy the best you can find and afford. Low-volume, practically handbuilt parts are extremely expensive, and these cars shouldn't be turned over to just any restorer. You'll need a real expert. The volume of parts and labor needed for a 600 restoration are bad enough, and the complex nature of the car only worsens the prospect.

108 and 109 Squareback Sedans 1965–1972 ★★

In 1965, Mercedes-Benz revealed the successor to the fin-back sedans, the New Generation. Sometimes called "squarebacks" because their trunk and rear fenders are squared-off, these cars are roomier than their predecessors, but they are also bigger, heavier, and more complex. Their W108 and W109 chassis are the same except for suspension; the 108 uses coil springs, the 109 uses air. (Some think that the difference is the wheelbase, but that's not so; some long-wheelbase SEL sedans—the 280SEL 4.5, for instance—have 108 chassis numbers.) For more rear legroom, all four inches of extra length are in the back seat area. These roomy, conservatively styled bodies still appear elegant.

Technical Specifications

Model	600	300SEL 6.3
Years	1964–1981	1968–1972
Engine		
Type	90-degree sohc V-8 (all)	
Engine # prefix	100.980	100.981
Displacement	6329cc (386.2ci) (all)	
Bore x stroke	103x95mm (all)	
Compression ratio	9.0:1 (all)	
DIN horsepower	250hp (300hp SAE) @ 4000rpm (all)	
Torque	369lb-ft @ 2800rpm DIN	434lb-ft @ 3000rpm SAE (all)
Fuel system	Mechanical fuel injection (all)	
Fuel required	Premium (all)	
Coolant capacity	24.3qt	19.0qt
Chassis		
Type	Unibody; steel	
Chassis # prefix	100.	109..018
Transmission	4-speed automatic (all)	
Rear-axle ratio	3.23:1 (limited-slip)	2.85:1 (limited-slip)
Rear suspension	Air, low-pivot swing-axle (self-leveling) (all)	
Front suspension	Air, unequal-length A-arms (self-leveling) (all)	
Wheels	6.5x15in	6.5x14in
Tires	9.00x15in	195x14in
Brakes	4-wheel disc, dual front calipers, air-assisted	4-wheel disc vacuum-assisted
Fuel capacity	29.6gal	27.7gal
Weight	5,732lb (SWB)	4,034lb; 6,107lb (Pullman)
Performance		
0-60mph	10sec (SWB)	7sec; 12sec (Pullman)
Top speed	115-129mph	137mph
Fuel consumption	9-12mpg	11-15mpg
Production and		

Model	Production
600	2,190
600 Pullman	428
600 Landaulette	59
300SEL 6.3	6,526

The Landaulet with top up for potentate protection; note the European lights. *DBAG*

Various models were powered by six- and eight-cylinder fuel-injected gasoline engines. First came the sixes: the 250S for the 1966 model year, followed by the 280SE, 280SEL, 300SE, and 300SEL. Both 280s use a 180hp single-overhead-cam six-cylinder engine similar to that of the 280SL, with decent performance. The 300's 185hp six was only slightly bigger but offered more torque.

The eight-cylinder models were DBAG's first mass-market V-8s, and most were sold in the United States, the 4.5 liter versions being the most common. The 3.5 liter is obviously smaller in displacement, but it shouldn't be overlooked. Thanks

to higher compression and less restrictive smog gear, its 230hp superceded the output of subsequent 4.5s, especially 1973 and later. Engines are thirsty by today's standards, consuming 11–15mpg.

Options included factory air conditioning (no longer dealer-installed), an electric sunroof, and vacuum door locks. Coil-spring suspension was fitted except for the 109 chassis 300SEL, 300SEL 3.5, 300SEL 4.5, 300SEL 6.3, which used air suspension.

Rear axles on some coil-sprung cars used a transverse spring above the differential as a self-leveling device. Called a compensating spring, it

Driving Impressions: 108 and 109

The 108 and 109 sedans are big, with plenty of space. Seats are not terribly supportive, and the heaters and air conditioning don't overwhelm, but the air conditioner makes up in fan noise what it lacks in effectiveness. You'll be comfortable inside what feels like a bank vault. The original nonretracting Kangol seatbelts are sloppy and easy to unfasten inadvertently, but a late 1980s service bulletin covers installation of factory-approved retracting units.

A V-8 should fire right off and easily peg the oil pressure needle at modest rpm levels. The sixes are not nearly as relaxed at highway speeds as the V-8s, which are downright lazy thanks to more torque.

Power steering should be precise, smooth, and quiet. Persistent steering play may indicate a cracked chassis where the steering box mounts. Brakes are excellent. At best, transmissions in these cars seem hard-shifting.

Fuel mileage of the big sixes varies widely, from 12 to over 20mpg, depending largely upon the condition of the engine, the carburetors, or the fuel injection pump. High compression demands high octane, not always available today. The V-8s are less picky, more thirsty.

Like most Mercedes-Benz cars, these are not at their best on snow or ice. Rear wheel-spin can be a problem for V-8s because of the combination of an automatic transmission and high torque at idle. Weight in the trunk helps.

can compress with age, resulting in excess negative camber, even with no load. Others used a hydro-pneumatic compensating unit; the hydraulic replacement is expensive, so the spring is sometimes substituted.

All 108- and 109-bodied cars used sliding heater and defroster controls with plastic levers, which break with age. Replacement with original levers is difficult, but an aftermarket lever replacement kit takes minutes to install. The heater cables may corrode, along with the coolant flow valves they control, making their action stiff. The remedy is to clean the valves and exercise the levers.

What to Look For

Rust is your main enemy. Most sedans are not worth spending a lot to restore, so find a rust-free example. If you'll use the car as a driver, you can tolerate a little rust in noncritical areas if the price is right. Check the front radiator support crossmember, around the headlights (for a better look, remove the headlight units from their buckets), and in the fenders behind the wheels. At the rear, rust eats at the wheel opening lip. Remove the trunk mat and check the side and rear edges of the trunk floor.

Used regularly, mechanical fuel injection is reliable. Nonuse typically causes dried-up seals, corrosion in the injection pump, and more. A common operating problem, vapor lock, can be fixed by modifying the system so that the cold-start injector squirts gasoline not only when the engine is cold (as designed), but also when it's hot. Some people do this with a switch under the dash, but Mercedes-Benz sells a factory relay and cable for the job.

The 600's engine compartment was filled with this mighty 6.3 liter, 300hp SAE powerplant, the first Mercedes-Benz passenger car V-8. *DBAG*

The Bosch fuel injection pump usually lasts at least 100,000 miles before needing overhaul. Overhaul is for specialists only. Keep yours away from anyone without proper equipment and experience.

Check for burned-smelling automatic transmission fluid, slow gear engagement, and leaks. Worn motor mounts allow the engine to sag and move under acceleration.

Restoration

Avoid it. You can buy a perfectly good example for half the cost of restoration.

Chassis and Engine Prefix Numbers

Years	Model	Chassis prefix	Engine prefix	Description
1965–1969	250S	108	180	6-cyl. gas, 146hp
1965–1968	250SE	108	129	6-cyl. gas, 170hp
1966–1967	300SE	108	189	6-cyl. gas, 195hp
1966–1967	300SEL	109	189	6-cyl. gas, 195hp
1968–1972	280S	108	130	6-cyl. gas, 157hp
1968–1972	280SE	108	130	6-cyl. gas, 180hp
1968–1971	280SEL	109	130	6-cyl. gas, 180hp
1968–1970	300SEL	109	189 (2.8)	6-cyl. gas, 180hp
1970–1972	300SEL 3.5	109	116	8-cyl. gas, 230hp
1971–1972	280SE 3.5	108	116	8-cyl. gas, 230hp
1971–1972	280SEL 3.5	109	116	8-cyl. gas, 230hp (rare)
1971–1972	280SE 4.5	108	117	8-cyl. gas, 230hp
1971–1972	280SEL 4.5	108	117	8-cyl. gas, 230hp
1971–1972	300SEL 4.5	109	117	8-cyl. gas, 230hp
1968–1972	300SEL 6.3	109	100	8-cyl. gas, 300hp

This typical 600 Pullman interior contains the first Mercedes-Benz power seats—hydraulically operated. A wide variety of options and custom features could be ordered. *DBAG*

The 300SEL 6.3 in original form. Bullet turn signals were later replaced by larger lamps resembling fog lights. Original hubcaps and wheels are often replaced by factory alloy wheels. *MBNA*

Working in the engine bay of the V-8 cars is more time and knuckle-consuming than on the sixes because more stuff is crammed in. Everything takes longer and costs more. Heater controls and blowers are especially tough to work on. The sliding heater levers harden and break, but a replacement is available that can easily be installed. Heater blower motors and windshield wiper mo-

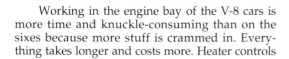

Technical Specifications			
Model	250SE Sedan	280SE Sedan	280SEL 4.5 Sedan
Years	1965–1968	1968–1972	1971–1972
Engine			
Type	Inline sohc six	V-8	V-8
Engine # prefix	129.980	130.980	117.984
Displacement	2496cc	2778cc	4520cc (276ci)
Bore x stroke	82x78.8mm	86.5x78.8mm	92x85mm
Compression ratio	9.3:1	9.5:1	8:1
SAE horsepower	170hp	180hp	230hp
Torque	22.0mkg	26.7mkg	38.5mkg (279lb-ft)
Fuel system	Mechanical fuel injection	Electronic FI	
Fuel required	Premium (all)		
Chassis			
Type	Unibody; steel (all)		
Chassis # prefix	108.014	108.018	109.068
Transmission	4-speed auto	4-speed auto	3-speed auto
Rear-axle ratio	3.92:1	4.08:1	3.23:1
Rear suspension	Swing-axle, coil springs		
Front suspension	Unequal-length A-arms (all)		
Wheels	6x14in	6x14in	6x14in
Tires	185x14in	185x14in	185x14in
Brakes	4-wheel disc (all)		
Fuel capacity	21.7gal	21.7gal	21.7gal
Weight	3,329lb	3,439lb	3,775lb
Performance			
0-60mph	12sec	11sec	12sec
Top speed	118mph	118mph	118mph
Fuel consumption	15mpg	15mpg	14-16mpg

tors are tough to reach, so make sure they work.

For an air-suspended car, air valves are expensive, so if the car shows any sign of sinking to its knees, proceed with caution. Unless the rest of the car is in exemplary condition, a 300 with air suspension problems is a car to be avoided for the normal restorer (or is that a contradiction?).

300SEL 6.3 1968–1972 ★★★

Looking at the 600's huge V-8, DBAG engineers Erich Waxenberger and Rudolf Uhlenhaut couldn't resist creating this factory hot rod. For 1968, they squeezed the V-8 into the 109 chassis, and thousands still thank them for the resulting 300SEL 6.3. This huge two-ton, four-door sedan managed 0–60mph in under seven seconds and topped out at about 135mph, impressive for an aerodynamic brick.

The M100 engine used a cast-iron block and aluminum alloy heads with a 9:1 compression ratio that demands today's highest octane premium fuel.

By 1960s Mercedes-Benz standards the 6.3 had a luxurious interior, but today it seems stark. Wood trim is minimal. Leather was standard on US cars, as was central locking, but the seats are manually adjusted, and a sunroof was optional. The 1968–1969 cars had power window controls on the doors plus a central wooden tray behind the shifter. For 1970–1971 the window switches moved to the console, replacing the tray. The 1968–1969 cars had small, bullet-shaped front turn signals, while 1970–1971 cars had larger, flatter orange lights shaped like driving lights.

Proper tires are a common question. Originally the 6.3 wore special 195x14in radials, but that size went out of production. Many now have 205/70VR14s, but Mercedes-Benz warns against that size; this is a heavy car, so load-carrying capacity is a factor. The best replacement size is 215/70VR14. Until the late 1960s tires were found wanting when it came to handling its speed and weight, the 6.3 was headed for a racing career. DBAG built several with roll cages, racing seats,

Driving Impressions: 300SEL 6.3

On hot days the 300SEL 6.3's fuel injection may suffer from vapor lock during hot-start attempts, but once you get it going, the engine should keep running. If you're stuck, let the engine cool. Turning the ignition key on and off for a few seconds at a time briefly activates the electric pump, moving cooler fuel from tank to engine. If you're in a hurry, spray the injection system with cold water. A simple factory fix for this problem is a relay (time switch, part number 001 545 16 24) and cable harness (part number 108 540 10 09). They fit on the rack next to the other electrical relays and turn on the cold-start injector even when the engine is hot.

A 6.3 is not much fun to drive at low speeds, but on the highway it comes into its own. Enjoying a good 6.3 on the open road will make you grin until your cheeks ache, but a bad one can make you cry. Low-speed ride is sharp over bumps, but speed up, and the car takes a set in a hard corner and goes around quickly in a surprisingly flat mode. If the steering wheel has a lot of play and the car wanders, the steering box mounting bolts may have loosened, and the chassis around them may have cracked.

The four-speed automatic transmission is typical of the era, with hard shifts the norm and a reluctance to downshift. The limited-slip differential is a liability in snow; low-rpm torque spins both wheels and may cause the entire rear of the car to slide sideways. On the track, the limited-slip gets you out of slow corners without spinning and frying the inside tire. During sharp turns at low speeds you'll hear groaning from the differential; that's normal. You may also hear gear whine, also normal; the differential mounts to the chassis, which transmits the sound.

Listen for noise from the power steering pump. Driveline vibrations indicate worn flex discs at each end of the driveshaft. You'll probably hear wind noise around the front vent windows, and by today's standards, the air conditioning and heating is mediocre. Engine vibration can signify a seizing air conditioning compressor.

The central locking may not work. Fixing it is usually a matter of discovering which door lock has the broken actuator diaphragm, involving more time than parts cost.

A good 6.3 will make at least 15mpg at highway speeds; around town you don't want to know. But no one buys these cars for fuel efficiency. Anyone who has driven one will tell you that.

The rarest 600 is this two-door Coupe, one of possibly two built. *FDB*

fender flares, and engine output bumped to around 350hp. The 6.3 originally had aluminum/steel wheels and hubcaps, but many have been retrofitted with factory alloy wheels.

The 6.3 was a hit on the autobahns and in the United States, then in the throes of the muscle-car era. Brock Yates drove one from New York to Georgia, thrashed it around Road Atlanta, then motored home before raving about it in *Car and Driver*. The 6.3 is a classic sleeper. You can pull up next to a Corvette at a light and act innocent. When the light turns green, you stay just far enough ahead to get the 'Vette driver to try harder...and harder...and harder!

What to Look For

Refer to the previous section dealing with potential rust areas in 108 and 109 bodies. That apart, maintenance records are important with 6.3s because they can be expensive to repair properly. Good, experienced, factory-trained mechanics are

fading, and previous owners sometimes attempt to fix things cheaply. Problem areas include the air suspension, the transmission, and the differential. If the expensive jobs have been done properly before you buy the car, that's good; most are once-in-a-lifetime procedures.

Some are wary of air suspension, but the system is simple. A compressor feeds air into a reservoir then through tubes to an air bag at each wheel. Four valves control airflow–one master valve, one level control valve at each front wheel, and one at the rear axle. Problems involve corrosion in the valves and air lines—or deteriorated air bags. A control knob is used to raise the car or lock the suspension (for jacking).

Alcohol in the reservoir behind the radiator is intended to dry the compressed air in the system, reducing condensation. Most owners let the reservoir run dry—finding any alcohol in it is a good sign. The metal air lines rust from the inside, but used ones can be found. Some control valves remain

The 6.3 engine compartment is nowhere for the novice mechanic to practice, but the engine is extremely reliable and durable. *FDB*

available new at stunning cost. They can be rebuilt.

The air reservoir, ahead of the left front wheel, has a drain valve in the wheelwell. Push up on the drain tube, and you'll be rewarded with a slimy ejaculation of a revolting mixture of oil, condensation, and God knows what else. Seeing and smelling this (and cleaning it off your hand) is all the more reason to keep after the air suspension.

Each wheel's rubber air bag ages due to heat and ozone, so with the car on a lift, check to see how badly cracked or hardened they are. Replacement is simple, but do it now rather than later. When an air bag fails, the suspension bottoms out, a nuisance if you're far from help. Emergency metal supports were provided for insertion into the suspension to hold it up; look inside the spare wheel. If the car is on its knees, the owner has obviously not taken care of it. Properly maintained air suspension should allow an undriven car to stay up almost indefinitely.

Forces on the steering box may crack the steel chassis. The cure is to remove the steering box, weld reinforcing plates to the chassis, and re-mount the box. With the car stationary and the engine running, watch the steering box for movement as the wheels are turned in each direction.

The differential can be a trouble spot, but they all make noise, so don't replace it until it literally screams at you. Check the lubricant level in the differential. The limited-slip unit uses special fluid, available at dealers. Make sure the axle and suspension mounts are solid and rust-free, especially where the trailing arms connect to the chassis.

A 6.3 engine (and other early V-8s) may leak oil from an oil passage near the rear of the heads, demanding a new head gasket. Easier to fix, warped valve covers also cause oil leaks. Overheating can warp the aluminum heads, but they can be straightened and/or machined.

When you turn on the radio, the automatic electric Hirschmann antenna should rise fully, lowering again when you switch it off.

Restoration

A 300SEL 6.3 can be neither as easy nor as hard to restore as it might seem. Bargains exist,

This 280SE sedan has the larger front turn signals. Painted door frames are common to the 108 body, and the air-suspended 109 bodies used chrome-plated door trim. *FDB*

This interior happens to be a 280SE, but apart from the column-mounted shifter it is similar to that of the 300SEL 3.5 and 6.3. Air conditioning was now integral with the dash. *FDB*

The 280SE engine is similar to that of the 280SL. Six-cylinder cars mounted the air conditioning compressor high instead of below the engine as in V-8 cars. *FDB*

114

The 300SEL 3.5 is quite rare, but at 230hp it is a surprisingly strong performer. *DBAG*

but here more than ever, avoiding them in favor of a better car can avoid a nightmare restoration. Buy a cheap 6.3, and you will end up using it as a parts car.

Rust thrives in rocker panels, lower doors, around headlights and fender openings, in the trunk, and in the closing panels behind the front wheels. Even a car that looks great can have plenty of rust under its shiny new paint. With many Mercedes-Benz restorations, the tendency is to dazzle the viewer with slick paint, but neglect the basics and the details. These big cars have a lot of glass and exterior trim, and a good restoration is often spoiled by poor metalwork or failure to replace pitted glass or scratched trim.

Luckily, most body parts and trim on a 6.3 are shared with 108- and other 109-bodied cars. A

good informal network of 6.3 owners and suppliers has evolved, so you are never alone.

Summary

Best bang for the buck is how we'll sum up these V-8s. You can enjoy their high performance, but it's in a cruder form than today's smoother cars. And be prepared to pay for it at the pump. Still, the big maintenance jobs are done only once per 100,000 miles, so long-term ownership can be reasonable.

The sixes and small V-8s are economical to buy and not expensive to maintain. A 600 or a 300SEL 6.3 is demanding to own, maintain, and restore, but it is sure to grow in value, kept in good condition. Few other old Mercedes-Benz cars are more fun to drive

Chapter 13

350SL, 380SL, 450SL, 500SL, and 560SL 1970–1989

The W107 chassis of the 350, 380, 450, 500, and 560SLs was one of Daimler-Benz AG's longest-running production bodies. With a variety of six- and eight-cylinder engines it bridged the considerable gap between the 1971 280SL and the 1990s SL models. Between April 1971 and August 1989 more than 237,000 W107 SLs were built; about two-thirds were sold new in the United States.

The 1971 350SL was completely different from the 1960s 230, 250, and 280SL that it replaced. The only recognizable carryover styling trait is the dip and the trim strips crossing the pagoda-shaped hardtop roof. Below that, everything was new.

Here was the first SL with a V-8, the 3.5 liter powerhouse that had made its debut in the 280SE 3.5. In the late 1960s, Daimler-Benz foresaw the conflict of performance and environmental controls. While customers craved power, the American government demanded lower emissions and proffered new rules about crashworthy bumpers. Meeting these conflicting demands meant bigger engines, heavier cars, and more fuel.

The new SL was not only faster and safer than the 1960s 280SL but also bigger, heavier, costlier, and thirstier. Like the old SLs, the new ones softened as the years passed, becoming more boulevardiers, and most owners used only a fraction of the car's performance. Thanks to gentle treatment and popularity, thousands survive in excellent condition.

350SL 1971–1980 and 450SL 1972–1980 ★★★

Confusion exists about engine displacement in the 350SL, sometimes called the 350SL 4.5. The new SL was introduced in Europe as a 1971 350SL with a 3.5 liter, iron-block M116 V-8. The first US 350SL, for 1972, actually had a low-compression 4.5 liter engine and bore the chassis number prefix 107.044. European 3.5 liter 350SL engine numbers (see the rear of the block) start with 116.982 (high-compression) or 116.992 (low-compression). All 4.5 liter engine numbers start with 117.

All 1971–1980 SLs sold in America had three-speed automatics. The 350SL (and later European SLs) had manual climate controls allowing driver and passenger to adjust heat or cooling separately, but the US 450SL soon got the complex Automatic Climate Control (ACC) system. With painted hubcaps and hand-cranked windows, a 1971 350SL sold for $11,059; its descendant, the 1989 560SL, cost $64,230.

The pre-1974 350SL and 450SL have the graceful original-design bumpers rather than the clumsy crash bumpers fitted to 1974 and later cars. Early-style bumpers continued on European cars and can be fitted to most US SLs. Alloy wheels became standard equipment by 1975.

The 450SL had excellent performance, but early emission controls strangled the engine. Performance, driveability, and fuel efficiency suffered, and vapor lock, caused hot-start problems. The 1972–1974 US models could use leaded or unleaded gasoline, but 1975 and later cars had catalytic converters, demanding unleaded. The 1975 and 1976 models had the most vapor lock problems because their catalytic converters were in the engine compartment, where airflow was restricted by the tight-fitting engine hood. For 1977, the catalytic coverters were moved back beneath the floor.

For 1976, CIS fuel injection replaced the earli-

The first and last of two decades: the 350SL, above, and the 560SL, below. Besides the obvi-ous powerplant changes, many other more subtle improvements were made. *MBNA*

Technical Specifications

	450SL	380SL	560SL
Model			
Years	1976–1980	1981–1985	1986–1989
Engine			
Type	Sohc V-8 (all)		
Engine # prefix	M117.982	M116.962	117.967
Displacement	4520cc (275.8ci)	3839cc (234.3ci)	5547cc (338.5ci)
Bore x stroke	92x85mm	88x78.9mm	96.5x94.8mm
Compression ratio	8.0:1 (1980)	8.3:1	9.0:1
SAE horsepower	180hp @ 4750rpm (to 1979)	155hp @ 4750rpm	227hp @ 4750rpm
	160hp @ 4200rpm (1980)		
Torque	230lb-ft @ 2500rpm (1980)	196lb-ft @ 2750rpm	279lb-ft @ 3250rpm
Fuel system	Bosch D or K-Jetronic fuel injection	K-Jetronic fuel injection	KE-Jetronic fuel injection
Fuel required	Unleaded, 91 octane		Unleaded, 92 octane
Chassis			
Type	Unibody; steel with aluminum		
Chassis # prefix	107.044	107.045	107.048
Transmission	3-speed auto	4-speed auto	4-speed auto
Rear-axle ratio	3.07:1 (to 1979)	2.47:1	2.47:1
	2.65:1 (1980)		
Rear suspension	Semi-trailing arm, coil springs (all)		
Front suspension	Unequal length A-arms, coils springs (all)		
Wheels	6.5x14in	6.5x14in	7x15in
Tires	205/70VR14	205/70HR14	205/65VR15
Brakes	4-wheel disc, power-assisted (all)		
Fuel capacity	23.8gal	22.5gal	22.5gal
Weight	3,615lb (+ hardtop)	3,495lb (+ hardtop)	3,670lb
Performance			
0-60mph	11.5sec (1980)	11.5sec	7.5sec
	10.7sec (to 1979)		
Top speed	112mph (1980)	110mph	130mph
Fuel consumption	12-19mpg (to 1979)	16-22mpg	15-17mpg
	16-22mpg (1980)		

Note: The 450SL figures are for a 1980 model; 380SL figures are for a 1985 model.

er electronic injection, accompanied by hydraulic valve lifters and breakerless electronic ignition. Some years ago Mercedes-Benz recalled all 450SLs and SLCs to weld a reinforcing bracket to the lower control arm mounting of the front suspension.

To avoid camshaft wear, all 4.5 liter V-8s require frequent oil changes and top-quality oil. The right-side camshaft usually wears first. If you're having a mechanic check the car, ask him to remove the valve covers and look at the cam lobes.

For the 1978 model year the 450SL (and SLC) were fitted with automatic climate control, never known for durability. Problems involve the electronic controls, the servo which directs coolant flow, and the vacuum-operated air flaps. A good Mercedes-Benz mechanic will be familiar enough with the system to fix it, but the work can require extensive diagnosis and labor.

To improve fuel economy the 1980 450SL's engine was detuned from 180 to 160hp SAE and a higher (lower numerically) rear axle was fitted, which cut performance. To help prevent vapor lock, for 1980, the air conditioner was used to cool fuel being fed to the engine. Earlier cars can be fitted with a switch to run the electric fuel pump and circulate cooler fuel from the tank before starting. It helps to keep the tank as full as possible. If vapor lock occurs, try turning the ignition switch on and off rapidly. This starts the fuel pump and may move cooler fuel into the injection system. If all else fails, pour cold water on the injection system.

Between 1971 and 1980, a total of 66,298 450SLs were produced, making it by far the most

Driving Impressions: SLs

Whoever dubbed these SLs "The German Corvette" was not mistaken when it came to interior space and highway performance (thankfully, quality is another matter). These cars are big outside, small inside. They go fast, but use lots of fuel. They make an indelible impression, but cost a lot. They are bold, not subtle, not even close to being politically correct. Owners love 'em.

The first thing you'll notice is the snugness. Doors and seats are thick, and the there's not much elbow room, but there is a child-sized rear seat (optional and still available via aftermarket suppliers) and a fair-sized trunk.

These cars feel heavy, but leverage provided by the huge steering wheel and the excellent power steering mask that. Spring rates were chosen for comfort, and the original tires were modestly sized, so cornering limits are less than inspiring, but the car handles safely and predictably. The 350 and early 450SL are the liveliest pre-1985 cars, but the 560SL's power makes it by far the quickest of all.

The most common complaint concerns the automatic climate control system, which lacks the flexibility of earlier manual systems and sometimes has a mind of its own. A good SL is remarkably smooth and quiet for a Convertible, without rattles and squeaks. You may hear differential whine from the rear axle, but because it is mounted to the chassis close behind you.

The 90lb hardtop requires a winch and a cart to remove and store safely. Soft tops were manually operated, right up to 1989, but you'll find it easy. An aftermarket kit to convert the top to power operation was not a success.

The biggest snag about an SL, like other recent Mercedes-Benz models, is that some observers classify you as a rich S.O.B. or the female equivalent. The vast majority though, reflecting the near cultlike following of the SL, will wish they were driving the car instead of you.

---

numerous SL. Next most popular was the 380SL, with 53,000 built from 1980 through 1985.

380SL 1981–1985 ★★★

Thanks to the new-for-1981 380SL's 3.8-liter V-8, some carefully added lightness, and a new four-speed automatic transmission, performance of the smaller engine was adequate, and the SL continued as a sales success in the United States despite its aging design.

The M116 aluminum-block V-8 had first appeared in the 450SLC 5.0 and was designed to work well with emission controls. Apart from the engine saving about 110lb, the 380SL was also lightened by its aluminum engine hood. Again, leather upholstery was an option. None of the US 450SLs or 380SLs had factory alarm systems or power seats, not to mention air bags or ABS brakes.

The 1981–1983 380SL had a mechanical quirk—it used a single-row cam chain instead of the usual dual-row chain. If the oil wasn't changed, friction under load could cause the chain to wear and stretch. If a single-row chain jumped a tooth on its sprockets, the valves could hit the pistons, with expensive consequences. For the 1984 model year, DBAG went to a duplex (double-row) chain that can be retrofitted to any older 380SL. If your car has a single-row chain,

check the tension every 10,000 miles; at the first sign of wear, convert to the dual-row chain. MBNA no longer sells the old chain, and we recommend the conversion rather than just replacing the single-row chain. Conversion won't be cheap, but it will cost far less than an engine overhaul, improve reliability, and enhance the car's value. If you're looking at a 1981–1983 SL, check the

The 350SL with soft top up, European headlights, short bumpers. Michelin XWX tires were standard equipment, and even today they look just right on a restored car. *DBAG*

market importers fed American desires for a more powerful SL, and hundreds of 500SLs were "unofficially" imported. (For more on gray-market cars, see chapter 2). Watching these private importers sell thousands of European SLs, Mercedes-Benz of North America acted...

560SL 1986–1989 ★★★★

For 1986, DBAG cured the 380SL's modest power and skewered the gray market by sending America the much stronger 560SL. The power and torque of its 47 percent larger engine better suited the big Roadster's personality, especially around town. This final iteration of the W107 chassis SL was sold only in North America.

The 560SL's 227hp M117 V-8 gave it a tremendous performance boost even over the 184hp (European only) 500SL. With a new double-wishbone rear suspension, a front air dam, and new-style 7x15in alloy wheels, the 560SL did 0-60mph in 8 seconds, down dramatically from the 11.5 seconds of the 500SL. Top speed leapt from the 380SL's 115 to 137mph. A third brake light was first required in 1986, so it was stuck onto the trunk lid in a blister-like enclosure. More importantly, the 560SL also had a limited-slip differential, leather upholstery, ABS brakes, and an alarm. To reduce rear-end squat and lift, a torque compensating arm braced the rear axle. Tire width stayed at 205mm, but wheels went from 6.5x14 to 7x15. The seats were still hand-adjusted, but a driver's side air bag was standard fare.

Given that it is the most powerful and best developed, the 560SL is the most desirable 1980s

This early 350SLC four-seater clearly shows the added length and louvered rear windows. See how good this car looks with the original bumper design? *DBAG*

records to see if the conversion was made, or ask the owner if you can have a mechanic pull a valve cover to see.

The 380SL was the least powerful of these US sports roadsters. For that reason, and because some still have the single-row timing chain, their values are lower than they might be. The 380SL's last model year was 1985.

Although the 500SL was popular in Europe, it was never sold as a US model. Early 1980s gray-

Chassis and Engine Prefix Numbers

Years	Model	Chassis prefix	Engine prefix	Description
1971–1980	350SL	107.043	116	8-cyl./230hp SAE
1972–1980	350SLC	107.	116	8-cyl./ 230hp SAE
1971–1980	450SL	107.044	117	8-cyl./160-230hp SAE
	(includes US 350SL 4.5)			
1973–1980	450SLC	107.024	117	8-cyl./160-230hp SAE
1974–1985	280SL	R107 E 28	110	6-cyl. gas, 177-185hp DIN
1974–1981	280SLC	C107 E 28	110	6-cyl. gas, 185hp DIN
1978–1980	450SLC 5.0	C107 E 50	117	8-cyl. gas, 240hp DIN
1980–1985	380SL	107.045	116	8-cyl. gas, 155hp (US)
1980–1981	380SLC	107.025	116	8-cyl. gas, 155hp (US)
1985–1989	300SL	R107 E 30	103 E 30	6-cyl. gas, 180-188hp DIN
1985–1989	420SL	R107 E 42	116 E 42	8-cyl. gas, 204-218hp DIN
1980–1985	500SL	107.	117	8-cyl. gas, 240-245hp DIN
1980–1981	500SLC	C107 E 50	117	8-cyl. gas, 240hp DIN
1986–1989	560SL	107.048	117	8-cyl. gas, 227hp (US)

Note: Models listed with DIN horsepower ratings were not officially imported to the United States, but are listed here because many arrived via the gray market.

By 1976 the SLC had grown 5mph crash bumpers and alloy wheels became standard equipment. *MBNA*

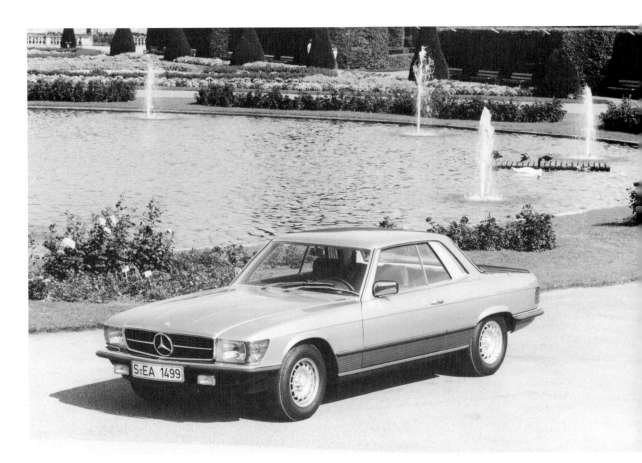

This rare 450SLC 5.0 has rocker panels of contrasting color and a small rear spoiler atop the trunk lid. *DBAG*

European SLs such as this 450SLC 5.0 continued with the original short bumpers. *FDB*

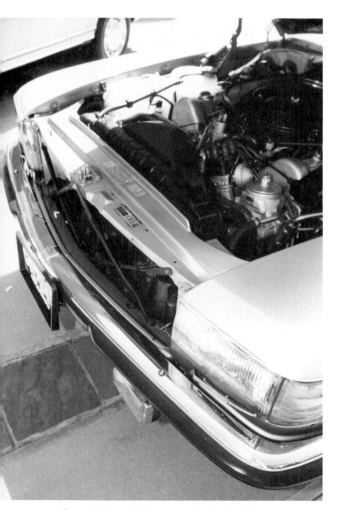

Smooth-faced European lights lent themselves to fitting headlight wipers. *FDB*

SL. The sole disappointment was that Mercedes-Benz never did heal those ugly bumpers.

The SLC ★★★

The four-seater SLC differs from the SL in having two habitable rear seats, a 14.2in longer wheelbase, and a slightly higher fixed steel top. First sold in America for 1972 as the 350SLC, this two-plus-two SL added the extra length right behind the door. To fill the longer quarter window, a unique set of vertical louvers was positioned to maintain visibility.

Air conditioning, power windows, central locking, a leather interior, and an automatic transmission were standard on the American SLC. An electric sunroof was optional, along with a heated rear window, and more.

As in the American 350SL, the 350SLC designation was a misnomer. Both had the M117 4.5 liter V-8, and in 1973 they officially became the 450SL and 450SLC. This engine first made about 195hp, but emission controls cut the 450SLC's output to about 160hp by 1980, the model's last year before being replaced by the 380SL and the rare 380SLC. The SLC's last model year in any form was 1981. The most popular SLC was the 450, with 31,739 made from 1972 to 1980. Only 3,789 380SLCs were built.

European Variations

Between 1967 and 1990, US and European safety and emission regulations at first diverged, then practically merged. At first, European cars got all the good stuff. Their headlights were more aerodynamic and attractive than the sealed-beams of US models. Their early bumpers were lighter and cleaner. Unburdened by emission controls, European engines generated far more power. But by the late 1980s, even German SLs had catalytic converters.

European SLs could be bought with six-cylinder engines (the 280SL) and four- or five-speed manual transmissions. Thousands of 107 chassis 280SLs and 500SLs were imported as gray-market cars. Even a 420SL was made, and from 1985 a 300SL used the 188hp M103 inline six of the 300E. These cars may offer excellent performance, but their low US prices now are a result of their low trade-in value and the potential difficulties of a gray-market car.

As the US 380SL grew more expensive, the European 500SL became popular on the gray market. With 240hp and a wide range of options (ABS brakes, velour interior, manual climate controls, limited-slip differential, rear spoiler, wider wheels, and so on) combined with lower prices, these 500SLs were attractive to Americans. But improper conversions and the reluctance of some US Mercedes-Benz dealers to even service gray-market cars limited their popularity and hastened depreciation.

An exception is the 450SLC 5.0, built as a 1978–1980 European model. A small rubber rear spoiler and a different front spoiler make the 450SLC 5.0 easy to spot. Its aluminum engine lid and trunk lid saved about 125lb, and the new M117 aluminum-block 5025cc engine was about 95lb lighter. Power went up to 240hp DIN, torque was 297lb-ft, and top speed was about 140mph. Compression ratio was 8.8:1.

Of fewer than 3,000 built, quite a few 450SLC 5.0s found their way to the United States, and because of their rarity, lower weight, and higher power, they remain highly regarded, especially since the model was the basis for a Mercedes-Benz factory rally team. Despite their rarity, they remain reasonably priced on the collector market.

What to Look For

Rust is a relatively minor problem with these cars, but look for it anyway. Besides the normal places under the fenders and around the headlights and wheelwells, open the metal tonneau cover and check the top well. The front valence may show damage from concrete curbs. Look for water and sun damage to upholstery, wood, and carpets. If you find significant rust or much accident damage, find a better car. So many good examples exist that there's no savings in buying and restoring a heap.

To avoid having to fix cam wear on the 450SL, pull the right-side (or both) valve covers and look closely at every cam lobe. Rotate the engine (using a wrench on the crankshaft, if possible) and look for pitting at the top of each lobe.

On a 1981–1983 380SL, check the cam chain to see whether it is the original single-row type or the desirable double-row replacement. If the car doesn't have a double chain, figure on substantial cost to install it. All 1984 and later 380SLs originally came with double-row chains, so there's no need to check them. All other things being equal, this is one reason to buy a 1984 or later car.

Despite the durability problems of some auto makers' aluminum blocks, the better-designed Mercedes-Benz blocks are at least as durable as their cast-iron equivalents. An SL is generally one of the most durable Mercedes-Benz cars.

In 1985, MBNA warned owners of the 350SL, 350SLC, 450SL, and 450SLC to have their cars inspected for cracks in the lower rear control arm mountings of the front suspension. Reinforcement brackets can be welded in. The 380SL and 560SL were unaffected.

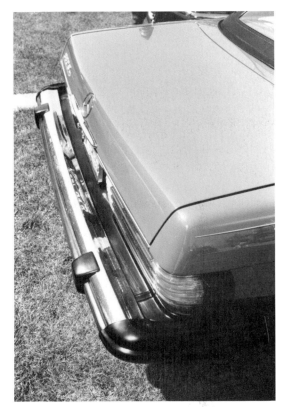

Whatever grace an SL has is severely compromised by these US bumpers. *FDB*

Older cars are somewhat prone to overheating and vapor lock, particularly with today's fuels and because the 450SL's catalytic converters were up front, under the tight-fitting engine hood. Hot-start problems are a sign of vapor lock; the engine will restart immediately when hot and when cold, but left standing for a few minutes while hot, it will not fire.

Examining the service records not only assures you that the proper service was done, but also that it was performed by a qualified mechanic. Look for mechanics' comments on invoices, particularly such phrases as "Customer declines..."

As a driver and a collector car, we suggest either the earliest or the latest—either a 1972 350SL (definitely collectible, with the small bumpers and perhaps a manual transmission) or a late-model 560SL. As a second choice we'd suggest a late 450SL, perhaps 1979 (before the 1980 power decrease) so that you get as many improvements as possible. A 380SL may be the least desirable, but it can make a fine daily driver, with better fuel mileage than the 450SL or the 560SL. As a high-performance rarity, try the 450SLC 5.0, but make sure this frequently abused European model hasn't been ridden hard and put away wet.

One final caution. If you're looking at a 560SL at a price within, say, 20 percent of that of an equally good 1990-on 300SL or 500SL, consider buying the newer car, especially if you'll drive it a lot. The newer car is more agile, spacious, safe, and enjoyable.

Restoration

Since thousands of excellent original examples still exist, restoration of these SLs has been limited. A new top is logical, but fighting rust, incorrectly repaired damage, or big mechanical problems makes little sense. Even if you already own the car, you're likely far better off finding a cleaner, original example.

Because they were more complex, bigger, and heavier than a 280SL, these cars cost more to restore properly. Later models have more complicat-

ed systems, especially the climate controls, but a 350SL is relatively simple. About the only W107 SL that justifies expensive restoration now is the 450SLC 5.0 because of its rarity and performance.

Operation of these cars will not be inexpensive, and neither will parts and repairs; you'll likely have to rely on a professional mechanic to maintain these sophisticated cars. Since they are too new to qualify for classic car coverage, insurance will be costly, too, and you'll need a garage to protect your investment. Check licensing and insurance costs before you commit.

Summary

As the earliest W107 SLs begin to be considered collectible, the latest are still in the early or middle stages of depreciation. Dating from the 1960s, their design may be ancient, but these SL models have served reliably. The 380SLs are good buys, and the 560 is the most fun for those who like to drive quickly, but none of these cars will disappoint you.

The 450SLC 5.0 did surprisingly well in long-distance international rallies; here Andrew Cowan approaches the finish of a 30,000km event in South America in 1978. *DBAG*

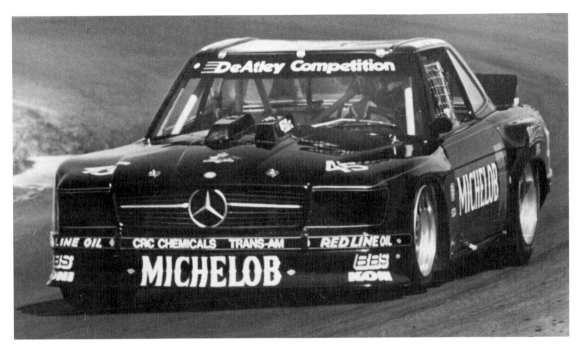

American racer Neal DeAtley entered an SL, driven by Loren St. Lawrence, in the Trans-Am series in 1981–1982, tuning the engine to around 450hp and paring weight to 2400lb. *DeAtley*

The 227hp 560SL, sold only in the United States, gained a new front air dam and ABS brakes. By then, leather upholstery and the hardtop were standard equipment. *MBNA*

Chapter 14

Sedans and Coupes 1968–1980

Safety and emissions assumed new importance in the late 1960s. As the flagship for the 1970s, the 450SE and SEL addressed these concerns and was regarded as the best sedan in the world. The new mid-range models joining it were equally successful.

Between 1967 and 1973, DBAG put almost every engine into almost every chassis, and some models were short-lived. Apart from the 1968–1973 V-8s described in chapter 12, let's look at the other sedans.

450SE and 450SEL ★★

In 1973 the world standard for luxury cars was reestablished by the new 450SE, soon followed by the 450SEL with a 3.9in longer wheelbase and more rear legroom. Although the W116 used practically the same V-8 engine as the preceding 1971–1973 4.5s, it was a completely different chassis.

Daimler-Benz finally abandoned the rear swing-axles in favor of trailing arms, which kept the rear wheels more upright throughout the range of suspension travel. Less drastic camber change improved stability, even in a straight line, by limiting rear toe-in and toe-out. The entire body was stronger, with additional interior padding and improved seatbelts. The 450SE and SEL strongly resemble a Mercedes-Benz safety car unveiled in 1971. The structure was designed to meet the new impact requirements.

Between 1973 and 1980 the 450SE and SEL were the world's best overall cars, combining the

In its first US model year, the 1973 450SE came with body-color hubcaps and short, European-style bumpers. *MBNA*

The 450SE had new suspension at each end. The front uses a MacPherson strut with separate coil springs and shock absorbers; the rear gave up on the swing-axle in favor of semi-trailing arms. *DBAG*

highest levels in safety, interior space, handling, performance, and ride.

The 1973 model was the only US 450 sedan to have the original, slim, European-style bumpers. Later US versions are protected by federally mandated 5mph battering rams that don't harmonize with the lines of the car. Mercedes-Benz left them that way for the life of the model.

Driving Impression:
450SE, 450SEL, and 450SEL 6.9

Because it lacks the smog clutter, an early 450SE or SEL is a good performer. The shorter wheelbase makes the SE more nimble than the SEL, which is more spacious for back-seat passengers. These are long-legged cars, about the earliest models that you can drive hard for a thousand miles without collapsing at day's end.

The 6.9 feels like driving your living room down the road at 130mph. The car is quiet, smooth, and astonishly fast, yet is totally unfussy. It demands only that you feed it massive quantities of fuel and maintain it in the manner to which it has become accustomed. Despite having power windows (controlled by switches awkwardly mounted on the console), the 6.9 had manually adjusted seats.

Comparisons with the 300SEL 6.3 are inevitable. The earlier car is less sophisticated and not as quiet and smooth, yet it's more fun. Most acknowledge that the 6.3 accelerates more quickly but that the 6.9 is better handling, more comfortable, and easier to drive fast. A good 6.3 will get slightly better gas mileage, and maintenance cost is probably a toss-up.

The 6.9 is a generation better than the 6.3. Its controls and transmission are smoother, and the steering is more precise. Besides having better heating and air conditioning, a 6.9 is safer, too. Even little things such as the windshield wipers work better.

Short of a 500E, the driver of 450SEL 6.9 will find that it is still one of the best sedans of all time.

Even the SE is a big car, so the SEL's extra rear legroom is not absolutely necessary. The SE is only slightly lighter than the SEL, so there's no real performance benefit; few can feel the slight handling difference due to the longer wheelbase. A good 1973 450SE is a joy to drive. It tracks down the road straight, smooth, and true, and you feel like Superman behind the wheel.

In its time, the W116 chassis was the best-driving sedan in the world. Credit for this goes to its suspension, especially the semi-trailing arms in the rear, which gave it great stability.

The loss suffered from the 450SEL's transition to US government-mandated bumpers was some- what offset by the appearance boost of alloy wheels. *MBNA*

The 450SE and SEL arrived just as the emissions and fuel crises struck, and both harmed the cars. Emissions technology was in its infancy, so driveability sometimes suffered. Fuel mileage rarely bettered the mid-teens. As the cars age, problems such as vapor lock, aging wiring, and fuel consumption worsen. The 1973–1975 450SEs and SELs used an early version of electronic fuel injection, but 1976 and later cars had the more reliable Bosch CIS injection, also called K-Jetronic. Its quantity matched to the amount of intake air, fuel enters the engine continuously, hence the name Continuous Injection System.

The 4.5 V-8 was a great engine with one weak point: its camshafts were susceptible to premature wear. Supposedly this was due to infrequent oil changes, but camshafts are difficult parts of any engine to lubricate. The oil lines to the camshafts were held by plastic clips, which become brittle and break. When you have a valve cover off, make sure these clips are in place, and check the peaks of the cam lobes for wear. A factory camshaft lubrication modification kit was made to fit 3.5 and 4.5 liter M116 and M117 engines.

A less serious problem is vapor lock on pre-1980 models. Today's fuels vaporize easily, so high underhood temperatures can boil fuel in the engine compartment while the car stands, hot, after running. Twenty minutes later the starter will crank, but the engine won't run. Spray water on the fuel lines—or wait for the engine to cool. For 1980, Mercedes-Benz used air conditioner refrigerant to cool the fuel, but we've never heard of anyone retrofitting this item. The CIS fuel injection also helped to solve this problem.

Other common problems include the automatic climate control servo (1976–1979) and the water pump. The 450SE and SEL were the first Mercedes-Benz models to use an automatic climate control; you set the desired temperature on a wheel, set the mode, and the system maintains the temperature. Before operating this system, read the owners manual. A seeming failure may be simply due to incorrect setting.

This system had weak spots. Chief of these was the electrically operated servo valve controlling coolant flow through the heating system, the same ex-Chrysler unit used in W123 (300D, 300TD, and so on) bodies. Repair kits and replacement servos are available.

The transmissions in these cars, all three-speed automatics, are also not noted for extreme durability.

These cars are so enjoyable that their owners never know when to stop driving them. Today it's hard to find a 450 with fewer than 100,000 miles behind it. The 1976 model year was the 450SE's last in the United States; from then until the end of the 1980 model year, only the 450SEL was available. Between 1972 and 1980, 41,604 450SEs and 59,578 450SELs were made.

450SEL 6.9 ★★★

Not until 1975 did DBAG got around to replacing the 300SEL 6.3—with the 450SEL 6.9. Its M100 engine was developed from the 6.3 liter unit but appeared only in this car; the 600 continued with the 6.3 liter. The 6.9's main advantages over the 450SEL included better performance, more advanced suspension, and slightly more luxury.

The 6.9's engine improvements included dry-sump lubrication and K-Jetronic fuel injection. A more sophisticated valve clearance method using oil to support the rocker arm fulcrum, eliminating the need for hydraulic lifters and quieting the valvetrain. The oil tank is alongside the engine.

Lead, follow, or get the hell out of the way—this 6.9 liter 450SEL means business! Bumper faces are all-black; tires are huge Michelin XWXs. *MBNA/John Lamm*

The 450SEL 6.9 was sold in Europe starting in 1975. Of 7,380 built, 1,816 were 1977–1979 US models. To meet emission laws, the US version had a tad less power, with minimal effect. A European version may have ABS brakes, albeit in elementary form. Quite a few found their way to the US unofficially, but your typical Serious German Motoring Enthusiast then bought the newest, biggest, fastest car and drove the living tar out of it. When the car would no longer pass the rigid German TUV safety inspection, he found a ready market among US enthusiasts. Hence, *caveat emptor* (let the buyer beware) when looking at any European 6.9.

Besides the chassis numbers, the easiest way to tell a European 6.9 is by its smaller bumpers, metric instruments, and possibly a cloth interior. European power was 286hp DIN with 405lb-ft of torque. US emission controls included air injection and a catalytic converter, cutting power to 250hp and torque to 360lb-ft. In US form the 4400lb car could reach 60mph in just over eight seconds, topping out at about 137mph.

Built before the days of traction control, a 6.9 (or a 6.3) can be kicked sideways by heavy throttle on a slick street. You could also outrun just about any production car from a standing start, looking re-laxed and comfy doing so. Part of the fun of owning these cars is that they may be the ultimate "sleeper."

The 6.9 is more stable than the 6.3 (and even the 450SE) because it has a sophisticated hydro-pneumatic suspension. Instead of the 6.3's air system or the 450SE's coil springs, the 6.9 uses nitro-

The 6.9's interior had a little more wood than the garden-variety 450SEL, but manual seats remained the only choice on this $50,000 car.

129

gen gas and hydraulic oil with a spherical pressure reservoir at each wheel. This provides better low-speed ride than the air system and responds better to changing suspension loads. Instead of the 6.3's rear swing-axle, the 6.9 uses semi-trailing arms, which better control camber change.

In a 6.9 the transmission handles a lot more torque than in the 450SE or SEL, so it is more likely to fail. Tires should be 215/70VR14 on 6.5x14in alloy wheels; the original Michelin XWXs are extremely expensive and short-lived. Standard features on US 6.9s included leather upholstery, central locking, four headrests, rear reading lamps, fog lights, a fully carpeted trunk, and a tachometer; options were an electric sunroof, velour seats, orthopedic and/or heated seats, and metallic paint. European 6.9s have a switch to increase ride height about 1.6in; US cars use the same switch to lock the suspension for jacking.

The market for 6.9s is unusual. American models sold new for $40,000–$50,000, a fortune at the time. Some cherry examples "meticulously maintained" (the Mercedes-Benz seller's favorite term) by original owners with delusions of great value top today's price scale, but others with obscure histories and lots of miles can be had for a fraction of the higher prices. Aim for the mid-range and be patient. Every time a 6.9 owner pays for service, he or she considers selling it. Time your offer accordingly!

European captains of industry could buy a 450SEL 6.9 with small bumpers, flush headlights, and headlight wipers. *DBAG*

The massive W116 body could still mix it up with the best of them; witness this modified 450SEL at a club driving event. *FDB*

What to Look For

Rusty 450SE and SEL sedans are uncommon. These cars, now growing old, are more likely to have suffered from improper maintenance. Some second or third owners can't afford to keep them up properly, so they postpone repairs or try a cheap patch job. The cars grow ever more tired and unkempt. Maintenance records mean a lot with these cars.

Because the cars are often owned by nonenthusiasts, they are more likely to be shabby. Be suspicious of fresh paint and undercoating. One clear indication of whether an owner cares about his car is its tires. Are they the right size and speed rating, or are they cheap substitutes for the genuine item?

Test every system, especially the heating and air conditioning and the instruments, power windows, power antenna, windshield wipers, and locks. The automatic climate control servo is notorious for failure, usually involving a cracked valve body. Left unattended, this can lead to coolant loss, with the usual serious consequences. A servo repair kit is available from Mercedes-Benz dealers, and aftermarket suppliers offer aluminum servo bodies. Look for coolant seepage around the water pump.

On the 6.9, check the suspension thoroughly. First, make sure it works properly. Use the level control to adjust the height, and invite a couple of people into the trunk to make sure the self-leveling does so. The trunk should contain four rubber blocks—two front and two rear—to support the car if the suspension fails. Should the car drop to its knees, you jack it up, take off each wheel, insert the block, and tie it in place with an attached wire. Often missing, these blocks are hard to find.

Since the 6.9 has a dry-sump oil system, its oil level is checked with the engine idling at normal operating temperature.

Restoration

Few of these cars have been restored much beyond a paint job. It's still simpler to sell your old one and find a fresher one. These are large and fairly complex cars, so they cost a lot in parts and labor to refurbish (or even to furbish, for that matter).

Technical Specifications			
Model	280S	450SE/SEL	450SEL 6.9
Years	1975–1979	1973–1979	1977–1979 (US)
Engine			
Type	Inline dohc six	V-8	V-8
Engine # prefix	117	100	
Displacement	2746cc (168ci)	4520cc (276ci)	6834cc (417ci)
Bore x stroke	86x78.8mm	92x65.8mm	107x95mm
Compression ratio	8:1	8:1	8:1
SAE horsepower	120hp (US)	190hp (1973 US) 250hp (US)	
Torque	143lb-ft	240lb-ft	360lb-ft
Fuel system	Solex 4-bbl carb fuel injection	Electronic fuel injection	K-Jetronic
Fuel required	Unleaded	Regular (1973)	
Chassis			
Type	Unibody; steel (all)		
Chassis # prefix	116	116	116
Transmission	4-speed auto	3-speed auto	3-speed auto
Rear-axle ratio	3.69:1	3.07:1	2.65:1
Rear suspension	Semi-trailing arms, coil springs	Hydro-pneumatic	
Front suspension	Lower A-arms, lateral links, coil springs		
Hydro-pneumatic			
Wheels	6.5x14in	6.5x14in	6.5x14in
Tires	185HR14	205/70VR14	215/70VR14
Brakes	4-wheel disc (all)		
Fuel capacity	25.4gal	25.4gal	25.4gal
Weight	3,890lb	4,030lb (1973)	4,300lb
Performance			
0-60mph	17sec	11sec	8sec
Top speed	103mph	125mph	140mph
Fuel consumption	15mpg	12–15mpg	

The 114 and 115 sedans (here in European form) were faithful daily drivers for hundreds of thousands of Mercedes-Benz owners. *DBAG*

The early electronic fuel injection was susceptible to bad wiring connections, especially with age. You might be able to make the car run better by methodically cleaning connections, but a new fuel injection wiring harness will probably help more. Apart from the cam lubrication problem, engines routinely last 150,000 miles or more before overhaul or replacement. If you decide to overhaul the engine, check out the replacement engines offered by Mercedes-Benz and other rebuilders.

Restoring a 6.9 is exceeded in cost only by restoring a 600 or a prewar classic. If you have to ask how much, forget it. Classified ad sections are full of owners who are financially buried in their

Chassis and Engine Prefix Numbers

Years	Model	Chassis prefix	Engine prefix	Description
1968–1976	200	115	115	4-cyl. gas, 105hp
1968–1976	200D	115	OM615	4-cyl. diesel, 61hp
1968–1973	220	115	115	4-cyl. gas, 116hp
1968–1976	220D	115	OM615	4-cyl. diesel, 65hp
1968–1976	230	114	180	6-cyl. gas, 135hp
1972–1976	230/4	115	115	4-cyl. gas, 85-95hp
1973–1976	240D	115	OM616	4-cyl. diesel, 62hp
1974–1976	300D	115	OM617	5-cyl. diesel, 77hp
1968–1972	250	114	114	6-cyl. gas, 146hp
1970–1976	250 (2.8)	114	130	6-cyl. gas, 157hp
1972–1976	280	114	110	6-cyl. gas, 120-180hp
1972–1976	280E	114	110	6-cyl. gas, 185hp DIN

Technical Specifications

Model	220 Sedan	250 Sedan	280 Sedan
Years	1968–1973	1969	1971–1976
Engine			
Type	Inline four	Inline sohc six	Inline dohc six
Engine # prefix	115.920	130.923 or 114.920	110.921
Displacement	2197cc (134ci)	2778cc (169ci)	2746cc (168ci)
Bore x stroke	87.0x92.4mm	86.5x78.8mm	86x78.8mm
Compression ratio 9:1	9:1	8:1	
SAE horsepower	116hp	157hp	120-160hp
Torque	19.7mkg (143lb-ft)	25.1mkg (182lb-ft)	23.0mkg (166lb-ft)
Fuel system	Stromberg (US)	Zenith carbs	Solex carbs
Fuel required	Premium	Premium	Premium or unleaded
Chassis			
Type	Unibody; steel (all)		
Chassis # prefix	115.010	114.010	114.060
Transmission	4-speed, automatic (all)		
Rear-axle ratio	4.08:1	3.92:1	3.69:1
Rear suspension	Semi-trailing arms, springs (all)		
Front suspension	Unequal-length A-arms (all)		
Wheels	5.5x14	5.5x14	6x14
Tires	175x14in	175x14in	185x14in
Brakes	4-wheel disc (all)		
Fuel capacity	17.2gal	17.2gal	17.2gal
Weight	2,890lb	3,179lb	3,200lb
Performance			
0-60mph	14sec	12sec	13sec
Top speed	100mph	118mph	118mph
Fuel consumption	18–22mpg	14–18mpg	14–18mpg

6.9s, and you needn't join them.

Because the W116 bodied cars are so numerous, the choice of a restorer is not as critical as it can be with a rare model. Most foreign car body shops have already seen plenty of these cars and have built up experience. All you need do is judge their previous work and communicate what you expect. Right.

280S and 280SE: A Six-Cylinder Variant

A twin-cam 2.8 liter six in the big W116 sedan chassis made the 280S. In Germany these engines sang unfettered at around 185hp, but in the United States, limited to 120hp by emission laws, the heavy sedans could barely get out of their own way. A four-speed automatic (instead of the 450's three-speed) helped, but the four-barrel Solex carburetor didn't. Gas mileage was disappointing.

For 1977, with fuel injection, the model became the 280SE, but Americans weren't used to revving an engine to redline, so first impressions caused many US sales prospects to think, "Gee, I could have a V-8." (Pun intended.) Few 280SEs were sold in the United States.

Summary

The 450SE and SEL's bang-for-the-buck factor is right up there, but if you drive in town much,

Chassis and Engine Prefix Numbers

Years	Model	Chassis prefix	Engine prefix	Description
1969–1972	250C	114	114	6-cyl. gas, 130hp DIN
1969–1976	250C	114	130	6-cyl. gas, 150hp DIN (2.8 liter)
1969–1972	250CE	114	130	6-cyl. gas, 157hp
1972–1976	280C	114	110	6-cyl. gas, 120-180hp
1972–1976	280CE	114	110	6-cyl. gas, 195hp DIN

The squared-off grille of the W114 and W115 nicely matches its US headlight units. *MBNA*

your gas bills may be higher than your car payments. Find a good one to start with; if and when you wear it out, find another.

The 450SE and SEL hold scant interest for collectors, but they can make great drivers. The 6.9 is incredible, but buy one only if you can afford to keep it properly. Best bets for future collector interest are the 6.9 and the 1973 450SE.

114 and 115 Sedans Fours and Sixes ★★

For 1968, a new sedan chassis was introduced for the four- and six-cylinder economy models. Many of these faithful workhorses were diesel-powered (see chapter 18). We'll cover the gasoline models here, but only the most unusual and pristine examples even begin to approach collectible status.

Besides the new body, the biggest chassis improvement was the semi-trailing arm rear suspension. Most powerplants were identical to those of the earlier fin-back models, but several US gasoline models used Stromberg carburetors. A four-speed manual transmission was standard; the optional automatic is best avoided on smaller-engined or diesel models.

Two chassis, eight engines, twelve models, eight years—no wonder Mercedes-Benz models are confusing. Besides that, a 250 is not always what it may seem: those sold in the United States in 1970 to 1976 model years had 2.8 liter engines. The 280s used a new M110 twin-overhead-cam six, but US output was strangled by emission controls. All 1974 and later US models had 5mph bumpers.

The 114 and 115 chassis are nearly identical. The 114 chassis used six-cylinder gas engines; the 115 had four-cylinder diesel, five-cylinder diesel, and four-cylinder gas engines. All were popular as daily drivers, with many still going after hundreds of thousands of miles.

The most common of these cars is the 200D, followed by the 1973–1976 240D. The smaller-engined gasoline models are slow but durable, and the 2.8 liter sixes are faster but shorter-lived. Parts are inexpensive and easy to find. Rust and poor carburetion are the main faults.

114 and 115 Coupes ★★

Early Coupe versions of the 114 and 115 chassis provided alternatives to the expensive 280SE

By 1975, the 280 Coupe had crash bumpers and was available with two-tone paint. Power came via a dohc six. *MBNA*

3.5 Coupe. All had gasoline engines, and convertibles were never offered, but a sunroof was optional. If any 114 or 115 model offers collector interest, it's these Coupes.

The squared-off W114 Coupe was first sold in the United States as the 1969 250C. Its proportions resemble those of a 300SEL 6.3 show car built by Pininfarina, but mechanically the Coupes are identical to their sedan brethren. Four-speed manual transmissions were available, but most US cars have automatics.

US models have the M130 2.8 liter engines. Again, because of the peculiarities of carburetors designed to stifle emissions, the electronic fuel injection models, designated CE, are your best bet. US models from 1974 onward had the unattractive extended bumpers, but in compensation these Coupes look quite attractive with alloy wheels, which by then had found their way down from the SL models.

W123 Mid-Range Models ★★

The mid-range W114 and W115 sedans were replaced by the W123. These were mostly fitted with diesel engines (see chapter 18), but gasoline models included sedans, wagons, and Coupes.

This list includes only the most popular models; some utilitarian models sold only in Europe—the 230, for instance—aren't shown. Few made it to the United States as gray-market imports, also the case with the 280, 230C and CE, and 280C. Be-cause MBNA offered no gasoline-powered wagon at the time, the 280TE wagon was a popular gray-market car.

The twin-cam six was a much better match to the 123 chassis than it was to the 300lb heavier 116 chassis. K-Jetronic injection boosted power to 142hp, except in the California version, where a catalytic converter held it to 137hp. Zero to 60mph took 11.5 seconds; top speed was about 110. US cars got four-speed automatics, but European versions offered five-speed manuals. Expect 16–20mpg with an automatic; a manual can do much better.

Because they were relatively expensive and a V-8 450SE and SEL could be had for little more, these sixes are almost rare. If you can find one, it can be a good buy today. Body and chassis were identical to those of the popular W123 diesels, so parts are easy to find.

Summary

Although numerous, the 1970s sedans are growing old, and some have been subjected to shoddy maintenance. Gas mileage is not their forte (even the sixes), but these cars are spacious and safe, and the V-8s can be quite rapid.

Prices are reasonable, and the parts supply is excellent, but restoration usually isn't warranted financially. Most collectors are interested only in the short-bumper 1973 450SE and SEL and the 450SEL 6.9, although any excellent example is worth preserving.

The gasoline-powered 1979 280CE Coupe was followed by a similar diesel version, the 300CD.
MBNA

Chassis and Engine Prefix Numbers

Years	Model	Chassis prefix	Engine prefix	Description
1976–1985	250	123	123	6-cyl. gas, 140hp DIN
1976–1981	280	123	110	6-cyl. gas, 156hp DIN
1976–1985	280E	123	110	6-cyl. gas, 137-142hp
1978–1986	280TE	123	110	6-cyl. gas, 177-185hp DIN
1977–1980	230C	123	115	4-cyl. gas, 109hp DIN
1980–1985	230CE	123	102	4-cyl. gas, 136hp DIN
1977–1980	280C	123	110	6-cyl. gas, 156hp DIN
1977–1985	280CE	123	110	6-cyl. gas, 137-142hp

Chapter 15

Sedans and Coupes 1980–1991

The 1980s saw huge progress in safety, emission controls, suspension, and performance. Mercedes-Benz also introduced new mid-range cars that some believe outshone even the S-Class.

During the 1980s, Mercedes-Benz made tremendous advances in design and construction. For instance, 1960s and even 1970s cars rust, but if there's even one rusty 300E out there, it's well hidden. Safety improvements involved air bags and seatbelts that tighten on impact (the Supple-

mental Restraint System). When you have an accident, you'll want the protection that these cars offer.

ABS brakes stop you no shorter, but they do let you steer under maximum braking. If you're buying a family car, it's worth saving up for. Electronic traction control systems also appeared on these cars.

Driveability improved incredibly during the 1980s and early 1990s. Engines start and run well

The W126 chassis was the basis for all S-class cars through 1991. This US 1981 380SEL has inset US headlights, but otherwise could pass for a 1991 560SEL. *MBNA*

For 1982 the United States got a new four-seater Coupe, the 380SEC, meant to replace the SLC. *MBNA*

in all temperatures. With electronic control, transmissions became smoother shifting. Electronic glitches did appear occasionally, but the refinement provided by microprocessors was worth the price.

The S-Class: 380 to 560

An S-Class Mercedes-Benz says that you've arrived. If that doesn't matter to you, they are still one hell of a car. From 1981 through 1991, the W126 chassis came with a variety of diesels

Technical Specifications			
Model	380SE/SEL	500SEL	560SEL
Year	1981–1985	1984–1985	1986–1991
Engine			
Type	Sohc V-8 (all)		
Displacement	3839cc	4973cc	5547cc (338.5ci)
Bore x stroke	88x78.9mm	96.5x85mm	96.5x94.8mm
Compression ratio	8.3:1	8.0:1	
SAE horsepower	155hp @ 4750rpm	185hp @ 4500rpm	238hp @ 4800rpm
Torque	196lb-ft @ 2750rpm	247lb-ft @ 2000rpm	287lb-ft @ 3500rpm
Fuel system	Electronic fuel injection (all)		
Fuel required	Premium (all)		
Chassis			
Type	Unibody; steel (all)		
Chassis # prefix	126.032	126.037	126.039
Transmission	4-speed automatic (all)		
Rear-axle ratio	2.47:1	2.47:1	2.47:1
Rear suspension	Semi-trailing arms, coil springs (all)		
Front suspension	Damper strut, coil springs (all)		
Wheels	6.5x14in	6.5x14in	7x15in
Tires	205/70HR14	205/70HR14	205/65VR15
Brakes	4-wheel disc (all)		
Fuel capacity	23.8gal	23.8gal	23.8gal
Weight	3,815lb	3,900lb	4,125lb
Performance			
0-60mph	10.5sec	9.0sec	7.4sec
Top speed	115mph	135mph	140mph (est.)
Fuel consumption	16-19mpg	14-18mpg	13-17mpg (est.)

(300SD, 300SDL), plus six-cylinder and eight-cylinder gasoline engines (380SE and SEL, 420SEL, 500SEL, 560SEL).

380 to 560SEL Sedans ★★

Sleeker than the old 450SE and SEL, the W126 body premiered in the United States as the flagship 1981 380SEL, with the 3.8 liter V-8 supplying a reasonable, if not exorbitant, 155hp with good fuel economy. The latter was also aided by added lightness and better aerodynamics, with the side effect of back-seat space that was practically decadent in the long-wheelbase SEL. The electrically powered seats were the first in any Mercedes-Benz (the 600's were hydraulic); an ingenious seat-shaped switch made adjustment intuitive.

Given regular oil changes, these V-8s are reliable. Given less, they are subject to camshaft wear. The 1981–1983 380 engines used a single-row timing chain. With age and neglected oil changes, the chain may wear and stretch. If it jumps on the sprocket, the valves can hit the pistons, with expensive results. For 1984 a double-row chain appeared, and it can be retrofitted. Mercedes-Benz recommends that timing chains be inspected regularly, and most mechanics replace them every 100,000 miles. If related work is needed, the single-row chain should be replaced with a double-row unit.

After customers requested more power, and as the gray market in European 500SEL sedans grew, Mercedes-Benz of North America responded with the 500SEL as a 1984 US model, relegating the 380 engine to the shorter-wheelbase 380SE for 1984 and 1985. With 184hp, the US 500 was faster than the 380 but not as hot as the European 500, so in 1986 the United States got the 238hp 560SEL, the final W126 sedan.

The 1986 and 1987 S-Class cars had 7x15in alloy wheels. For a smoother ride, rim width was decreased to 6.5in for 1988–1991; tire sizes remained the same. Electronic traction control (ASR), was first made available on 1991 S-Class models.

The 420SEL, using a 201hp, 4.2 liter version of the M116 engine, was built as a 1986–1991 model. With 17 more horsepower than the US 500, it topped out at 135mph and reached 60mph in nine seconds. A six-cylinder 300SEL, using the 300E's 177hp engine in the S-Class body, was sold as a 1988–1991 model, accompanied by the virtually identical but 5.5in shorter 300SE.

From 1986 through 1991 the 560SEL topped the line. Its catalyst-equipped 238hp V-8 was the final development of the alloy M117 engine. A 54hp boost from the 500SEL and SEC chopped 0–60 times to 7.5 seconds, fully 2.5 seconds faster than the US 500. Bosch's electronically controlled

To allow occupants easier access to seatbelts, the SEC used an automatic seatbelt arm which presents the belt when the engine is started. *DBAG*

fuel injection had matured into the KE-III, a blend of electronic and mechanical systems with a limp-home mode should electrons cease. The headlights were made flush, like the 300's, and flatter alloy wheels (similar to those on the 190) appeared. In-

Driving Impressions: S-class

An S-class model gives you that King of the Road feeling, and your passengers will be equally comfortable and impressed. Like all 1980s Mercedes-Benz models, their controls are instantly familiar. Even the transmission shift-gate design dates back to the early 1960s, but it makes it easy to manually override the automatic transmission.

Rear passengers can play with a power back seat on some sedans, and an SEL provides limousine legroom. The 560 has a huge power advantage over the 380 and the US 500 that you can feel instantly on the road. The car sometimes feels as if its going 20mph slower than it really is. Thanks to 200lb less weight and slightly better aerodynamics, the Coupes are a bit quicker and less thirsty than the sedans.

Go for a car with ABS, but traction control isn't a necessity. Fuel mileage is nothing to write home about, but that's the price of all this space, luxury, and safety. The forte of these V-8s is their ability to effortlessly cruise the interstates at any safe speed.

The SEC could form the basis for a personalized hot rod. Wider tires and European headlights were popular. *FDB*

terior options included a suede-like synthetic called Amaretta, and a memory for the driver's seat and steering wheel position.

The 560SEL was the ultimate 1980s "businessman's express." For 1992, it was replaced by the all-new W140 S-Class.

380 to 560SEC Coupes ★★

These grand touring Coupes filled the void left by the demise of the SLC. The 380SEC was first built for the 1981 model year (1982 in the United States). Mechanically it was identical to the equivalent sedan. Inside, a pair of electrically driven seatbelts automatically offered themselves to driver and passenger after the doors were closed.

For 1984 the 380SEC became the 500SEC, gaining 29hp; for 1986 it became the 560SEC with 238hp. Production was low, so if kept in excellent condition, collector potential is excellent, especially for the higher-powered versions. Many still serve their original owners, occasionally becoming available as used cars at reasonable prices.

What to Look For

Problem areas on the 380, 500, and 560SEL and SEC include the radio, air conditioning, and power windows. The 1981–1983 380s with single-row timing chains have already been discussed; the fix is expensive, but it's a one-time deal.

The 1980–1991 S-Class models are almost bulletproof except for the radio and automatic climate control. Listen for rear-axle whine, but even if you hear it, chances are that everything is OK; since the differential is on the chassis, noise travels readily.

If you're looking at a pre-1984 500 sedan or Coupe in the United States, it's a gray-market car. Be wary of silly spoilers, deeply tinted windows, and elaborate audio or alarms. The best buys are the original cars, whose conservative owners gave them the best care and modest use. Plenty are out there, so take your time.

Summary

The 560SEL is the finest and the final 1980s S-Class car. The 380 and 500 engined cars were less expensive and will remain so. Collectors don't find much of interest here, but they may aim for low-production models such as the late S-Class Coupes. Great bang for the buck here if you can spare the admission fee.

300 Mid-Range Models

For most people, a 300E or one of its derivatives is the best car in the world. A clean, used

300E is your best buy in a luxury sedan. Its ABS, air bag(s), and advanced rear suspension are complemented by a willing yet economical six-cylinder engine. The car is unostentatious, nimble, safe, reasonably fast, durable, and fun to drive.

300E 1986–1993 ★★

Introduced for 1986 in the United States, the mid-range 300E's W124 chassis replaced the venerable but bluff W123. Its new body incorporated safety features developed with decades of experience. A five-link rear suspension (similar to that of the 190) provided stability and excellent handling under any load. The single-arm windshield wiper works well, and the interior has almost everything except a cupholder.

The 300E came to the United States with the new M103 3.0 liter, single-cam six making 177hp. A four-speed automatic transmission or a five-speed manual could be ordered, but few had the latter, and only in 1986 and 1988. Fifth gear was really an overdrive (0.80:1). The lower four gears are in an H-pattern with fifth and reverse off to the right. Automatic transmissions in 1986 through 1990 cars started in second gear, but in 1991 this was changed to a first-gear start with a higher-ratio rear end (2.87:1 vs. the previous 3.27:1).

The 1986 300E outperformed the 380 and 500 engined S-Class cars plus the contemporary Porsche 944 and IROC Z28 Camaro. Top speed was 140mph, with 60mph reached in about 8 seconds. Even so, highway fuel mileage could easily reach the mid-twenties, and 30mpg was possible.

The 300E's biggest weakness is the automatic climate control system. Effective and reliable heating and air conditioning systems have long eluded Mercedes-Benz, costing thousands of repeat sales in America. The complicated system is ridden with potential failures. The switch pad on the console can fail. Vacuum-operated air flaps fail. Air conditioning compressors fail. Climate control problems apply to all post-1980 models, but don't let that put you off. It's just part of the price for the excellence of the rest of the car.

Technical Specifications			
Model	300E	300E 2.6	300E
Year	1986–1992	1986–1992	1993–
Engine			
Type	Inline sohc six		Inline dohc six
Engine # prefix	103.	103.	104.
Displacement	2962cc (180.8ci)	2794cc (170.5ci)	3190cc (194.7ci)
Bore x stroke	88.5x80.3mm	89.9x73.4mm	89.9x83.8mm
Compression ratio	9.2:1	10:1	10:1
SAE horsepower	177hp @ 5700rpm	194hp @ 5500rpm	217hp @ 5500rpm
Torque	188lb-ft @ 4400rpm	199lb-ft@3750rpm	229lb-ft @ 3750rpm
Fuel system	Electronic fuel injection (all)		
Fuel required	Premium (all)		
Chassis			
Type	Unibody; steel (all)		
Chassis # prefix	124.	124.	124.
Transmission	4-speed automatic (all) 5-speed manual option		
Rear-axle ratio	3.07:1	2.65:1	2.65:1
Rear suspension	Multi-link, coil springs (all)		
Front suspension	Damper strut, coil springs (all)		
Wheels	6.5x15in (all)		
Tires	195/65VR15 (all)		
Brakes	4-wheel disc (all)		
Fuel capacity	18.5gal (all)		
Weight	3,295lb	3,460lb	3,525lb
Performance			
0-60mph	7.8sec (manual) 8.3sec (auto)	8.8sec	8.0sec
Top speed	140mph (manual) 137mph (auto)	125mph	140mph (est.)
Fuel consumption	19-25mpg	19-25mpg	19-25mpg

Because it was available in Europe several years before it came to the United States, the 500 was a popular gray-market model; this is a European 500SEC engine. *FDB*

Driving Impressions: 300 Series

The modest 300E hides its capabilities. The 300s offer much more space than the 190s. They are as fast as an S-class car with an equivalent engine, practically as luxurious, and just as durable.

Pre-1992 automatic transmissions start in second, so they feel sluggish off the line. Press down your right foot, and they downshift to first. The 1991 and later 300s start in first and shift more smoothly. The five-speed manual transmission is fun, but has a rubbery wind-up under hard acceleration. Fifth is tall—60mph yields only 2100rpm on the tach—so it saves fuel.

The four-valve engine, seen first in the 1990 300CE and the 1993 300E and 300TE, transforms the car. All 300Es require premium gas, but mileage is in the mid-twenties at modest highway speeds, and a heavy foot is required to earn less than 20mpg.

The 300E is among the world's best cars for the driver. Precise steering and comfortable ride make them particularly good long-distance cars. The 300CE's subtle speed makes it almost a stealth bomber.

Discussing the handling of these cars is academic. Anything that you can do to break them loose on the public road is not only irresponsible and illegal, but also highly unlikely. The only thing better than a 1986–1992 300E is the later version with the more powerful engine.

The 300E evolved quietly. A passenger-side air bag was offered for 1989. For 1990, the sedan and wagon got new lower body cladding and a less austere interior. Better sound systems arrived for 1991, along with optional ASR traction control. For 1993 the 300E underwent other drivetrain changes that vastly improved performance; see chapter 17 for more on those. Chapter 18 contains information on the 300 diesel models.

300TD and 300TE Wagons ★★

The first Mercedes-Benz wagon officially imported to the United States, the turbo-diesel 300TD wagon (on the W124 chassis) showed up as a 1986 model. The 177hp 300TE gasoline wagon replaced it for 1988. Both came only with an automatic transmission and hydro-pneumatic self-leveling. The wagon was taller than the sedan, with more headroom; empty weight was nearly 300lb more, so 0–60mph took about nine seconds. For 1991 ASR traction control was optional, and for 1993 the 300TE got the four-valve 227hp engine.

The wagon's most popular option was a rear-facing third seat for two passengers. The second row of seats folds flat, expanding cargo space. A 300TE has a payload of about 1,250lb but will easily carry more. The self-leveling rear suspension helps it to handle well even with a load. One serves as our business car, so we're biased, but if you want a "different" Mercedes-Benz that's eminently practical, a 300TE is hard to beat.

Many 300TEs were used as Roadside Assistance vehicles by dealers. If you need a low-priced wagon and don't mind white, these can be good buys; you'll pay a premium for a "civilian" wagon.

300CE Coupe ★★

The subtle 300CE Coupe is underappreciated. Making its debut as a 1988 model using 300E mechanical pieces, it rides on a 3.3in shorter wheelbase. In 1988 the Coupe was the first mid-range model to use the plastic lower body cladding, and it uses the automatic seatbelt feeders. Velour upholstery was optional; few US cars had it.

For 1990 the 300CE became the first non-SL to enjoy the variable-intake valve timing and the four-valve head. These four-valve Coupes fly. Because a 300CE is lighter than a 300SL, it beats the sports car to 60mph. Like the 300E and TE, the CE got a first-gear start plus a higher rear-end ratio in 1991.

260E, 300E 2.6, and 300E 2.8 ★★

The 260E and 300E 2.6 are one and the same. Marketed as an economical alternative to the 300E, the 260E came with the 158hp six. To minimize price, it had few standard luxuries, but a long op-

Coincidence or not, the 300E appeared in the company's 100th year, 1986. *DBAG*

tion list. The connotation of "260E" made the car hard to sell, so in 1990 its model designation changed to 300E 2.6. For one model year, 1993, the 300E 2.8 was built.

These smaller-engined cars require the same power as the 300E to maintain a given speed, so no substantial fuel savings are involved. Lower initial cost was the main advantage; trade-in value will be lower than a comparable 300E. These are cars for using, with almost no potential collector interest.

300E 4Matic and 300TE 4Matic ★★

Introduced at the 1985 Frankfurt Auto Show and appearing first in the United States on 1990 models, the 300E 4Matic sedan and 300TE 4Matic wagon were equipped with MBAG's first passenger car four-wheel-drive system. Until mid-1993, when the 4Matic system was discontinued for the United States, these were the only two models to use it.

What to Look For

The 300s share the weak automatic climate control and the Becker Grand Prix radio. Read the owners manual and test the climate control system. Set the horizontal push-buttons to full automatic (hit the button with arrows up and down), set the fan to automatic, and crank the temperature wheel to Min. The air-conditioning should blow cold air. Set the wheel to Max, and it should blow hot air. A gurgling noise in the dash is just coolant flow; an "anti-gurgle kit" is available.

Valve seals on pre-1988 cars should have been replaced with new seals of viton material. The automatic transmission can leak, usually evidenced by smoke at sustained high speed. Some leaks can be fixed with the unit in the car, but usually it must come out. The radiator's top outlet pipe is plastic and can crack if the narrow hose clamp is too tight. Look for excessive oil leaks from the valve cover gasket and the timing cover at the front of the 300E engine; most seep a bit, which doesn't hurt. Make sure the accessory drive belt isn't cracked or worn; changing it is no roadside job. When looking at a 300TE, make sure the self-leveling system works.

Pay attention when shifting at full throttle or on high-speed curves. Age and use can harden and wear driveshaft flex disks plus the bushings in the rear suspension, causing loose handling under high torque and loads. At idle, shift the transmission back and forth between Reverse and Drive; if you notice a clunk, the flex disks are probably worn.

To test the ABS, find a road with no traffic, and punch the brakes hard. Don't squeeze them, punch them! You should feel a slight pulsing in the pedal, and the car should stop in a straight line. Get used to the feeling—when ABS engages, some people think something is wrong and lift off the brakes.

Summary

Mercedes-Benz has always built terrific inline sixes, and this one is their best. If you can't find what you want in this 3.0 liter gasoline sedan, try one of its variations: diesel, wagon, Coupe, Convertible, four-wheel drive. The market has an excellent supply of well-maintained 300 models at a good discount from their original prices. A 300E is

The 300CE soon joined the 300E sedan. Mechanically, the two were virtually identical until 1990, when the Coupe got the four-valve engine.

your best overall buy in a used Mercedes-Benz. Period. End of discussion.

Traction Control Systems

Three traction control systems were developed by Mercedes-Benz during the 1980s. One (ASD) is a simple mechanical/electronic system, the second (ASR) uses more sophisticated electronics and is more effective, and the third (4Matic) was excellent but too much for the market. By maintaining traction, these systems improve stability, helping to prevent skids.

All three traction control systems share hardware with ABS brakes, which preceded them. If an indivdual brake begins to lock, ABS automatically "pumps" it, preventing the tire from skidding and allowing you to steer the car. ABS is most useful on slick pavement. If you're wondering, ABS can't be retrofitted practically.

Mercedes-Benz began fitting ABS in 1978, but it didn't appear on their US cars until the 1985 model year. By 1986 it was standard on all but the 190E 2.3 and the 190D 2.5, where it was a popular option. Since 1989, ABS has been standard on all US models. To determine whether a car has ABS, look for the small circular red ABS warning light or symbol below the instruments or the hydraulic valve marked "ABS" under the hood.

ASD

The Automatic Locking Differential (ASD) was the simplest of MBAG's traction control systems. Using the ABS wheel sensors to detect rear wheelspin at speeds under 21mph, a microprocessor signals hydraulically actuated clutches to lock the differential, so that both rear wheels turn at the same speed. A light in the speedometer indicates that the system is working. Traction regained, ASD disengages when the car reaches 22mph. The simple system has similar limits to a mechanically locking differential—if traction is equally bad at both rear wheels, both may spin.

The 300TE wagon has a slightly higher roof than the sedan, self-leveling rear suspension, and an optional third, rear-facing seat. *DBAG*

ASD saw only brief use as a US option on the 190E 2.3, 190E 2.6, turbo-diesels, and the 300SL. It was superceded by ASR, which took matters beyond the differential.

ASR

Acceleration Skid Control (ASR) is more sophisticated and effective than ASD, especially at improving stability, and was more widely used. Instead of locking the differential, ASR uses the brake to slow a spinning wheel. If two wheels spin, ASR brakes them both and reduces engine torque. Even with throttle mashed to the floor, ASR prevents wheelspin. As the system engages, an indicator light comes on in the speedometer face.

Put two wheels in mud or snow, and ASR allows steady acceleration without swerves. Turning and applying heavy power may also engage ASR. In snow, ASR gives you some of the advantages of four-wheel drive without the drawbacks. In the United States, ASR first appeared as an option for the 1991 model year on six- and eight-cylinder gasoline-engined models.

A criticism of ASR is that on models through 1994 it can't be switched off, as might be desirable under some winter conditions or by enthusiasts who use power to provoke oversteer. A dash switch allows the wheelspin rate to increase to accommodate tire chains or snow clumps on the tires.

4Matic

4Matic means automatic four-wheel drive. In two-wheel-drive mode, this automatic system senses wheelspin via the wheel sensors then goes through three stages. First, front-wheel drive is engaged, with rear, center, and front differentials left disengaged. If wheelspin continues, the center differential is engaged. If that's not enough to stop

Four-valve head boosted power from 177 to 217hp in the 1990 300CE, but sedans and wagons had to wait until 1993. *FDB*

The 300CE inspired tuners such as AMG to create high-performance alternatives, this one with a thirty-two-valve, 6.0 liter V-8. *AMG*

wheelspin, the rear differential locks. Disengagement also occurs in stages unless the brakes are applied, whereupon 4Matic uncouples so that ABS can work.

The process is automatic, beyond control of the driver, who sees only the 4Matic indicator light, a safety feature in itself, telling unwitting drivers that they are entering low-traction conditions. The system senses steering angle and engages 4Matic sooner if the car is turning. All four tires should be the same type and size, but 4Matic accommodates wear by compensating for slight differences in diameter.

Although heavy (300lb), expensive (over $6,500 new), and complicated, 4Matic was judged the best of contemporary four-wheel-drive traction control systems. Whether or not you need it depends upon where and how you drive. In ski country it's useful. In Los Angeles, it's not. 4Matic was discontinued during the 1993 model year. Even though the system was effective, cost made many buyers think twice, especially when ASR functioned almost as well.

Becker Grand Prix Radio

The most common failure in 1980s models in-

volves the Becker Grand Prix Electronic radio. The tiny controls are complicated and difficult to operate, reliability is poor, and sensitivity and sound quality are inferior. Even the automatic antenna can fail.

The radio was once a popular target for thieves, so an anti-theft feature was added, but it could backfire. If power to the radio was cut off with the alarm system on, the radio scrambled its controls, requiring at least a trip to the dealer to have it descrambled.

In 1986–1987 models, a supplementary lithium battery maintains power to the radio, but if the standby battery fails, the radio may scramble. The batteries weren't used in 1988–1989 models, and 1990–onward models provide the owner with a code to punch in to reactivate the radio. Descrambling a pre-1990 radio can be arranged through dealers or through Becker North America. The radio scrambling device can be disabled.

The Grand Prix radio's sensitivity was low, so it wouldn't pick up many stations, and sound quality was only fair. The tape deck and controls were subject to failure. Many Grand Prix radios were replaced. If the car you're considering has a Sony or an Alpine, that's probably a plus.

Chapter 16

The 190 1983–1993

As an entry-level model for the 1980s, Mercedes-Benz developed its first new compact sedan in three decades, the 190. This series successfully encompassed uses from taxicab to racer. It had been nearly thirty years since Mercedes-Benz had built a small car, so the new one was designed entirely from scratch.

In 1983, the 190 appeared in Europe, named for the 1.9 liter engine of the base model. For 1984, two entry-level four-cylinder sedans, the diesel 190D 2.2 and the gasoline 190E 2.3, came to the United States. Both were well-equipped but could have used more torque. Later displacement increases met this need, and more standard equip-

The 190E 2.3 and 190D 2.2 in original US form had new alloy wheels (easier to clean) and inset headlights. *MBNA*

ment and options appeared. The 201 chassis was built only as a four-door sedan. Its potential was best realized in the 190D 2.5, the 190D 2.5 Turbo, the 190E 2.6, and the 190E 2.3–16 sports sedan.

Handling improvements came with the 190's totally fresh rear suspension. The computer-designed five-link system better controlled track width, toe-in, and rear wheel camber, providing more stable handling under a variety of loads and while accelerating or braking. Front suspension is by MacPherson strut; coil springs are fitted all round, as are disc brakes. The 190 introduced the "new-style" alloy wheel, easier to clean than the more intricately shaped alloy wheel dating from 1971.

The 190's limitations involve rear legroom and a few early build quality snags. Advantages include low price, light weight, high fuel efficiency, a choice of manual or automatic transmission, and nimble yet stable handling. Over a million 190s were built before the C220 and C280 replaced them for the 1994 model year.

190E 2.3 ★★

The gasoline-powered 190E 2.3 combined light weight with 113hp, increased to 121hp for 1985. At 2500lb, the 2.3 was the lightest Mercedes-Benz sedan since the 1930s. Drag coefficient was 0.33, compared to the 0.36 of the contemporary S-Class sedans. Four-speed automatic and five-speed manual transmissions were offered. In the lower four gears, the latter's shift pattern forms an H; fifth and reverse are off to the right.

The 190s introduced the single-arm windshield wiper, which sweeps 86 percent of the glass area. A few problems occurred with climate control systems and power windows. Even though the automatic climate controls appear similar, 190s used a completely different system than did earlier models. Still, they had similar problems—with controls, compressor, and so forth—but nothing that an experienced Mercedes-Benz mechanic can't handle.

A 1991 factory service bulletin covered a parking brake modification to prevent accidental release; the parts can be retrofitted to 1984–mid-

The four-valve Cosworth head of the 190E 2.3–16 makes it the choice for an enthusiast driver. Note the front air dam, modest fender flares, aerodynamic lower body molding, and rear spoiler. *FDB*

148

1988 190s. The 1984 and 1985 190s used 14in alloy wheels; later models used 15in wheels. Steel wheels were sold in Europe but not in the United States.

Driver's side air bags were optional on 1984 and later 190s. ABS braking became an option for 1986 and was made standard for 1989. Other options were an alarm system, power seats, sunroof, metallic paint, and more.

For the 1987 model year, all 190s (gasoline and diesel) were fitted with better headlights and a slightly revised climate control system; when the difference between inside and outside air temperatures exceeded a certain level, the system switched to recirculated air. The 1987 190E 2.3 had a power boost to 130hp. For 1989 the 190s got new lower body cladding, plus new front and rear valences. Starting with the 1990 model year, an Alpine radio replaced the trouble-prone Becker Grand Prix Electronic unit.

In 1991, after two model years when only the 190E 2.6 came to the United States, the 190E 2.3 returned with a new head and improved fuel injection. The 190E's final American fling was as the 1993 Limited Edition 190E 2.3 and 2.6. The 2.3 came only in metallic green with creme beige leather and burl walnut; the 2.6 was black with black and red leather interior and cross-hatch pattern trim. The package also included a power sunroof, headlight washers and wipers, and rear seat headrests. Eight-hole alloy wheels were fitted, and the trunk lid carried no model identification. The 2.6 is interesting to enthusiasts because it has stiffer shocks, shorter springs, larger wheels and tires, a faster steering ratio, and a smaller steering wheel. About 700 of each were built exclusively for the US market.

With long-lived engines and rust-free bodies, a well-kept four-cylinder 190E 2.3 can be a bargain today. Still, if you can stretch your budget a bit,

Technical Specifications			
Model	190E 2.3	190E 2.3–16	190E 2.6
Year	1984–1988	1986–1987	1987–1993
	1991–1993		
Engine			
Type	Inline sohc four	Inline dohc four, four valves per cyl.	Inline sohc six
Displacement	2299cc (140.3ci)	2299cc (140.3ci)	2599cc (158.6ci)
Bore x stroke	95.5x80.3mm	95.5x80.3mm	82.9x80.3mm
Compression ratio	8.0:1	9.7:1	9.2:1
SAE horsepower	121hp @ 5000rpm	167hp @ 5800rpm	158hp @ 5800rpm
Torque	136lb-ft @ 3500rpm	162lb-ft @ 4750rpm	162lb-ft @ 4600rpm
Fuel system	Electronic fuel injection (all)		
Fuel required	Premium unleaded (all)		
Chassis			
Type	Unibody sedan; steel (all)		
Chassis # prefix	201.024	201.034	201.029
Transmission	4-speed auto or 4-speed auto	5-speed manual or 4-speed auto	4-speed auto or 5-speed manual
Rear-axle ratio	3.23:1	3.27:1	3.27:1
Rear suspension	Multi-link, coil springs (all)		
Front suspension	Damper strut, coil springs (all)		
Wheels	6x15in	7x15in	6x15in
Tires	185/65x15	205/55VR15	185/65VR15
Brakes	4-wheel disc (all)		
Fuel capacity	14.5gal + 1.8	18.7gal + 2.3	14.5gal + 1.8
Weight	2,745lb	3,030lb	2,880lb
Performance			
0-60mph	10.0sec	8.6sec (auto) 8.3sec (manual)	9.5sec (auto) 9.1sec (manual)
Top speed	121mph	134mph (auto) 137mph (manual)	126mph (auto) 129mph (manual)
Fuel consumption	22-30+mpg	20-30mpg (est.)	22-30+mph (est.)

Note: Specifications for the 190E 2.3 are for the 1985 model year; those for the 190E 2.3–16 are for US models.

The rear spoiler of the 190E 2.3–16 also accommodates the high-mounted brake light. *DBAG*

you'll like the six-cylinder 190E 2.6, introduced as a 1987 model, even better. And then there's the high-performance 190E 2.3–16.

190E 2.3–16 ★★★

The most collectible 190 is this four-door pocket rocket. Sold in the United States only for 1986 and 1987, the 190E 2.3–16 was a sporting version of the 190E 2.3. The four-valve head by Cosworth in England improved gas flow, so power jumped to 185hp in Europe. With a compression ratio of 9.7:1 instead of the European car's 10.5:1, American cars had 167hp, but a lower rear-axle ratio compensates. Redline is 6800rpm, up 600

over the 190E 2.3, and an external engine oil cooler was added. Suspension improvements, wider wheels and tires, supportive leather seats, bigger (vented) brakes, and a Getrag five-speed manual transmission make this car a joy to drive.

American "sixteen-valves" were available in two colors, smoke silver and black pearl, both with black leather upholstery. In Europe the model was sold only with a close-ratio five-speed manual transmission, but about half of US cars came with a four-speed automatic. All had hydropneumatic self-leveling and a mechanical limited-slip differential.

DBAG took several slightly modified 190E 2.3–16 cars to the high-speed Nardi test track in Italy in 1983 and set fifteen world speed records. The highest was 154.06mph for 50,000km, just over 31,000 miles. A taller rear-axle ratio allowed this; European production cars top out at 140, American versions hit 135 or so.

The car was a hit among Mercedes-Benz performance fans, who used them successfully in club driving events. A squadron of 190E 2.3–16s, piloted by renowned race drivers, christened the new Nürburgring in 1985. The factory entered several teams in the German Touring Car Championship races. In the United States, Rick Hurst Racing ran a tuned 190E 2.3–16 in IMSA's International Sedan Series. A stock 190E 2.3–16 could whip any other Mercedes-Benz on an autocross course.

European 190E 2.3–16 models quickly appeared on the US gray market. MBNA first

---

Driving Impressions: 190 Series

The compact, nimble, and economical 190s make good city cars. With the front seats occupied, back seat legroom is less than spacious, but it's sufficient for kids.

The normally aspirated diesels are slow, but the 190D 2.5 Turbo can be fun. The 190E, which brought the words "sports sedan" back to Mercedes-Benz, is excellent in 2.6 liter form. A five-speed 190E 2.6 is practically the equivalent of the 190E 2.3–16. Enthusiastics should avoid the automatic transmission, which can have a mind of its own. The 1992 and later 190E models with the Sportline option are even closer to a 190E 2.3–16.

Agility is the 190E 2.3–16's most enjoyable attribute. Relatively light weight, great suspension, and good tires make it respond instantly. Braking is excellent, and ABS keeps

you out of trouble. The limited-slip differential (mechanical, not the ASD or ASR electronic traction control that couldn't be switched off) lets you get the power down early and smoothly in tight corners without melting the inside tire. Supportive seats hold you firmly in place during all this fun.

The five-speed's shift pattern has first dog-legged to the left, below reverse, so the four top gears are in an H-pattern, best suited to high-speed driving. (Other five-speeds put reverse to the right, leaving the lower four gears in an H, easier in town.)

All 190Es need lead-free premium gasoline. Highway fuel mileage of the 190E 2.3 could exceed 40mpg at 55mph and is unlikely to drop below 22. A 190D 2.2 normally gets 35—40mpg on the open road. In a 190E 2.3–16, you just don't care.

Sportline-equipped 1992–1993 190E 2.6 stands lower, has wider wheels and tires, logo behind front wheels, and other features. All 1988 and later

US 190s had these improved headlights; the lower body molding first appeared on 1989 models.

brought the car over for 1986, but it became clear that it would sell in limited numbers in America. It was expensive (over $40,000), and conservative Mercedes-Benz buyers were put off by its spoilers and air dams. Although Mercedes-Benz performance models were renowned in Europe, Americans had been taught to consider them as luxury cars instead.

After 1987 the 190E 2.3–16 was dropped as a US model, fewer than 2,000 having been imported officially. In Europe, though, spurred by the burgeoning German Touring Car Championship, the 2.3 liter version grew into the 190E 2.5-16 and eventually the limited-production, high-winged Evolution II, neither of which came to the United States. The 197hp 190E 2.5-16 made 0–60mph in 7.5 (manual) or 7.8 seconds (automatic) and could hit 146mph.

Few changes occurred during 190E 2.3–16 production. A 1987 version differs from a 1986 car only in its more aerodynamic headlights (with standard washers and wipers) and the revised air conditioning. The engine eschews hydraulic valve adjustment in favor of mechanical shims requiring cam removal for adjustment. Fuel capacity increased to 18.7gal plus 2.3gal reserve, up from the 14.5 and 1.8 of the 190E 2.3.

The 190E 2.3–16 is an exceptional value for an enthusiast. The time to buy a recent collector car is just as depreciation ends and appreciation begins, when prices dip to their lowest. The 190E 2.3–16 is now a prime candidate. Because of their low volume and high performance, the 190E 2.3–16, the European 190E 2.5-16, and the Evolution II are the only 190s generating collector interest.

The 190E 2.3–16 engine made 167hp in US form; higher-compression European version made 185hp. *FDB*

A factory team of modified 190E 2.3–16 sedans set several world speed records at Nardo, Italy, in 1983. *DBAG*

190E 2.6 ★★

The biggest-engined 190E was the 190E 2.6, which appeared for 1987 with a 159hp inline six; either a four-speed automatic or a five-speed manual transmission; ABS brakes; and a revised front air dam. Much less expensive than the 190E 2.3–16 but with only slightly less power, it became quite popular. Increased torque made the car easier to drive.

Rear seat legroom grew a bit in 1989 when the front seatbacks were re-shaped. For 1992 the factory's Sportline option became available, bringing the 190E 2.6 even closer to its sixteen-valve brother. With Sportline and the right tires, a good driver can at least equal the times of a 190E 2.3-16.

190D ★★

At 72hp, the 1984–1986 190D 2.2, especially with an automatic transmission, is only for the devoted diesel fan. Even though it starts in first gear, acceleration is sluggish. Entering a freeway via a short, uphill ramp can be tense. The five-speed manual transmission allows better performance. On the plus side, fuel mileage often exceeds 40mpg, and these cars are affordable. The 190D 2.2 was the first Mercedes-Benz to employ an engine encapsulation system to decrease interior and exterior engine noise.

Displacement was boosted to 2.5 liters in the

93hp 1986-87 190D 2.5 (automatic only), and for 1987 a turbocharger was added, creating the sprightly, 123hp 190D 2.5 Turbo. For more on the diesel 190s, see chapter 18.

Sportline ★★★

Mercedes-Benz has a strong performance image in Europe but not in the United States. For the 1992 model year, MBNA's new option, Sportline, made the cars more appealing to enthusiasts. To the 190E 2.6 (and the 300E and 300CE), Sportline brought stiffer springs and shock absorbers, wider eight-hole alloy wheels, wider tires, a quicker steering ratio, more supportive seats, and a smaller-diameter steering wheel. For models without leather seats, Sportline added them, too. No changes were made in the engine or transmission. Cars with Sportline stand slightly lower and bear a blue and silver logo on their front fenders and their shift knobs.

Without sacrificing comfort, Sportline brings out these cars' inherent handling abilities, and we highly recommend it. Few cars were sold with Sportline, and because it was an expensive and desirable option, it can be expected to increase the value of a used car.

Apart from the factory-installed gear, AMG spoilers and wheels for SLs, 190s, and 300 class models became available through US Mercedes-Benz dealers in 1993.

What to Look For

As with any recent model, service records are critical. Some early 190s experienced high oil consumption, traced to valve seals, which were replaced under warranty. In 1985, because of possible cracking, MBNA issued a recall on 14in alloy wheels with date codes between 3583 and 4983.

The most likely snag will be in the automatic climate control, so read the owners manual and test the ACC at all settings. The power windows weren't the most reliable, so make sure they all work smoothly; try the sunroof, antenna, and power seats, too. Manual transmissions should make no bearing noise; look for leaks from automatics. Check to see that the ABS works correctly. If the Becker Grand Prix Electronic radio has been replaced, you're one step ahead, but late models have better sound systems.

That's about it. The basic car is sound, and we've yet to see a rusty 190. For a completely new design, the 190 got off to an excellent start.

With the latest eight-hole wheels, the 1993 Limited Edition 190E 2.3 and 190E 2.6 were the final

US versions; the 2.6 has wider wheels and stiffer springs. *MBNA*

The high-winged Evolution 190E 2.5–16 proved extremely successful in the German Touring Car Championship. *DBAG*

The interior of a 1993 Limited Edition 190E 2.3, laid out similarly to other models. *MBNA*

Chapter 17

The Latest: C, E, S Class and SL

Current models are entering the used car market, and although few are inexpensive, these are the best Mercedes-Benz cars ever. Several are already collectible.

During the early 1990s, competition proved strong, and US luxury and gas guzzler taxes didn't help sales, so Mercedes-Benz broadened their range with niche models appealing to special buyers; twenty years hence these will be collector cars.

Mercedes-Benz competed at the low end, too. The C-Class cars were more than a refinement of the preceding 190s. For 1994, just as the C-Class was introduced, Mercedes-Benz simplified its model designations. The new names were based on three classes: C (Compact), E (Executive), and S ('Spensive?), plus engine displacements—220 (2.2 liter), 320 (3.2 liter), and so on.

The E320 is a refined and polished 300E. This 1994 model has the updated grille and headlights, eight-hole wheels, lower body cladding, and a 221hp engine. *MBNA*

1993 Models	1994 Models
190E 2.3	C220
190E 2.6	C280
300E 2.8	—
300E	E320
300TE	E320 Wagon
300CE	E320 Coupe
300CE Cabriolet	E320 Cabriolet
300D 2.5 Turbo	—
—	E300 Diesel
400E	E420
500E	E500
300SD	S350 Turbodiesel
300SE	S300
400SE	S420
500SEL	S500
600SEL	S600
500SEC	S500 Coupe
600SEC	S600 Coupe
300SL	SL300
500SL	SL500
600SL	SL600

The letter indicates the class; the number indicates the displacement.

400E 1992–1993 and E420 1993–on ★★

For 1992, Mercedes-Benz offered a new mid-range sedan as a Lexus-fighter for the United States, the V-8-powered 400E. For not much more than the cost of a 300E, Americans could enjoy more power and torque. With an improved transmission, the 4.0 V-8 gives strong performance.

The 400E actually has a 4.2 liter engine. Peak power from the thirty-two-valver is 268hp, about 90 more than the original 300E and almost 50 more than the 3.2 liter 300E. Suspension and brake im-

This 1994 E320 Cabriolet is the same as the 1993 300CE Cabriolet. The screen behind the seats folds up to prevent air turbulence; the rear headrests serve as an automatic roll bar. Top on US version is power-operated. *MBAG*

provements accompanied this extra power, but tire size stayed the same as the 300E at 195/65VR15. (Given the 400E's potential, they could have been wider.) Variable intake cam timing spread torque over a wider rpm range; the car feels strong whenever you punch it. A leather interior is standard, ASR traction control optional.

Since 60mph came up in seven seconds and its speed ran to 149mph, the 400E approached 500E performance at a savings of more than $20,000. This is what the 300E should have been all along! A slightly restyled body (new grille, headlights, engine hood) came in the 1994 model year.

500E 1992–1993 and E500 1994 ★★

Once a decade, Mercedes-Benz builds the world's fastest and finest sedan. In the 1960s it was the 300SEL 6.3. In the 1970s it was the 450SEL 6.9. In the 1980s—well, we had to wait until 1992, for the astonishing 500E.

Anybody can plunk a big, powerful engine into a small chassis, but MBAG created a well-integrated, tractable, and safe super-sedan by re-designing and strengthening the W124 chassis and suspension, improving the brakes, fitting wider wheels and tires, and upgrading the seats. AMG had tried this earlier with their Hammer, but at $150,000 a copy, few were sold. The far more refined 500E was available at your local Mercedes-Benz dealer for around $80,000, and it could be serviced there, too.

A lowered and strengthened body shell was designed and assembled with Porsche's help. The 5.0, thirty-two-valve V-8 produced 322hp and 354ft-lb of torque, exceeded only by the V-12. All US 500Es had ASR traction control (optional on European versions) and self-leveling rear suspension. Tires were 225/55ZR16 front and rear. The 3,750lb sedan reached 60mph in under six seconds, with a governed top end of 155mph. Ungoverned, a 500E would be capable of at least 165mph.

Between 500 and 600 cars reportedly came to the United States as 1992 models, and although sales slowed, the model continued through 1994. The 500E is the prime Mercedes-Benz collector car of the early 1990s.

This E420 interior is typical of the 1990s cars with dual air bags, center console. *MBAG*

300CE Cabriolet 1993 and E320 Cabriolet 1994–on ★★★

If you had bought a new 280SE 3.5 Convertible in 1971 and kept it, today it would be worth

---

Driving Impressions: 300E, 400E, and 500E

In a sedan, a 300E or E320 is your best buy. This car will last nearly forever and remain fun to drive. The 1986–1992 300Es are good, but if you can, pick the more refined 3.2 liter, four-valve (1993 and later) version. The better-shifting transmission is worth a lot, but even the older version performs well if you shift by hand, made easy by the excellent shift gate.

Mercedes-Benz has stuck to recirculating ball steering, which you might guess would be less precise than rack and pinion, but given good tires that's not so. The 300E goes exactly where you point it, every time.

The 400E adds power, and the 500E is the driver's instant favorite. Buying either V-8 is a no-brainer. If you can afford it, just do it and be happy. These cars will cover more miles in a day than you can, but we give the edge to the 500E for its better seats and its stunning performance. The new Bose sound system is far better than the old Becker rig. The other attraction to these cars is their highway stealth capability.

---

many times its original price, and meanwhile you'd have enjoyed a great car. Well, our advice is to find yourself a 1993 or later 300CE Cabriolet, and do just that.

Like the 1993 300E, the Cabriolet incorporates all the modern amenities, with the power soft top as a bonus. It's a safe Convertible—thanks to pop-up rear headrests, side door beams, and engineers who design for real-world crash requirements rather than government standards.

The four-valve, 3.2 liter, 217hp six pushes the Cabriolet to 60 in 8.6 seconds, slower than other 300s because it is 500lb heavier than a 300CE Coupe. Chassis reinforcements avoid body twist and vibration, also discouraged by rubber and lead dampers in the windshield header, on the left front shock tower, and in the trunk.

This car is a low-production luxury model with a folding top, so as a future classic, it's a no-brainer. Cash in that sluggish mutual fund. You're not getting any younger.

300E 1993 and E320 1994–on ★★

We said good things about the original 300E, but for 1993, Mercedes-Benz made the car even better. Displacement was nudged from 3.0 to 3.2 liters, and a new four-valve head utilized variable intake cam timing. Power jumped from 177hp to 221. Peak torque increased, and variable cam timing provided a flatter and fatter torque curve. The four-speed automatic transmission, which had normally started in second gear, was altered to start in first gear, improving take off. The transmission is electronically linked to the ignition system so that timing is momentarily adjusted to smoothen shifts.

These changes make a 1993 300E or later E320 more enjoyable. Given some right foot, the car steps out smartly. Keep your foot down, and at redline the transmission powershifts silkily into the next gear. Downshifts are far quicker than in older models. This transmission works just the way you think an automatic transmission should work. For the enthusiast, the Sportline option provided wider wheels and tires, shorter and stiffer springs, more supportive seats, and more.

For 1994 the 3.2 liter 300E got a truer name, E320, and styling was updated with an grille resembling the S-Class. Other changes included new headlights, taillights, and trunk lid center panel.

E300 Diesel 1994–on ★★

So that its new diesels could again be sold in highly regulated states, Mercedes-Benz reverted to a non-turbocharged, three-liter diesel for the 1994 E300 Diesel. See the next chapter for details.

Aggressive even when standing still, the E500 is sure to be a future collector car. *MBAG*

Technical Specifications

Model	300E	400E	500E
Year	1993–	1992–	1992–
Engine			
Type	Inline dohc six	Dohc V-8	Dohc V-8
Engine # prefix	M104.992	M119.975	M119.974
Displacement	3199cc (195ci)	4196cc (256ci)	4973cc (303ci)
Bore x stroke	89.9x84.0mm	92.0x78.9mm	96.5x85.0mm
Compression ratio	10:1	11:1	10:1
Horsepower	221hp @ 5500rpm	275hp @ 5700rpm	315 @ 5,600
Torque	229lb-ft @ 3750rpm	295lb-ft @ 3900rpm	347lb-ft @ 3900rpm
Fuel system	Electronic fuel injection (all)		
Fuel required	Premium (all)		
Chassis			
Type	Unibody; steel (all)		
Chassis # prefix	W124.032	W124.034	W124.036
Transmission	4-speed automatic (all)		
Rear-axle ratio	2.65:1	2.24:1	2.82:1
Rear suspension	Multi-link, coil springs (all)		
Front suspension	Damper strut, coil springs (all)		
Wheels	6.5x15in	6.5x15in	8x16in
Tires	195/65VR15	195/65VR15	225/55ZR16
Brakes	4-wheel disc (all)		
Fuel capacity	18.5gal	18.5gal	23.8gal
Weight	3,525lb	3,745lb	3,855lb
Performance			
0-60mph	8.0sec	7.1sec	6.3sec
Top speed	140mph	149mph	155mph (governed)
Fuel consumption	19-25mpg	18-24mpg	16-19mpg

Technical Specifications

Model	300SL	500SL	600SL
Years	1990–	1990–	1993–
Engine			
Type	Inline dohc six	Dohc V-8	Dohc V-12
Engine # prefix	M104.981	M119.960	M120.981
Displacement	2962cc (180.6ci)	4973cc (303.5ci)	5987cc (365.4ci)
Bore x stroke	88.5x80.25mm	96.5x85mm	89x80.2mm
Compression ratio	10:1 (all)		
DIN horsepower	228hp @ 6300rpm	315hp @ 5600rpm	389hp @ 5200rpm
Torque	201lb-ft @ 4600rpm	347lb-ft @ 3900rpm	420lb-ft @ 3800rpm
Fuel system	Electronic fuel injection (all)		
Fuel required	Premium unleaded (all)		
Chassis			
Type	Monocoque, power soft top, automatic roll bar		
Chassis # prefix	R129.061	R129.067	R129.076
Transmission	5-speed auto	4-speed auto	4-speed auto
	5-speed manual (option)		
Rear-axle ratio	3.69:1 (auto)	2.65:1	
	3.46:1 (manual)		
Rear suspension	Multi-link, coil springs (all)		
Front suspension	Damper strut, coil springs (all)		
Wheels	8x16in (all)		
Tires	225/55ZR16 (all)		
Brakes	4-wheel disc, ABS (all)		
Fuel capacity	21.2gal (all)		
Weight	4,035lb	4,165lb	4,455lb
Performance			
0-60mph	8.3sec (auto)	6.4sec	5.9sec
Top speed	149mph	149mph	155mph (governed)
Fuel consumption	15-22mpg	16-20mpg	13-18mpg

300SL and 500SL 1990–on, and 600SL, 1993–on ★★★

Introduced for 1990, the R129 SL was a revolutionary step beyond the aging 560SL. Its totally fresh chassis was powered by a 3.0 liter, 228hp inline six, the 300SL, or a 5.0 liter, four-valve 322hp V-8, the 500SL. For 1993 these were joined by the 6.0 liter V-12 600SL.

All three SLs shared significant advances including an automatic power top (the first on any SL) and the world's first automatic roll bar. Automatically adjusting shock absorbers (ADS) and electronic traction control (ASR) were options on the 1991 500SL, standard on the 600SL. All SLs had self-leveling rear suspension, dual air bags, remote locking, an electrostatic air filter to capture smog and dust particles, and more. Leather upholstery is standard on US models.

Although other convertibles had used them for years, the first power top for a Mercedes-Benz was impressive. No fiddling with latches or panels. Just rock the switch, and the top goes up or down in about thirty seconds, automatically, including latching and unlatching at the windshield header. This engineering tour de force uses fifteen hydraulic cylinders, eleven solenoids, and seventeen proximity switches.

While the 300SL offered the world's first five-speed automatic transmission, the torque of the 500SL and 600SL allowed them to use four-speeds instead. For the first time in two decades an SL offered a manual transmission in America. The 300SL's manual five-speed was delightful, but since Americans were inured to automatics in previous SLs, it is rare.

Both 500SL and 300SL had automatic intake valve timing for better power and torque over a wider rpm range. Zero to 60 times were 8.3 seconds for the 300SL, 6.3 seconds for the 500. The V-12 600SL cut this to 5.9 seconds.

One styling feature of the SL took a while to catch on. The plastic lower body molding, including front and rear bumpers, was painted a color slightly different from the body color. The red combination wasn't well received, so MBAG began painting the moldings on red cars in body color.

ADS first became available on the 1991 300SL

In 1993, AMG's links with Mercedes-Benz strengthened, so more cars were originally fitted with wider wheels and tires, aerodynamic aids, and similar features. *MBAG*

and 500SL. The system allows a comfortable ride yet maintains maximum tire contact with the road. Judging a road's bumpiness (through vertical wheel acceleration sensors), driving speed, steering wheel angle, and load, ADS adjusts individual shock absorber damping between taut, normal, soft, and comfort settings.

How do you spot a V-12 600SL? Besides the model number on the trunk, a V-12 emblem adorns each front fender vent. Because of its longer engine, the 600SL's front bumper projects 2in farther forward than those of the 300 and 500SL. The V-12 has a few deluxe interior trim touches, including a leather and wood shift knob and a wood-trimmed shift gate panel. A cellular telephone and a CD changer are standard equipment, as is ASR traction control.

S-Class Sedans 1992–on ★★

The first new S-class sedan in more than a decade, the W140 S-Class appeared at the 1991 Geneva show. Normal and long-wheelbase versions were powered by gasoline engines from a 3.2 liter inline six to a 6.0 liter V-12 or a turbo-diesel. US 1992 S-Class models included:

Model	Engine type	Engine # prefix
300SD	3.5 liter six (diesel), 150hp	OM603.971
300SE	3.0 liter six, 231hp	M104.990
400SE	4.2 liter V-8, 286hp	M119.971
500SEL	5.0 liter V-8, 326hp	M119.970
600SEL	6.0 liter V-12, 408hp	M120.980

For 1993 the 400SE was replaced with the longer-wheelbase 400SEL. For 1994, model designations changed as shown.

These interstate cruisers offer unparalleled space, safety, and comfort for four. Elbow, head, and leg room seem limitless, with your personal environment enhanced by individual climate controls and an elaborate air filtering system. Innovations include double-paned side windows to reduce heat transfer and noise, self-latching doors, reverse-sighting rods, and even a retracting trunk lid handle to keep your fingers clean. The W140 used computers to control everything from ignition timing to rear brake bias. It introduced a new Bose sound system far better than anything previously fitted. It was the first car to substitute non-polluting R134a for the old freon (R12) air conditioning medium.

159

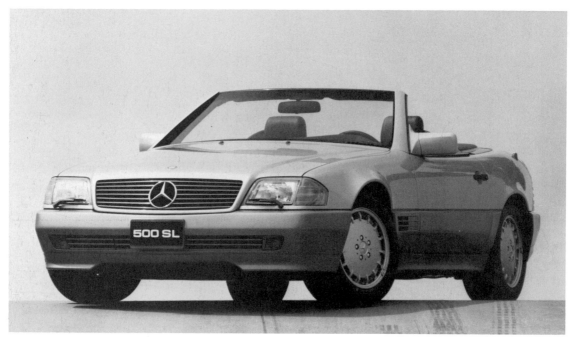

Introduced for 1990, the 315hp, V-8-powered 500SL is a twin to the 228hp, six-cylinder 300SL. *MBAG*

These S-Class sedans are more daily drivers than collector cars, but the 600SEL may be an exception. Production of the V-12 sedan was low (1,000 in 1993 worldwide, 600 for the United States), and price was high. Look for the V-12 emblem on the rear pillar. It's no coincidence that this car bears the famous 600 number.

New 1992 S-Class cars included free maintenance covering almost everything but tires for three years, but the program was dropped for 1993. You can buy a cheaper car, but if and when you and your family have The Big One, what would you rather be in?

Driving Impressions: 300SL, 500SL, and 600SL

A 300SL, 500SL, or 600SL will allow the enthusiast to explore his or her full driving ability. They'll go faster than you can—or should—drive on any public road. These cars all offer seamless competence. Far more contemporary than the old 560SL, they offer the latest in ergonomics and safety.

The best buy is the 300SL with the excellent five-speed manual gearbox. Even the automatics are more enjoyable than older versions, shifting more smoothly and more quickly. The most responsive six-cylinder SL is the 1994 SL320 with the 3.2 liter engine.

The 500SL has ample power for far less money than the 600SL, but being rarer, the latter is a sure collector's item. The 600SL's huge helpings of smooth torque make speed effortless. When new, it was the fastest Mercedes-Benz to 60mph—at 5.9 seconds.

More sporting and aggressive than previous SLs, these cars accelerate, handle, and stop two generations better. Some new 300SL owners, accustomed to lazy V-8s, felt it sluggish. It isn't. Rather than being lugged like an old V-8, to realize its performance a 300SL must be revved to redline.

500SEC and 600SEC Coupes 1993–on ★★

The V-8 500SEC and V-12 600SEC Coupes introduced for 1993 are blessed with 315 and 389hp, respectively, with fresh headlight and taillight treatments. Mechanically they are similar to their sedan counterparts, with slight power differences due to exhaust system changes.

Standard equipment includes ASR traction control. The ADS adaptive damping system is standard on the 600SEC, optional on the 500SEC. Both have pneumatically self-closing doors. The V-12's sculpted intake manifold makes opening the hood a pleasure. The performance produced by the engine is elegantly amazing. The 5,075lb 600SEC can reach 60mph in 6.3 seconds, and both cars are governed to a top speed of 155mph.

The 500SEC and 600SEC may be the last big luxury Coupes from Mercedes-Benz. Priced at $98,900 and $132,000, their obvious luxury tested the political correctness then in vogue. Fewer than 1,000 of each came to the United States in 1993. Ever since the first 380SEC, owner loyalty has been excellent for luxury Coupes. These newest versions are sure to be collectible cars.

Driving Impressions: S-Class

The S-Class was criticized for its size and weight, but the cars feel more at home in the open spaces of America than in crowded European streets. With four seats filled an S-Class sedan offers your family or business the most comfortable, safe, efficient, and rapid long-distance motoring. And frankly, if you're going to be in an accident, this is the car to be in. These are the best long-distance cars of all time, and it is unlikely that they will be surpassed for a very long time.

Sportline ★★

For 1992, a new option, Sportline, appealed to the enthusiast. On the 300E, 300CE, and 190E 2.6, Sportline brought stiffer springs and shocks, wider eight-hole alloys, wider tires, quicker steering, more supportive seats, and a smaller-diameter steering wheel. For models with MB-tex seats,

Technical Specifications			
Model	500SEL	600SEL	600SEC
Years	1992–	1993–	1993–
Engine			
Type	Dohc V-8	Dohc V-12	Dohc V-12
Engine # prefix	119.970	120.980	120.980
Displacement	4973cc (303ci)	5987cc (365.4ci)	5987cc (365.4ci)
Bore x stroke	96.5x85mm	89x80.2mm	89x80.2mm
Compression ratio	10:1	10:1	10:1
DIN horsepower	315hp @ 5600rpm	389hp @ 5200rpm	389hp @ 5200rpm
Torque	347lb-ft @ 3900rpm	420lb-ft @ 3800rpm	420lb-ft @ 3800rpm
Fuel system	Electronic fuel injection (all)		
Fuel required	Premium unleaded (all)		
Chassis			
Type	Monocoque (all)		
Chassis # prefix	140.051	140.057	140.076
Transmission	4-speed automatic (all)		
Rear-axle ratio	2.64:1 (all)		
Rear suspension	Multi-link (all)		
Front suspension	Double wishbone, coil springs (all)		
Wheels	7.5x16in (all)		
Tires	235/60ZR16 (all)		
Brakes	4-wheel disc, ABS (all)		
Fuel capacity	26.4gal (all)		
Weight	4,830lb	5,095lb	5,075lb
Performance			
0-60mph	7.2sec	6.3sec	6.3sec
Top speed	155mph (governed) (all)		
Fuel consumption	13-17mpg	12-16mpg	12-16mpg

Sportline added leather upholstery. No drivetrain changes were made. Cars with Sportline are slightly lower; a blue and silver logo appears on their front fenders and shift knobs.

Without sacrificing comfort, Sportline brings out the cars' inherent handling abilities, and we recommend it. To some buyers, Sportline will increase the value of a used car. Apart from this factory-installed option, AMG spoilers and wheels for SLs, 190s, and E-Class models were sold through US Mercedes-Benz dealers from 1993.

What to Look For

The newer the car, the more important its provenance. A 1990s model will probably be owned by its original buyer. Service records tell you how the car was treated. Make sure that all services were carried out by an authorized dealer. Run the car by a dealership and pay them to check it thoroughly, including a leakdown test on the engine.

Make sure that all power accessories work properly, especially the automatic climate control system. The 1991–on S-Class cars use a new design, but the 300 series continues with the older system. The new S-Class cars have a good track record, but tires may suffer from flat spots when cold, and the cars are susceptible to improper front-end alignment and tire wear. The car should track properly and shouldn't wander over "ruts" worn into the asphalt.

On an SL or 300CE Cabriolet, check power top operation. Be sure that the mechanism works smoothly and that windows and seals fit tightly. A few teething troubles occurred, and this is no simple device to repair. Continually raising and lowering the top without running the car will eventually drain the battery. Try the switch raising the automatic roll bar, too.

Recent models came with a factory-installed alarm, and some had factory-installed cellular telephones. Improper installation of aftermarket electronics can cause problems, so if you see evidence of rewiring, make doubly sure that every electronic system works properly.

Many of these cars were leased rather than bought, so if you seek a specific model, ask a dealer or leasing company if a good car will be coming off lease. If you're buying from a dealer, ask about MBNA's used car warranty.

Technical Specifications

Model	C220	C280
Years	1994–	1994–
Engine		
Type	Inline dohc four	Inline dohc six
Engine # prefix	111.961	104.941
Displacement	2198cc (134.1ci)	2798cc (170.7ci)
Bore x stroke	89.9x86.6mm	89.9x73.5mm
Compression ratio	10:1	10:1
SAE horsepower	147hp @ 5500rpm	194hp @ 5500rpm
Torque	155lb-ft @ 4000rpm	199lb-ft @ 3750rpm
Fuel system	Electronic fuel injection (all)	
Fuel required	Premium unleaded (all)	
Chassis		
Type	Unibody; steel (all)	
Chassis # prefix	202.022	202.028
Transmission	4-speed automatic (all)	
Rear-axle ratio	3.07:1	2.87:1
Rear suspension	Multi-link (all)	
Front suspension	Upper and lower control arms, coil springs (all)	
Wheels	6.5x15in (all)	
Tires	195/65x15	
Brakes	4-wheel disc, ABS (all)	
Fuel capacity	16.4gal (all)	
Weight	3,173lb	3,293lb
Performance		
0-60mph	10.2sec	8.3sec
Top speed	125mph (est.)	130mph (governed)
Fuel consumption	21-28mpg	20-26mpg

A current production car may allow you to rent an example and try it out, using it the same way you'll use your new car later. This isn't cheap, but it can avoid disappointment if you discover that your dream car just isn't for you.

C-Class Sedans 1994–on ★★

For 1994, a new compact sedan series replaced the 190s. Although European versions were powered by a wide range of engines and came in four trim levels, the US started with two gasoline-powered models, the four-cylinder, 147hp C220 and the six-cylinder, 194hp C280. Both brought big improvements in performance, space, safety, and value.

Key to the performance increases were the four-valve heads and variable intake cam timing on both engines, also improving fuel efficiency. The back seat is roomier, and an optional drop-down seatback allows long items to fit inside the car. Standard dual air bags and more high-strength steels offer additional protection. The rear suspension is the proven five-link system; the front's

By the 1990s, Mercedes-Benz stylists had cleaned up the engine compartment, as in this 500SL. *FDB*

The 500SL and 300SL were the first Mercedes-Benz models to have a power-operated Convertible top and an automatic roll bar. *MBAG*

163

Four-valve V-12 makes around 400hp and looks great doing it. *MBAG*

upper link design is adapted from the S-Class.

Standard equipment included a sunroof, wood trim, driver's side power seat, power windows, central locking, and an improved AM/FM/cassette radio with provision for a CD unit in the trunk. A Bose sound system was standard on the C280, optional on the 220. US C220s and C280s had a four-speed automatic transmission, with no manual transmission option. Climate controls are simplified, and the system uses CFC-free R134a refrigerant. Even though the C-cars were substantially better in every way, their new car prices came within three percent of those of the 190s.

Summary

If you want the conveniences, safety, comfort, seamless performance, and the latest engineering, these are the cars for you. Their high price when new is beaten down by a few years of depreciation, so used examples can be excellent investments as well as dependable and enjoyable cars.

The S-Class may be the last new big sedan from Mercedes-Benz for decades, so don't wait for anything better. The 500E offers performance to take you well beyond the turn of the century in more ways than one. The C-Class is the world's most sophisticated compact car. The SLs are amazing. All of these cars will serve you seamlessly in many roles. If you want the best, Mercedes-Benz offers it.

The V-12 600SEL is distinguished by a "V-12" logo on the C-pillar, but other S-class cars look virtually identical. *MBAG*

New headlight (and taillight) styling makes the 600SEC (nee S600 Coupe) easy to identify. The similar S500 Coupe is powered by a V-8. *MBNA*

The 1994 C280 set new standards in compact car performance, comfort, and safety. *MBNA*

Chapter 18

The Diesels

First to build and sell a diesel-powered passenger car, in 1936, Daimler-Benz is the acknowledged leader in that field. In 1978, DBAG developed the first turbo-diesel car, the 300SD. Since then, DBAG has engineered low-emission engines offering the advantages of diesel power yet practically matching the performance of gasoline-powered models.

Early diesels are covered in the chapters on their gasoline-fed brethren. Here we'll look at the most popular diesels, from 1968 onward. Whichever you choose, consider it as transportation. Few diesels even approach collector status. Of course, many owners still become enamored with their favorite diesel car.

114 and 115 Diesels ★

Developed since the 1950s, the four-cylinder diesels are pretty basic cars. Although dependable and economical, they required the driver to acti-

Until 1979, Mercedes-Benz diesels were normally-aspirated, that is, not turbocharged. In 1968, this four-cylinder 220D was the most popular diesel model. *MBNA*

Technical Specifications

Model	220D	240D	300D
Years	1968–1976	1974–1985	1975–1985
Engine			
Type	Inline ohc four	Inline ohc four	Inline ohc five
Engine # prefix	615.912	616.916 or 616.912	617.910 or 617.912
Displacement	2197cc	2404cc (146.7ci)	3005cc (183.4ci)
Bore x stroke	87x92.4mm	91x92.4mm	90.9x92.4mm
Compression ratio 21:1	21:1+	21:1+	
SAE horsepower	65hp @ 4200rpm	67hp @ 4000rpm	83hp @ 4200rpm
Torque	92.6mkg @ 2400rpm	97mkg @ 2400rpm	120mkg @ 2400rpm
Fuel system	Mechanical injection (all)		
Fuel required	Diesel (all)		
Chassis			
Type	Unibody; steel (all)	115.117 or 123.123	115.114 or 123.130
Chassis # prefix	115.110	123	123
Transmission	4-speed manual or 4-speed auto	4-speed auto	
Rear-axle ratio	3.92:1	3.69:1	3.46:1
Rear suspension	Semi-trailing arms, coil springs (all)		
Front suspension	Strut, coil springs (all)		
Wheels	5.5x14in	5.5x14in	5.5x14in
Tires	175SR14	175SR14	175SR14
Brakes	4-wheel discs (all)		
Fuel capacity	17.2gal	17.2gal	17.2gal
Weight	3,000lb	3,164lb	3,296lb
Performance			
0-60mph	27sec	25-27sec	20-21sec
Top speed	83mph	83-86mph	90-93mph
Fuel consumption	25-35mpg	24-30mpg	20-24mpg

vate a pre-glow circuit before starting and were sluggish performers even when new. These cars are simpler than the latest diesels, but they are only for the serious diesel fan.

220D 1968–1976 ★

Starting in 1968 a new body, the W114/W115, appeared as the 220D, a three-box, four-door sedan replaced the old round-body and fin-back diesels. Visibility, comfort, handling, and safety were all much improved. Unfortunately, performance wasn't. This is the slowest car that you should consider driving regularly on today's highways. Uphill freeway on-ramps are a challenge, and it's easy to get into dangerous positions in busy, fast traffic. In-town and secondary road per-formance is acceptable, but if you drive in heavy freeway traffic, consider a 240D or a 300D instead.

Of the more than 420,000 220Ds built, one has gone over a million miles, a 1968 model used for eleven years to commute in Oregon. Now owned by Mercedes-Benz, the car is in remarkably good original condition. Despite this, it remains second in the high-mileage department to a 1957 180D which reportedly ran 1,184,000 miles.

The five-cylinder engine improved the diesel's appeal. The 300D, first sold as a 1975 US model, was easier to start, had more power, an automatic transmission (the 240's was optional), and air conditioning. Its more luxurious atmosphere satisfied those who might not have considered earlier diesels, so the car was a huge success.

Chassis and Engine Prefix Numbers

Years	Model	Chassis prefix	Engine prefix	Description
1968–1976	200D	115	OM615	4-cyl. diesel, 61hp
1968–1976	220D	115	OM615	4-cyl. diesel, 65hp
1973–1976	240D	115	OM616	4-cyl. diesel, 62hp
1974–1976	300D	115	OM617	5-cyl. diesel, 77hp

In 1976 the 240D switched to this roomier and more modern W123 body, which served it until the end of the model run in 1983. *MBNA*

W123 Sedans, Wagons, and Coupes ★

The mid-range W123 sedans, first sold in the United States for 1976, were the company's most successful diesels. Before being replaced in 1986 by the W124 300D, hundreds of thousands were built.

For 1977 the W123 five-cylinder diesels (300D, 300TD) got the automatic climate control system pioneered on the 450SE and SEL. For 1979, so did the 240D. For 1981 a revised ACC system went into the W123 chassis, lasting through the final model year, 1985.

Unfortunately, these ACC systems give trouble. They rarely fail completely but may blow hot air when you want cold and vice versa. Failure can involve the electronic controls, the servo valve that controls coolant flow, and the vacuum system that operates air flaps. Failure is often related to faults in the circuit board in the control head. If the coolant is dirty, the valve may jam (causing the battery to run down as the servo motor tries to operate it), or the plastic center section may crack and leak (causing coolant loss). Servo rebuilding kits and replacement

Chassis and Engine Prefix Numbers

Years	Model	Chassis prefix	Engine prefix	Description
1976–1985	240D	123	OM616	4-cyl. diesel, 62-67hp
1976–1985	300D	123	OM617	5-cyl. diesel, 77-83hp
1982–1985	300D	123	OM617A	5-cyl. turbo-diesel, 118-123hp
1978–1986	300TD	123	OM617	5-cyl. diesel, 77-83hp
1980–1986	300TD	123	OM617A	5-cyl. turbo-diesel, 118-123hp
1978–1981	300CD	123	OM617	5-cyl. diesel, 77-83hp
1981–1985	300CD	123	OM617A	5-cyl. turbo-diesel, 118-123hp

This list includes only the most popular models; some utility models sold only in Europe are not included.

In 1979, the five-cylinder 300D was the most popular US diesel. Thousands still serve owners everywhere. *MBNA*

aluminum center sections are available. Vacuum hoses harden and break with age, and air flaps may jam. (No bad rap on diesels—the gasoline models' ACC is similarly afflicted.)

If the car has cruise control, make sure that it works properly. Because these systems have electrical, mechanical, vacuum, and electronic components, failure potential is high. Because of their vacuum situation, failure seems more frequent in

diesels. This snag is so common that most Mercedes-Benz mechanics can diagnose and repair it efficiently.

240D 1974–1983 ★

Eschewing the traditional subframe, the W123 mid-range body mounted the engine and front suspension directly to the chassis. With the same OM616 normally aspirated, four-cylinder 2.4 liter

In 1978 the S-class 300SD was the world's first turbo-diesel production car, but its W116 chassis was soon replaced by the W126. *MBNA*

Even a diesel Coupe was available; the 120hp 300CD had EPA fuel mileage figures of 27mpg city, 33mpg highway. *MBNA*

engine as its W115 predecessor, the 240D was a reliable workhorse.

The pre-1980 240D got along with 62hp; 1980 and later engines made 67hp. A 1980s 240D gets over 30mpg on the highway and can reach 80–85mph. Reliable, the 240D had a few problems with water pumps, air conditioning, and the auto-

Starting in 1981, the turbocharged W126-bodied 300SD led the line of diesels for almost a decade. *MBNA*

matic transmission, but overall it's one of the most dependable cars ever. Used examples are numerous and economical to maintain, but they lack the turbo-diesel's appeal.

300D Sedan ★

This five-cylinder diesel W123 chassis sedan was extremely popular, normally-aspirated (1976–1981) or turbocharged (1982–1985). US cars came with air conditioning, power windows, vacuum locking, power brakes and steering, cruise control, and tinted glass. Options usually included a sunroof, leather seats, power seats, heated seats. This was the first Mercedes-Benz diesel to give up the pre-glow knob in favor of a key start similar to a gasoline-engined car.

A normally-aspirated 300D was faster than (or not as slow as) the 240D, taking 20 seconds to hit 60mph. The turbo 300D shortened this to 14 seconds; its top speed is just over 100mph.

The 300D's strength was as a basic transportation system. Its weaknesses were in ancillary, comfort-oriented devices. The air conditioning could not always cope with America's humid heat. The climate control servo leaked, as did the vacuum lines and door lock actuators. The Becker Grand Prix Electronic radio (a mandatory option) often required repair or replacement.

On any old diesel, check the fuel line cap in the rear-most cylinder's injector fuel leak-off fitting. As the plug ages, it will eventually blow out; replace it as a precaution or carry a spare. The newest type has a metal plug in the end.

Best mid-range turbo-diesel is the 1990–1993 300D 2.5 Turbo, which controlled turbo boost via computer; slots in fender are for engine air intake system. *MBNA*

300CD Coupe ★★

A diesel luxury Coupe? Only Mercedes-Benz could pull it off. Their first was the 1978 300CD, using the same body as the gasoline-fueled 280C and CE Coupe. A wheelbase 4.3in shorter than the sedan's made the 300CD nimble. Only an automatic transmission was available, and 0–60mph took seventeen seconds in the 77hp non-turbo version, about thirteen seconds in the 123hp turbocharged 1981–1985 300CD. The stylish Coupe was attractive, but its price, diesel clatter, and low performance deterred prospective buyers who expected more from a luxury car. Sales were low.

300TD and 300TDT Wagon ★

In 1978, DBAG began building diesel station wagons on the W123 chassis, and these roomy, utilitarian vehicles were popular. From the B-pillar forward the four-door wagon is identical to the sedan, but it's about 300lb heavier. The five-cylinder, normally-aspirated diesel pushed only 77hp into the four-speed automatic transmission, so we recommend a turbo-diesel, the 300TDT, with 123hp. The tailgate lifts upward, and a folding, rear-facing third seat (for two children) was optional. The split backs of the rear seats fold down, so space is generous. The spare tire is tucked into the left quarter panel (incidentally, Mercedes-Benz has always used full-sized spare tires for all models).

Performance of the 300TDT turbo-diesel wagon befits a 3800lb car with 123hp, but handling and ride are excellent. The self-leveling rear suspension uses nitrogen gas to help it handle normally under heavy loads. If the suspension is unusually stiff, the nitrogen has probably leaked out. Highway mileage was usually 25–30mpg.

Turbo-Diesels

In 1982, at the height of the diesel's popularity, MBNA sold 79 percent diesels vs. 21 percent gas-powered cars. General Motors' attempt to transform gasoline engines into diesels gave Rudolf's pride a sour reputation, and by 1990 the percentages had reversed. Too bad, because the late 1980s and 1990s diesels are good, thanks to turbocharging.

Turbo-diesels are quieter, more powerful, more efficient, lose less power at altitude, and emit less smoke and soot than normally-aspirated diesels. A turbocharger uses exhaust gas to drive a turbine which squeezes more air into the engine. This denser mixture makes more power. Despite a weak durability record on gasoline engines, turbochargers are far more successful on diesels, where exhaust temperatures are lower, meaning less heat stress.

Complaints of harsh shifting or slippage are not unusual. The 1982 and later turbo-diesels have an adjustable vacuum modulator, allowing shifts to be smoothened. Proper adjustment requires adherence to the factory-specified procedure.

300SD: First Turbo-Diesel ★★

The 1978 300SD was the world's first turbocharged diesel car. Combining the big W116 sedan chassis with the 110hp, 3.0 liter, five-cylinder *oel* motor, it was sold only in the United States for 1978 and 1979. Unless you've just *got* to have one, there's no reason to seek one out. The later W123 turbo-diesels were better developed, sprightlier performers, and are more numerous.

The 300SD turbo-diesel brought the performance of a modest gasoline engine to an efficient diesel car. Zero to 60mph took 13 seconds, about the same as the contemporary gasoline-fueled 280SE, and top speed was about 110mph. The W116 300SD was soon upgraded to the newer S-Class chassis, the W126.

300SD, 300SDL ★★

That S means S-Class, the same body as the big gas sedans. If you need maximum space at minimum cost, these are the cars for you. The 300SD made its debut with the W126 chassis for 1981 and ran through 1987. The stretched-wheelbase 1986–1987 300SDL was a one-year shot, but its 148hp pushed it to 60mph in thirteen seconds, then onward and upward to 120mph. The L's back seat legroom is downright sinful.

California versions of the 1986–1987 300SDL and the 1985–1987 300SD have trap oxidizers. These emission devices can be troublesome (see below).

Compact Diesels: 190D 2.2 ★

The new W201 compact sedan which came along for 1984 was a good diesel candidate, but the naturally aspirated 190D 2.2 was slow, especially with an automatic transmission. At least it was quieter. A new engine encapsulation system enclosed the powerplant and helped to contain the typical rattle.

This model's big advancement was not its engine but its chassis, which included the new multi-

Technical Specifications			
Model	190D 2.5	190D 2.5 Turbo	300D (Turbo)
Years	1986–1988	1987	1987
Engine			
Type	Inline ohc five	Inline ohc five	Inline ohc six
Engine # prefix	602.	602.	603.
Displacement	2497cc (152ci)	2497cc (152ci)	2996cc (183ci)
Bore x stroke	87.0x84.0mm	87.0x84.0mm	87.0x84.0mm
Compression ratio 22.0:1	22.0:1	22.0:1	
SAE horsepower	93hp @ 4600rpm	123hp @ 4600rpm 1	43hp @ 4600rpm
Torque	122lb-ft @ 2800rpm	168lb-ft @ 2400rpm	195lb-ft @ 2400rpm
Fuel system	Mechanical injection	Turbo	Turbo
Fuel required	Diesel (all)		
Chassis			
Type	Unibody; steel		
Chassis # prefix	201.	201.	124.
Transmission	4-speed manual or 4-speed auto	4-speed auto	
Rear-axle ratio	3.07:1	2.65:1	2.65:1
Rear suspension	Multi-link, coil springs (all)		
Front suspension	Strut, coil springs (all)		
Wheels	6x15in	6x15in	6.5x15in
Tires	185/65R15	185/65R15	195/65HR15
Brakes	4-wheel disc, power-assisted (all)		
Fuel capacity	14.7gal + 1.8	14.7gal + 1.8	18.5gal
Weight	2,845lb	3,010lb	3,540lb
Performance			
0-60mph	14.8sec (manual) 15.2sec (auto)	10.0sec	10.5sec
Top speed	107mph (manual) 104mph (auto)	120mph	100mph (est.)
Fuel consumption	25-32mpg	22-30mpg	22-30mpg

In 1992, the 300SD brought diesel advantages to the W140 S-class models. *MBNA*

link suspension. By now these cars have seriously depreciated, so a low-mileage example can be a bargain. The problem with diesels, though, is that they usually get driven a lot. Performance was, shall we say, basic. All things being equal, we recommend that you step up to the 190D 2.5.

190D 2.5 ★

Introduced for 1986 to replace the 190D 2.2, the 190D 2.5 boosted performance. With 300cc more displacement, power jumped to 93hp, cutting 0–60mph time to about 15 seconds and extending top speed to 107mph. The rest of the car remained virtually the same as the 190D 2.2. ABS brakes were an option, and buyers could have either a four-speed automatic or a five-speed manual transmission.

By 1989 an interior update had improved rear legroom, but the 190D 2.5 was not sold in California because it no longer met that state's tightening diesel emissions regulations. Late that year the model was dropped from the US line.

190D 2.5 Turbo ★★

If you want the fastest and best 190 diesel, there's only one choice. For one model year, 1987, American diesel fans could buy this unusually peppy, five-cylinder turbo-diesel, the only turbo engine used in the 190 (W201) body. Sporting for a diesel, the car should have been a success, but, thanks to GM, diesels took big hits in 1987.

The 190D 2.5 Turbo made 123hp, and torque was up almost 40 percent. Zero to 60mph took only ten seconds, and top speed was 120mph, yet normal fuel mileage was around 30mpg. Cruising range was nearly 500 miles.

All 190D 2.5 Turbos had four-speed automatics. Six louvers behind the right headlight draw in air for the intake system. Driver's side air bags and seatbelt tensioners joined ABS and a full complement of optional comforts (leather upholstery, electric sunroof, power seats, headlight washers and wipers). These cars were not sold new in California (tougher smog laws) and were only available as 1987 models.

300D Turbo 1986–1987 ★★

Built on the same W124 mid-range chassis as the gasoline 300E, this six-cylinder diesel first came to the United States as a 1986 model. With 148hp, enough to take it to 127mph, it was then the world's fastest diesel-powered production car. A wagon, the 300TD Turbo, was available for 1987.

Other than their OM603 engine and their drivetrain, these cars are practically identical to the gasoline-powered 300E. The only transmission sold in the United States was a four-speed automatic. The Achilles heel of these cars was their trap oxidizer.

Trap Oxidizer

To enable its 1985 turbo-diesels to meet tighter California standards for diesel particulate emissions in western states, Mercedes-Benz equipped them with a trap oxidizer. This metal cannister, in the exhaust pipe upstream of the turbocharger, trapped particles in a ceramic honeycomb. Benefits included less smoke and exhaust odor, at the cost of about 1mpg and about 4 percent of power.

The self-regenerating device used hot exhaust gases to burn off the particles. If performance dropped, you simply ran at full throttle to burn off the particles in the filter.

The clever device didn't always work properly. Its ceramic mesh could fracture and enter the turbocharger, damaging its blades. In other cases the trap oxidizer clogged and would not burn off accumulated particles. When a trap oxidizer clogs, the engine loses power, fuel consumption increases, and overheating may occur. MBAG rapidly developed an improved unit for 1986 and 1987 models. They also installed the new units free on every 1985 trap oxidizer-equipped car and provided for free replacement at 30,000 mile intervals.

The remedy's effectiveness has not been universal. Some turbo-diesels are now on their third trap oxidizer and/or turbocharger. Cases have been reported where debris from a trap oxidizer somehow entered the cylinders, causing bore wear. As time passes, some dealers are reportedly reluctant to honor the warranty, especially for second or third owners. Use of nonapproved fuel additives can also cause problems for trap oxidizers. At the end of the 1987 model year, Mercedes-Benz halted production of trap oxidizer-equipped cars.

US models with trap oxidizers include the 1985 300D, 300CD, 300TD, and 300SD (California versions, sold in eleven western states); the 1986 300SDL (California version); and the 1987 300D Turbo, 300TD Turbo, and 300SDL (federal and California versions).

Should you buy a turbo-diesel with a trap oxidizer? Theoretically, the problem was solved, but because of their real-world record, their current warranty situation, and the considerable financial risk involved, we can't recommend it. Why invest your money in a car likely to have a major mechanical failure? Even if you do avoid problems, a car with a trap oxidizer will always be worth less as a trade-in.

Technical Specifications

Model	300D 2.5 Turbo	350SDL Turbo	300SD
Years	1990–1993	1990–1991	1992–
Engine			
Type	Inline ohc five	Inline ohc six	Inline ohc six
Engine # prefix	602.	603.	603.
Displacement	2497cc (152.4ci)	3449cc (210.5ci)	3449cc (210.5ci)
Bore x stroke	87.0x84.0mm	89x92.4mm	89x92.4mm
Compression ratio	21.5:1	22:1	22:1
SAE horsepower	121hp @ 4600rpm	134hp @ 4000rpm	148hp @ 4000rpm
Torque	165lb-ft @ 2400rpm	229lb-ft @ 2000rpm	229lb-ft @ 2000rpm
Fuel system	Mechanical fuel injection, turbo (all)		
Fuel required	Diesel (all)		
Chassis			
Type	Unibody; steel		
Chassis # prefix	124.	126.	140.
Transmission	4-speed auto (all)		
Rear-axle ratio	2.65:1	2.82:1	2.82:1
Rear suspension	Multi-link, coil springs (all)		
Front suspension	Shock strut, coil springs	Double wishbones, coil springs	
Wheels	6.5x15in	6.5x15in	7.5x16in
Tires	195/65HR15	205/65HR15	225/60VR16
Brakes	4-wheel disc, vacuum-assisted		
Fuel capacity	18.5gal	23.8gal	26.4gal
Weight	3,390lb	3,850lb	4,610lb
Performance			
0-60mph	12.4sec	11.4sec	12.5sec
Top speed	121mph	109mph	115mph
Fuel use	26-40mpg	20-30mpg	20-23+mpg

1990s Diesels

In early 1990, MBNA bounced back with two excellent new turbo-diesels without trap oxidizers, the 300D 2.5 Turbo (in the mid-range body) and the 350SD Turbo (in the S-Class body). Neither was sold in California, but they were highly regarded for their performance and quiet operation. For 1991 a 350SDL Turbo joined them, on the 5.5in longer wheelbase.

The 1990–1993 300D 2.5 Turbo used a computer to control intake air pressure and prevent overboosting. Along with the 350SD Turbo, the 300D 2.5 drives and performs like a gasoline-engined car; it demands effort for an occupant to hear diesel knock. Alas, California diesel emission requirements were impractical for DBAG to meet, so new Mercedes-Benz diesels were not sold there.

The 300D 2.5 is distinguished by slots in its right front fender, used to deliver intake air to the five-cylinder engine. Its 121hp sounds humble, but low-end torque was excellent, and since the transmission was programmed to start in first gear instead of second, the car felt reasonably quick. The 300D 2.5 Turbos are renowned for fuel efficiency, easily reaching 35mpg on the highway.

The big-bodied 350SD and 350SDL Turbos used a six-cylinder 3.5 liter engine, the largest diesel ever in a Mercedes-Benz car. Peak power was only 134hp, but torque, at 228lb-ft, matched the 4.2 liter V-8 gasoline engine. Zero to 60mph took 11.4 seconds.

E300 Diesel 1994–on ★

When the naturally-aspirated six-cylinder E300 Diesel arrived as a 1995 model, Mercedes-Benz diesels were once again sold in all US states. Its six-cylinder engine is remarkable for its 134hp—more than the 300D 2.5 Turbo's 120hp—and for its fuel efficiency. The keys to its performance lie in its four-valve head, the first in a diesel passenger car, and its advanced electronic control of fuel mixtures.

Thanks to a 23.8 gallon fuel tank, the E300 Diesel's range can approach 800 miles. Since it shares creature comforts with the E320 gas sedan,

The rain-soaked million-mile 1968 220D rests along Highway 1 near Big Sur in California. *FDB*

this mid-range diesel will keep you comfortable for that distance, too.

Summary

If you want a diesel, save up and buy the latest model possible, avoiding those with trap oxidizers. While these diesels are not collector items, they provide excellent transportation value, and you might even find one that becomes endearing to you.

Chapter 19

The Rarest Models

Although they aren't titled that way, the next two categories are distinguished by the rarity and cost of their subjects. This chapter could be divided into two sections: Impossible to Buy and Somewhat Available.

Museum Material

You'll probably never get a chance to buy these cars, but who knows? We wouldn't want you to overlook one. More details are available elsewhere, so we won't go into detail here about these extremely rare cars. We just want to be sure you'll recognize the bargain of a lifetime when you see it.

Silver Arrows ★★★★★

Mercedes-Benz Grand Prix racing cars are among the world's most renowned and valuable

Early Mercedes and Benz racing cars were widely raced in the United States. In 1915 Ralph De-Palma won the Indianapolis 500 in this Mercedes. *Indianapolis Motor Speedway*

automotive artifacts. The best known early cars are the 1908 and 1914 versions, but other successes came in the 1930s with the W125 and W154, and in the 1950s with the W196. Most of these rare cars are safely ensconced in museums. Still, it's conceivable that one or two might remain hidden away.

Although rumors persist of examples surviving in Eastern Europe, practically every Mercedes-Benz Grand Prix car made since 1934 is accounted for. Only a few are in private hands. Arguably the best to drive was the postwar W196, the car that carried Juan Manuel Fangio to a world championship. The 2.5 liter straight-eight is renowned for its desmodromic valves and mechanical fuel injection, making it easier for you and your mechanic to maintain than the more complicated prewar supercharged cars!

300SLR ★★★★★

Derived from the postwar 2.5 liter W196 Grand Prix car, the W196S 300SLR was a tube-framed, 3.0 liter racer contesting the sports car world championship but used only for 1955. Its 302hp inline eight boasted desmodromic valve gear and was matched to a five-speed transmission, with inboard drum brakes all around. Its legendary successes in the Mille Miglia (Stirling Moss/Denis Jenkinson) and elsewhere were tempered by its tragic crash at Le Mans in 1955. Ten chassis numbers were issued, but only nine cars were built, including two Coupes. All are accounted for.

300SLS ★★★★★

Ah, the mystery of the two disappearing 300SLS race cars. If they survive, somewhere in the world are two factory-built, lightweight race ver-

This early Benz racer is being raced on the sand at Daytona Beach, Florida. *MBNA*

sions of the 300SL Roadster, specially built for Paul O'Shea to use in SCCA races in 1957. The team, backed by George Tilp, entered everything in sight, and while they didn't win everywhere, they swept the championship. Cagey SCCA rules makers legislated this factory race car out of contention for 1958, and the two cars, chassis numbers 8467198106/2 and 8442620070/1, were reportedly sold in the United States for $5,000–$6,000 each. They promptly disappeared, and no one has admitted seeing them since. If you find one, it will be one of the most desirable Mercedes-Benz cars ever.

C111 ★★★★★

Developed in the 1960s as a showcase for the Wankel rotary engine, the C111 appeared in 1969.

The W125 swept the 1937 Grand Prix season; at least one is in private hands. *DBAG*

Juan Manuel Fangio at the wheel of a W196 Grand Prix car. *DBAG*

Rally Cars ★★★★

Mercedes-Benz often used rallying to demonstrate the durability and strength of its cars. To do so, they stuck quite closely to production cars. Before World War II, rally versions of most small-engined models existed, especially the 170s. After the war and through the early 1960s, sedans were frequently entered.

The most frequently recognized rally car is the 450SLC 5.0, which in modified form was moderately successful during the 1979 European rally season. No production models, these Coupes were fitted with a roll cage as well as being extensively strengthened and lightened. First entered in that year's Rally of Portugal and driven by Bjorn Waldegaard and Hannu Mikkola, a competition 450SLC 5.0 won the 1979 Bandama Rally.

Other successful rally cars included the 1961–1962 300SE sedans of Eugen Bohringer and several 280E sedans that placed well in the 1978 London to Sydney Marathon.

C112 ★★★★★

At the 1991 Frankfurt show, amid a boom in super-car design, Mercedes-Benz unveiled the C112, a mid-engined Coupe with Gullwing doors, powered by the production 408hp V-12. Despite such advanced features as moveable spoilers, active body control, and electronic brake balancing, the car appeared ready for production, but pragmatism ruled, and the C112 joined the C111 as an example of what might have been.

Sauber-Mercedes Race Cars ★★★★★

Rather than jump back into racing in the late 1980s, Mercedes-Benz eased back in, sponsoring an independent team run by Peter Sauber. Combining his management skills with MBAG support, Sauber did well, so the team evolved into a factory effort. Sauber built quite a few racers, and while it's unlikely that you'll see one for sale, it is conceivable.

Sauber's first Mercedes-Benz powered car was the C8, remembered for a 150mph backflip on the Mulsanne Straight at Le Mans in 1985. It used a stock-block 5.6 liter V-8 fed by twin turbos to make 650hp in race trim. Kouros, a Yves St. Laurent perfume, was the sponsor, at least on the surface.

The team's first win was at the Nürburgring 1,000km in 1986. For 1987, Sauber built the C9, which became such a great success that in 1988 the cars were painted silver and finally bore the name "Sauber Mercedes." In 1989 the team won Le Mans and the World Sportscar Championship. The C9's weak link was the Hewland transmission, which had trouble surviving heavy power

Its four-rotor motor made up to 350hp. Only six Gullwing-doored Coupes were built, the first with a primitive "mule" body of aluminum, the rest with sleeker fiberglass bodies. The first, even with a steel platform chassis, weighed under 3000lb and had a top speed beyond 185mph.

This early super car came close to production but was destined instead to be a concept vehicle and a record-setter. In 1976 and 1978, rebodied C111-IIs set world speed records using a souped-up, five-cylinder, turbo-diesel engine. In 1979 a C111-IV with a 500hp, twin-turbo gasoline V-8 set a new world closed-course record of 250.918mph at Nardo, Italy.

All C111s were retained by DBAG, so your chances of buying one are presently low. Still, maybe if you could find something that DBAG *really* wanted...

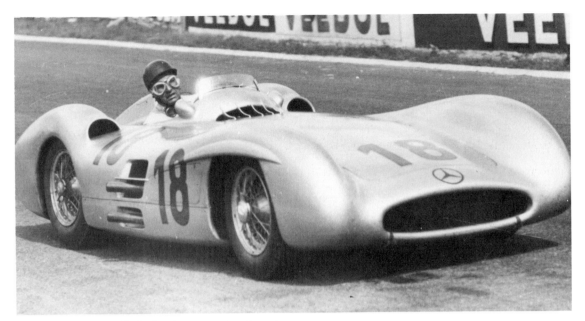

The W196 was built in both open-wheel and fendered versions. *DBAG*

on rough tracks.

The C11, built for 1990, was the last thundering V-8. Its 720hp, 5.0 liter M119 engine worked through a new Mercedes-Benz five-speed manual transmission. For reasons of racing politics, the team declined to enter Le Mans in 1990, and Jaguar won, but the C11 handily repeated as world champion.

Mercedes-Benz still enters some of its prize racing cars in historic events; here Stirling Moss exercises a 300SLR at Monterey in 1986. *FDB*

A great road car would be this Wankel-powered C111, posed here next to the factory's fiberglass-bodied 300SL. *DBAG*

For 1991, FISA mandated 3.5 liter, normally aspirated engines, requiring new cars—and earplugs. Mercedes-Benz and Sauber created the new C291 with a radical flat-twelve engine and a six-speed gearbox set as low as possible between two ground effects ducts. The C291 had teething troubles, mostly involving bad engine castings, so a planned active suspension program took second priority to finishing races. The C11s were used for Le Mans; the C291s ran everywhere else but won only the final event. MBAG then ended its sports car racing program, and development of another new car, the C292, halted.

Sedan Racers ★★★★

While the World Sportscar Championship was becoming a poor investment, the German Touring Car Championship drew record crowds, so Mercedes-Benz shifted to racing cars resembling production models. The 190E 2.5-16 was run by three factory-supported teams. Judging by the rac-ing's ferocity, they must have used up a fair number of cars, so surplus examples must exist. The stock-block engines developed ungodly power (up to 375hp from a normally aspirated 2.5 liter four), so you'd need a race mechanic to keep one running. Emissions laws would never allow the cars to be street-licensed, but what fun on a track.

In Europe, a 190E 2.5-16 Evolution production model was introduced in 1990, and 500 were sold to the public as a homologation special for the race cars. Distinguished by a huge rear wing and ovoid fender flares, the 235hp Evo II got to 60 in 7.1 seconds and could hit 155mph. Even this street version can't be licensed in the United States.

Speaking of sedan racers, an American team led by Rick Hurst, a Mercedes-Benz dealer, entered a 190E 2.3–16 in IMSA's International Sedan series. The team, including driver Bob Strange, was experienced in SCCA Showroom Stock racing, so the car was successful, at least until the rules writers favored other brands. The car still exists.

Limousines, Station Wagons, Ambulances, and Hearses ★★★

In Germany, Mercedes-Benz is not only the favorite taxi but also the favorite limousine, ambulance, even hearse. In the United States such commercial cars are rare, mostly imported examples.

Special-purpose cars were built by outside coachbuilders based on chassis supplied by Daimler-Benz. During the 1950s, the most popular coachbuilder was Binz (not a typo), who built wagons on round-body 190 and 220 chassis. Another was Miesen, in Bonn. Fin-back station wagons were built by the Belgian firm of D'Ieteren and first offered in 1965 by Daimler-Benz in Europe as the "Universal." Gasoline and diesel power were equally popular, but most vehicles were on the low-end chassis with small engines. Only a few 220 and almost no 300 models were built as ambulances or hearses.

During the 1970s several hundred long-chassis 240D limousines were built and sold, reportedly in Canada. These use a wheelbase 24.8in longer than the normal car, plus 15.0in wheels.

Most 1980s stretch limousines you'll find were built not by Mercedes-Benz, but by German and American body shops of varying talent. Quality is inconsistent. We've seen stretched cars obviously bent at the joint.

Geländewagen ★★★

This off-road, all-wheel-drive Mercedes-Benz is an amazing dual-purpose vehicle. A 280GE won the 6,000 mile 1983 Paris-Dakar Rally. It's a German concept of a better Range Rover. What began as a utilitarian vehicle (we can't call it a car) is softening. In 1990 a more luxurious version was developed, and the latest version is now being sold in the US.

A Geländewagen could be custom-tailored—short or long wheelbase, diesel or gasoline engines, various roofs and seating arrangements, and any number of serious accessories for storming the shrubbery.

Most of those in the US were imported through special importers and modified to meet US safety and emissions regulations. Most US Mercedes-Benz dealers don't know much about

How about a custom-bodied European Mercedes-Benz ambulance? It would make a great camper. *FDB*

181

The super car that never was. A production 408hp V-12 was to drive the C112 to 190mph speeds, aided by ABC (Active Body Control) and slowed by EBV (Electronic Brake Balance). *MBAG*

them, so you must rely on others for service, which works well. Parts are available promptly, and a good Mercedes-Benz mechanic can handle service and most repairs.

A Geländewagen isn't a collector car in the normal sense, but it breaks every other rule, so we've got to give it respect with a mention here.

Buses and Trucks ★★

Daimler-Benz passenger cars are just the tip of the iceberg; buses and trucks make up much of the company's worldwide business. DBAG has tried to crack the US bus and truck market, but the nature of the business has been a formidable barrier.

The most commonly seen buses in this country were the upright diesel-powered "airport bus" O319D types of the 1950s and 1960s. Frequently used hard, few survive.

In the early 1980s, after Daimler-Benz purchased US truck-builder Freightliner, Mercedes-Benz trucks began to appear on US streets and highways. Most were diesel-powered "straight" trucks with van bodies, used for city delivery and short-distance hauling. DBAG established a network of over 200 truck dealers, but in 1992 the system was severely cut due to slow demand.

A series of Class 7 (semi-tractor) trucks was introduced in the mid-1980s but never became popular. The cab-over-engine LPS 1525 was powered by a 250hp, 10 liter, five-cylinder turbo-diesel with a six-speed transmission and a two-speed overdrive. Like the straight trucks, this model was assembled in Hampton, Virginia, from components made in Germany, Brazil, and North America.

Even the fin-backs were good racers; here Bohringer throws a 300SE sedan around the Nürburging in 1964. *DBAG*

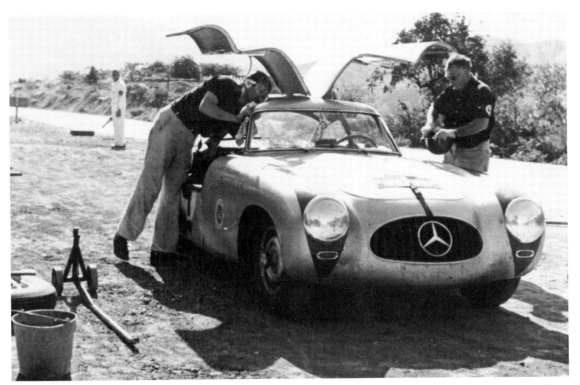

In the early stages of the 1952 Carrera Panamericana, a buzzard broke the windshield of this early 300SL racer. As a result, vertical "buzzard bars" were added, but why not restore it with a broken windshield? *DBAG*

This 190E 2.3–16 racers was entered by Rick Hurst and driven by Bob Strange in IMSA's International Sedan class. *Rick Hurst Racing*

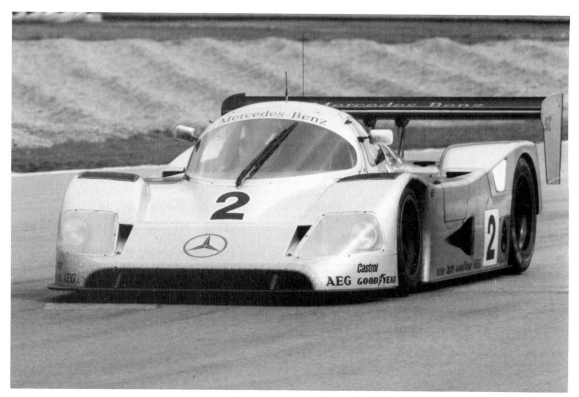

The 720hp, V-8 powered C11, racing here at Montreal in 1990, went on to take the World Sportscar Championship that year. *FDB*

The four-wheel-drive Geländewagen can be had with diesel or gasoline engines; new and used ones are available in the United States. *DBAG*

Unimog ★★

No other company makes anything like the Unimog. A cross between an all-wheel-drive truck and a tractor, it was developed after World War II as a multi-purpose tractor. In the United States these expensive, versatile vehicles are found mostly in cold climes serving ski areas and municipalities. The ability to switch between a variety of implements (snowblowers and plows in the winter, mowers and backhoes in the summer) makes the Unimog more efficient than dedicated vehicles.

The diesel-powered Unimog appeared in 1948. The first officially imported into the United States came over in 1959, followed by the 90hp U900 in the late 1960s. In 1983 a bigger version, the five-ton 120hp turbo-diesel U1200, appeared. A modified version of the 168hp U1700 won the 1982 Paris-Dakar Rally. Eight-speed manual transmissions with high and low range offer up to twenty-four gear ratios forward and reverse. A Unimog can climb a 70 percent grade and go anywhere

Tour with your family and friends in a restored
1950s Mercedes-Benz sightseeing bus. *DBAG*

you can stand. Early models are too slow for interstate use; current models hit 60mph, but you
wouldn't want to do that all day.

After using Case and MBNA as importers,
DBAG switched to Schmitt Engineering and
Equipment in New Berlin, Wisconsin. Unimogs
were sold to many armies, but cost limited civilian
sales. Used examples are available at modest
prices.

You might not think of a Unimog as a collector car, but we've seen several restored examples,
so interest exists. Remember, when the going gets
tough, the tough get Unimogs!

With a Unimog, you can pretty much go wherever
you like. *FDB*

Appendices

Model Numbers

Mercedes-Benz model numbers are confusing, at least at first sight. To work your way through the maze, you need remember only a few simple truths.

The first three numbers (190, 300, 560, and so on) usually indicate engine displacement (1.9 liters, 3.0 liters...). If a second number is present (190D 2.2, 280SE 3.5, 300SEL 6.3), it indicates displacement in liters, as when an existing model grew a bigger engine. For example, the 190D came out in Europe with a 1.9 liter engine, but in the United States it had the 2.2 liter motor, so it was the 190D 2.2.

Capital letters, single or in combination, indicate bodystyle and/or engine type:

C: Coupe, as in 280C, 300CD
D: Diesel; typical examples are the 190D, 300TD (turbo-diesel)
E: Gasoline fuel injection, from Einspritzer
G: Gelandewagen; off-road, all-wheel-drive vehicle
SD or SDL: Sedan, normal or long wheelbase, diesel power
SE or SEL: As above, except gasoline power
SL: Two-seater Convertible, from Sports Light (often loosely applied, as SLs tend to be anything but)
SLC: Four-seater sports Coupe (a stretched SL with fixed steel top)
T: Station wagon, from Touring, as in 280TE (2.8 liter gasoline wagon), 300TDT (3.0 liter turbo-diesel wagon), 300TE 4Matic (3.0 liter gasoline wagon with all-wheel drive)
TD: Turbo-diesel, as in 300TD

Lower-case letters indicate updates within a model series, so they're fairly redundant if you know the year:

a, b, c, d: 300, 300b, 300c, 300d; or 190D, 190Db, and so on

Older Cabriolets are the A (two-seater), B (four-seater, two side windows on each side), and C (four-seater, one side window). The Cabriolet D is a four-seater with four doors, and the Cabriolet F is a long-wheelbase four-seater with four doors.

In a fit of corporate evolution, Mercedes-Benz dazed the automotive world in 1993 by announcing that henceforth, rather than being numbered and lettered, its models would be lettered then numbered. The 1994 compact sedans were thus the C220 and the C280. The Executive mid-range cars are the E320, E420, E500, and so forth. The top-rung S-Class encompasses the S320, S420, S500, and S600. Body variations were addenda to numerical designations: E320 Cabriolet, S500 Coupe, S600 Coupe, et al, and the SL models were re-dubbed SL320, SL500, and SL600.

Clubs

Car clubs provide historical, technical, and restoration information. Their publications contain useful articles plus advertisements for prod-

ucts and services. Experts can answer your questions. National clubs and local branches hold tech sessions, tours, and car shows.

Mercedes-Benz Club of America
(23,000 members)
1907 Lelaray St.
Colorado Springs, CO 80919

The Gull Wing Group
(700 members)
15875 Oak Glen Ave.
Morgan Hill, CA 95037

190SL Group
(700 members)
16 Theodore Dr.
East Brunswick, NJ 08816

Finding the Part Number

You can still walk into a dealership and buy most mechanical parts for a postwar collectible Mercedes-Benz. Still, when you go in, you'd better have the chassis number and engine number, and it doesn't hurt to have the part number, too.

Number	Location
Chassis	Since 1969, on windshield post (US models); prior to that, usually on driver's doorpost
Engine	On left rear upper corner of engine
Transmission	Stamped into main transmission housing
Axle	Stamped into rear-axle housing; on front spindle
Steering	Stamped into steering box
Paint	Three-digit code number on front radiator support, followed by a "G" or "H"
Upholstery	From mid-1985, same as paint code without "G" or "H"; before then, on vehicle data card or warranty ID plate
Key	On one vehicle data card; older cars may have number stamped on locks

Part numbers are in the Parts Picture Catalog for your model.

Chassis and Engine Numbers

An entire book could be written about Mercedes-Benz chassis and engine numbers. Prewar chassis numbers usually matched the original engine numbers. Since 1946, DBAG has used two basic systems, the most drastic change occurring in 1981 in response to US regulations.

Chassis Numbers

The first part of the chassis number describes the model. Throughout a given model run, regardless of model year or production date, cars were assigned individual 5- or 6-digit consecutive "serial numbers" at the end of their chassis numbers, identifying individual cars. Until the 1984 model year, each model had its own serial number series.

Cars from 1946–1950 bore 11-number engine and chassis numbers. For 1951 and 1952, the last two numbers of the production year were added, for a total of 13 digits. For 1953 through 1959, code letters were added for clutch and transmission types, and the production year digits were reversed.

From 1960 to 1980, 14 digits were used. The production year digits were eliminated, and the codes were changed from letters to numbers. Generally, pre-1981 chassis numbers used 0 or 1 as the fourth digit; 0 indicated fitment of a gasoline engine, 1 indicated a diesel.

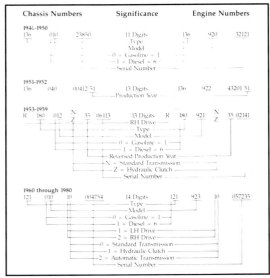

For model year 1981, a 17-digit system was started, with VIN on a plate on the left (driver's) side windshield post and on the left front door pillar. The VIN indicates whether a car is to US or other specification, its original passenger-restraint system, its city of manufacture, its model year, and its place in the production run.

Although 1983 and earlier models each had their own individual serial number progression, starting with the 1984 model year, the two main cities of manufacture, Bremen and Stuttgart, each got their own chassis number series (F and A, respectively). Thus it's possible to find two post-1983 cars of the same model with identical last 6-digit chassis numbers—but they should have different assembly plant codes! Check the 11th digit from the left.

Of course, model year and production (i.e., calendar) year can differ. Since the 1940s, Mercedes-Benz has traditionally shifted to production of the next model year's cars in early September. Thus a car of one model year may have been built during the last four months of the previous calendar year. Some US states titled cars in the year they were sold, so a leftover car's title date may not agree with the model year according to the its chassis number. In any case, the chassis number governs.

Registration Years

Registration Years		Registration Years	
1980	A	1991	M
1981	B	1992	N
1982	C	1993	P
1983	D	1994	R
1984	E	1995	S
1985	F	1996	T
1986	G	1997	V
1987	H	1998	W
1988	J	1999	X
1989	K	2000	Y
1990	L		

Engine Numbers

Postwar engine numbers typically used 9 as the fourth digit, the first digit of the engine type number. Note that gasoline engine numbers begin with the digit 1, and diesels begin with a 6.

This list of chassis and engine type prefixes, arranged by model and year, allows you to check the car you're looking at to be certain, for instance, that a 560SEL is nor really a reincarnated 380SEL. Asterisks indicate sunroof models.

Model	Years	Chassis Prefix	Engine Prefix	Description
170V	1947-50	136.010	136.920	sedan, gasoline
170Va, Vb	1950-53	136.060	136.923	sedan, gasoline
170Va, Vb*	1950-53	136.072	136.923	sedan, gasoline
170S	1949-52	136.040	136.922	sedan, gasoline
170S*	1949-52	136.049	136.922	sedan, gasoline
170S Cabriolet A	1949-51	136.042	136.922	Convertible, gasoline
170S Cabriolet B	1949-51	136.043	136.922	Convertible, gasoline
170Sb	1952-53	191.010	136.922	sedan, gasoline
170Sb*	1952-53	191.018	136.922	sedan, gasoline
170Sb Cabriolet A	1952-53	191.011	136.922	Convertible, gasoline
170Sb Cabriolet B	1952-53	191.012	136.922	Convertible, gasoline
170S-V	1953-55	136.081	136.926	sedan, gasoline
170S-V*	1953-55	136.082	136.926	sedan, gasoline
170D	1949-50	136.110	636.915	sedan, diesel
170Da, Db	1950-53	136.160	636.916	sedan, diesel
170Da, Db*	1950-53	136.172	636.916	sedan, diesel
170Ds	1952-53	191.110	636.918	sedan, diesel
170Ds*	1952-53	191.113	636.918	sedan, diesel
170S-D	1953-55	136.181	636.981	sedan, diesel
170S-D*	1953-55	136.182	636.981	sedan, diesel
220	1951-53	187.011	180.920	sedan, gasoline
220*	1951-53	187.014	180.920	sedan, gasoline
220 Cabriolet A	1951-55	187.012	180.920	Convertible, gasoline
220 Cabriolet B	1951-54	187.013	180.920	Convertible, gasoline
220 Coupe	1954-55	187.014	180.920	Coupe, gasoline
300, 300b	1951-55	186.011	186.920	sedan, gasoline
300, 300b*	1951-55	186.015	186.920	sedan, gasoline
300, 300b Cab. D	1951-55	186.014	186.920	Convertible, gasoline
300c manual trans	1955-57	186.016A	186.920	sedan, gasoline

Model	Years	Chassis Prefix	Engine Prefix	Description
300c manual trans*				
—		186.017A	186.920	sedan, gasoline
300cmanual trans, Cab. D				
—		186.033A	186.920	Convertible, gasoline
300c auto trans				
—		186.016	186.921	sedan, gasoline
300c auto trans*				
—		186.017	186.921	sedan, gasoline
300c auto trans, Cab. D				
—		186.033	186.921	Convertible, gasoline
300d auto trans				
	1958-62	189.010	189.980	sedan, gasoline
300d auto trans*				
	1958-62	189.011	189.980	sedan, gasoline
300d auto trans Cab. D				
	1958-62	189.033	189.980	Convertible, gasoline
300d manual trans				
	1958-62	189.010	189.981	sedan, gasoline
300d manual trans*				
	1958-62	189.011	189.981	sedan, gasoline
300d manual trans Cab. D				
	1958-62	189.033	189.981	Convertible, gasoline
300S Cabriolet				
	1951-55	188.010	188.920	Convertible, gasoline
300S	1951-55	188.011	188.920	Coupe, gasoline
300S	1951-55	188.012	188.920	Roadster, gasoline
300Sc Cabriolet				
	1955-58	188.013	199.980	Convertible, gasoline
300Sc	1955-58	188.014	199.980	Coupe, gasoline
300Sc	1955-58	188.015	199.980	Roadster, gasoline
180	1953-57	120.010	136.925	sedan, gasoline
180*	—	120.011	136.925	sedan, gasoline
180a, 180b	1957-61	120.010	121.923	sedan, gasoline
180a, 180b*	—	120.011	121.923	sedan, gasoline
180c	1961-62	120.010	121.927	sedan, gasoline
180c*	—	120.011	121.927	sedan, gasoline
180D, 180Db				
	1953-61	120.110	636.930	sedan, diesel
180D, 180Db*				
	1953-61	120.111	636.930	sedan, diesel
180Dc	1961-62	120.110	621.914	sedan, diesel
180Dc*	1961-62	120.111	621.914	sedan, diesel
300SL	1954-57	198.040	198.980	Coupe, gasoline
300SL (light alloy)				
	1955-56	198.043	198.980	Coupe, gasoline
300SL	1957-63	198.042	198.980	Roadster, gasoline
300SL engine, light alloy crankcase, post-3/62				
			198.982	
190SL	1955-63	121.040	121.921	Roadster, gasoline
190SL	1955-63	121.042	121.921	Roadster, gasoline
190SL engine, newer valve gear, post-8/61				
			121.928	
190, 190b	1956-61	121.010	121.920	sedan, gasoline
190, 190b*	1956-61	121.011	121.920	sedan, gasoline
190c	1961-65	110.010	121.924	sedan, gasoline
190D, 190Db				
	1958-61	121.110	621.910	sedan, diesel
190D, 190Db*				
	1958-61	121.111	621.910	sedan, diesel
190Dc	1961-65	110.110	621.912	sedan, diesel
220a	1954-56	180.010	180.921	sedan, gasoline
220a*	—	180.011	180.921	sedan, gasoline
219	1956-59	105.010	180.920	sedan, gasoline
219*	1956-59	105.011	180.920	sedan, gasoline
220S	1956-59	180.010	180.924	sedan, gasoline
220S*	1956-59	180.011	180.924	sedan, gasoline
220S	1956-59	180.030	180.924	Convertible, gasoline
220S	1957-59	180.037	180.924	Coupe, gasoline

Model	Years	Chassis Prefix	Engine Prefix	Description
220SE	1958-59	128.010	127.980	sedan, gasoline
220SE*	1958-59	128.011	127.980	sedan, gasoline
220SE	1958-60	128.030	127.984	Convertible, gasoline
220SE	1958-60	128.037	127.984	Coupe, gasoline
220 (220b)	1959-65	111.010	180.940	sedan, gasoline
220S (220Sb)				
	1959-65	111.012	180.941	sedan, gasoline
220SE (220SEb)				
	1959-65	111.014	127.982	sedan, gasoline
220SE (220SEb) Coupe				
	1960-65	111.021	127.984	Coupe, gasoline
220SE (220SEb) Conv.				
	1960-65	111.023	127.984	Convertible, gasoline
230SL	1963-67	113.042	127.981	Roadster, gasoline
250SL	1966-68	113.043	129.982	Roadster, gasoline
280SL	1967-71	113.044	130.983	Roadster, gasoline
600	1963-81	100.012	100.980	sedan, gasoline
600 Pullman, 4-dr				
—		100.014	100.980	limousine, gasoline
600 Pullman, 6-dr				
		100.016	100.980	limousine, gasoline
600 Landaulet				
—		100.615	100.980	Convertible, gasoline
200	1965-68	110.010	121.940	sedan, gasoline
200D	1965-68	110.110	621.918	sedan, diesel
230	1965-66	110.011	180.945	sedan, gasoline
230 w/INAT carbs, 7/66-68				
—		110.011	180.949	sedan, gasoline
230S	1965-68	111.010	180.947	sedan, gasoline
250S	1965-69	108.012	108.920	sedan, gasoline
250SE	1965-68	108.014	129.980	sedan, gasoline
250SE Coupe				
	1965-67	111.021	129.980	Coupe, gasoline
250SE Convertible				
	1965-67	111.023	129.980	Convertible, gasoline
300SE	1961-65	112.014	189.984	sedan, gasoline
300SEL	1963-65	112.015	189.984	sedan, gasoline
300SE, 160hp				
	1962-63	112.021	189.985	Coupe, gasoline
300SE, 160hp				
	1962-63	112.023	189.985	Convertible, gasoline
300SE, 170hp				
	1964-67	112.021	189.987	Coupe, gasoline
300SE, 170hp				
	1964-67	112.023	189.987	Convertible, gasoline
300SEb	1965-67	108.015	189.989	sedan, gasoline
300SEL	1965-67	109.015	189.988	sedan, gasoline
300SEL	1967-70	109.016	189.981	sedan, gasoline
300SEL	1971	109.016	130.981	sedan, gasoline
280S	1967-72	108.016	130.920	sedan, gasoline
280SE & SEL				
	1967-72	108.018	130.980	sedan, gasoline
280SE	1967-71	111.024	130.980	Coupe, gasoline
280SE 3.5	1969-71	111.026	116.980	Coupe, gasoline
280SE 3.5	1969-71	111.027	116.980	Convertible, gasoline
280SE/SEL 3.5				
	1970-72	108.018	116.980	sedan, gasoline
300SEL 6.3	1968-72	109.018	100.981	sedan, gasoline
300SEL 3.5	1969-72	109.056	116.981	sedan, gasoline
200/8	1967-76	115.015	115.923	sedan, gasoline
200D/8	1967-76	115.115	615.912	sedan, diesel
220/8	1967-73	115.010	115.920	sedan, gasoline
220D/8	1967-76	115.110	615.912	sedan, diesel
230/8	1967-76	114.015	180.954	sedan, gasoline
250	1967-72	114.010	114.920	sedan, gasoline
250	—	114.011	130.923	sedan, gasoline
250C	1968-72	114.023	114.920	Coupe, gasoline
250C	—	114.023	130.923	Coupe, gasoline

Model	Years	Chassis Prefix	Engine Prefix	Description
280C (single cam)				
	1969-73	114.073	130.921	Coupe, gasoline
280C (twin cam)				
	1974-76	114.073	110.921	Coupe, gasoline
280 (single cam)				
	1970-73	114.060	130.921	sedan, gasoline
280 (twin cam)				
	1974-76	114.060	110.921	sedan, gasoline
*With sunroof				

The above includes some European models. Unless stated otherwise, the following are US models, by model year.

Model	Years	Chassis Prefix	Engine Prefix	Description
1971: (US and other models)				
220D	115.110	615.912		sedan, diesel
220	115.010	115.920		sedan, gasoline
230 (6)	114.015	180.954		sedan, gasoline
250	114.010	114.920		sedan, gasoline
250	114.011	130.923		sedan, gasoline
250C	114.023	130.923		Coupe, gasoline
280S	108.016	130.920		sedan, gasoline
280SE	108.018	130.980		sedan, gasoline
280SE	111.024	130.980		Coupe, gasoline
280SE	111.025	130.980		Convertible, gasoline
280SEL	108.019	130.980		sedan, gasoline
280SE 3.5	111.026	116.980		Coupe, gasoline
280SE 3.5	111.027	116.980		Convertible, gasoline
280SE 4.5	108.067	117.984		sedan, gasoline
280SEL 4.5	108.068	117.984		sedan, gasoline
300SEL	109.016	130.981		sedan, gasoline
300SEL 3.5	109.056	116.981		sedan, gasoline
300SEL 4.5	109.057	117.981		sedan, gasoline
300SEL 6.3	109.018	100.981		sedan, gasoline
600	100.012	100.980		limousine, gasoline
600 Pullman, 4-dr	100.014	100.980		limousine, gasoline
600 Pullman, 6-dr	100.016	100.980		limousine, gasoline
600 Landaulet	100.615	100.980		landaulet, gasoline
280SL	113.044	130.983		Roadster, gasoline
350SL	107.044	117.982		Roadster, gasoline
1972: (US and other models)				
220D	115.110	615.912		sedan, diesel
220	115.010	115.920		sedan, gasoline
230 (6)	114.015	180.954		sedan, gasoline
250	114.010	114.920		sedan, gasoline
250	114.011	130.923		sedan, gasoline
250C	114.023	130.923		Coupe, gasoline
280	114.060	110.921		sedan, gasoline
280C	114.073	110.921		Coupe, gasoline
280SE 4.5	108.067	117.984		sedan, gasoline
280SEL 4.5	108.068	117.984		sedan, gasoline
300SEL 3.5	109.056	116.981		sedan, gasoline
300SEL 4.5	109.057	117.981		sedan, gasoline
300SEL 6.3	109.018	100.981		sedan, gasoline
450SE	116.032	117.983		sedan, gasoline
450SEL	116.033	117.983		sedan, gasoline
450SL	107.044	117.982		Roadster, gasoline
450SLC	107.024	117.982		Coupe, gasoline
600	100.012	100.980		limousine, gasoline
600 Pullman, 4-dr	100.014	100.980		limousine, gasoline
600 Pullman, 6-dr	100.016	100.980		limousine, gasoline

Model	Years	Chassis Prefix	Engine Prefix	Description
1973: (US models only)				
220D	115.110	615.912		sedan, diesel
240D	115.117	616.916		sedan, diesel
220	115.010	115.920		sedan, gasoline
230 (4)	115.017	115.951		sedan, gasoline
280	114.060	110.921		sedan, gasoline
280C	114.073	110.921		Coupe, gasoline
450SE	116.032	117.983		sedan, gasoline
450SEL	116.033	117.983		sedan, gasoline
450SL	107.044	117.982		Roadster, gasoline
450SLC	107.024	117.982		Coupe, gasoline
1974:				
240D	115.117	616.916		sedan, diesel
230 (4)	115.017	115.951		sedan, gasoline
280	114.060	110.921		sedan, gasoline
280C	114.073	110.921		Coupe, gasoline
450SE	116.032	117.983		sedan, gasoline
450SEL	116.033	117.983		sedan, gasoline
450SL	107.044	117.982		Roadster, gasoline
450SLC	107.024	117.982		Coupe, gasoline
1975:				
240D	115.117	616.916		sedan, diesel
300D	115.114	617.910		sedan, diesel
230 (4)	115.017	115.951		sedan, gasoline
280	114.060	110.921		sedan, gasoline
280C	114.073	110.921		Coupe, gasoline
280S	116.020	110.922		sedan, gasoline
450SE	116.032	117.983		sedan, gasoline
450SEL	116.033	117.983		sedan, gasoline
450SL	107.044	117.982		Roadster, gasoline
450SLC	107.024	117.982		Coupe, gasoline
1976:				
240D	115.117	616.916		sedan, diesel
300D	115.114	617.910		sedan, diesel
230 (4)	115.017	115.951		sedan, gasoline
280	114.060	110.921		sedan, gasoline
280C	114.073	110.921		Coupe, gasoline
280S	116.020	110.922		sedan, gasoline
450SE	116.032	117.986		sedan, gasoline
450SEL	116.033	117.986		sedan, gasoline
450SL	107.044	117.985		Roadster, gasoline
450SLC	107.024	117.985		Coupe, gasoline
1977:				
240D	123.123	616.912		sedan, diesel
300D	123.130	617.912		sedan, diesel
230	123.023	115.954		sedan, gasoline
280E	123.033	110.984		sedan, gasoline
280SE	116.024	110.985		sedan, gasoline
450SEL	116.023	117.985		sedan, gasoline
450SEL 6.9	116.036	100.985		sedan, gasoline
450SL	107.044	117.985		Roadster, gasoline
450SLC	107.024	117.985		Coupe, gasoline
1978:				
240D	123.123	616.912		sedan, diesel
300D	123.130	617.912		sedan, diesel
300CD	123.150	617.912		Coupe, diesel
230	123.023	115.954		sedan, gasoline
280E	123.033	110.984		sedan, gasoline
280CE	123.053	110.984		Coupe, gasoline
280SE	116.024	110.985		sedan, gasoline
300SD	116.120	617.950		sedan, turbo-diesel
450SEL	116.033	117.985		sedan, gasoline
450SL	107.044	117.985		Roadster, gasoline

Model	Years	Chassis Prefix	Engine Prefix	Description
450SLC	107.024	117.985		Coupe, gasoline

1979:

Model	Years	Chassis Prefix	Engine Prefix	Description
240D	123.123	616.912		sedan, diesel
300D	123.130	617.912		sedan, diesel
300CD	123.150	617.912		Coupe, diesel
300TD	123.190	617.912		wagon, diesel
230	123.023	115.954		sedan, gasoline
280E	123.033	110.984		sedan, gasoline
280CE	123.053	110.984		Coupe, gasoline
280SE	116.024	110.985		sedan, gasoline
300SD	116.120	617.950		sedan, turbo-diesel
450SEL	116.033	117.985		sedan, gasoline
450SL	107.044	117.985		Roadster, gasoline
450SLC	107.024	117.985		Coupe, gasoline

1980:

Model	Years	Chassis Prefix	Engine Prefix	Description
240D	123.123	616.912		sedan, diesel
300D	123.130	617.912		sedan, diesel
300CD	123.150	617.912		Coupe, diesel
300TD	123.190	617.912		wagon, diesel
280E	123.033	110.984		sedan, gasoline
280CE	123.053	110.984		Coupe, gasoline
280SE	116.024	110.984		sedan, gasoline
300SD	116.120	617.950		sedan, diesel
450SEL	116.033	117.985		sedan, gasoline
450SL	107.044	117.985		Roadster, gasoline
450SLC	107.024	117.985		Coupe, gasoline

1981:

Model	Years	Chassis Prefix	Engine Prefix	Description
240D	123.123	616.912		sedan, diesel
300D	123.130	617.912		sedan, diesel
300CD	123.150	617.912		Coupe, diesel
300TD	123.193	617.952		wagon, turbo-diesel
280E	123.033	110.984		sedan, gasoline
280CE	123.053	110.984		Coupe, gasoline
300SD	126.120	617.951		sedan, diesel
380SEL	126.033	116.961		sedan, gasoline
380SL	107.045	116.960		Roadster, gasoline
380SLC	107.025	116.960		Coupe, gasoline

1982–1983:

Model	Years	Chassis Prefix	Engine Prefix	Description
240D	123.123	616.912		sedan, diesel
300D	123.133	617.952		sedan, turbo-diesel
300CD	123.153	617.952		Coupe, turbo-diesel
300TD	123.193	617.952		wagon, turbo-diesel
300SD	126.120	617.951		sedan, turbo-diesel
380SEL	126.032	116.963		sedan, gasoline
380SEC	126.043	116.963		Coupe, gasoline
380SL	107.045	116.962		Roadster, gasoline

1984:

Model	Years	Chassis Prefix	Engine Prefix	Description
190E 2.3	201.024	102.961		sedan, gasoline
190D 2.2	201.122	601.921		sedan, diesel
300D	123.133	617.952		sedan, turbo-diesel
300CD	123.153	617.952		Coupe, turbo-diesel
300TD	123.193	617.952		wagon, turbo-diesel
300SD	126.120	617.951		sedan, turbo-diesel
380SE	126.032	116.963		sedan, gasoline
500SEL	126.037	117.963		sedan, gasoline
500SEC	126.044	117.963		Coupe, gasoline
380SL	107.045	116.962		Roadster, gasoline

1985:

Model	Years	Chassis Prefix	Engine Prefix	Description
190E 2.3	201.024	102.985		sedan, gasoline
190D 2.2	201.122	601.921		sedan, diesel
300D	123.133	617.952		sedan, turbo-diesel
300CD	123.153	617.952		Coupe, turbo-diesel
300TD	123.193	617.952		wagon, turbo-diesel
300SD	126.120	617.951		sedan, turbo-diesel
380SE	126.032	116.963		sedan, gasoline
500SEL	126.037	117.963		sedan, gasoline
500SEC	126.044	117.963		Coupe, gasoline
380SL	107.045	116.962		Roadster, gasoline

1986:

Model	Years	Chassis Prefix	Engine Prefix	Description
190E 2.3	201.024	102.985		sedan, gasoline
190E 2.3-16	201.034	102.983		sedan, gasoline
190D 2.5	201.126	602.911		sedan, diesel
300E	124.030	103.983		sedan, gasoline
300SDL	126.125	603.961		sedan, diesel
420SEL	126.035	116.965		sedan, gasoline
560SEL	126.039	117.968		sedan, gasoline
560SEC	126.045	117.968		Coupe, gasoline
560SL	107.048	117.967		Roadster, gasoline

1987:

Model	Years	Chassis Prefix	Engine Prefix	Description
190E 2.3	201.028	102.985		sedan, gasoline
190E 2.6	201.029	103.942		sedan, gasoline
190E 2.3-16	201.034	102.983		sedan, gasoline
190D 2.5	201.126	602.911		sedan, diesel
190D 2.5 Turbo	201.128	602.961		sedan, turbo-diesel
260E	124.026	103.940		sedan, gasoline
300E	124.030	103.983		sedan, gasoline
300D	124.133	603.960		sedan, turbo-diesel
300TD	124.193	603.960		sedan, turbo-diesel
300SDL	126.125	603.961		sedan, turbo-diesel
420SEL	126.035	116.965		sedan, gasoline
560SEL	126.039	117.968		sedan, gasoline
560SEC	126.045	117.968		Coupe, gasoline
560SL	107.048	117.967		Roadster, gasoline

1988:

Model	Years	Chassis Prefix	Engine Prefix	Description
190E 2.3	201.028	102.985		sedan, gasoline
190E 2.6	201.029	103.942		sedan, gasoline
190D 2.5	201.126	602.911		sedan, diesel
260E	124.026	103.940		sedan, gasoline
300E	124.030	103.983		sedan, gasoline
300CE	124.050	103.983		Coupe, gasoline
300TE	124.090	103.983		wagon, gasoline
300SE	126.024	103.981		sedan, gasoline
300SEL	126.025	103.981		sedan, gasoline
420SEL	126.035	116.965		sedan, gasoline
560SEL	126.039	117.968		sedan, gasoline
560SEC	126.045	117.966		Coupe, gasoline
560SL	107.048	117.967		Roadster, gasoline

1989:

Model	Years	Chassis Prefix	Engine Prefix	Description
190E 2.6	201.029	103.942		sedan, gasoline
190D 2.5	201.126	602.911		sedan, diesel
260E	124.026	103.940		sedan, gasoline
300E	124.030	103.983		sedan, gasoline
300CE	124.050	103.983		Coupe, gasoline
300TE	124.090	103.983		wagon, gasoline
300SE	126.024	103.981		sedan, gasoline
300SEL	126.025	103.981		sedan, gasoline
420SEL	126.035	116.965		sedan, gasoline
560SEL	126.039	117.968		sedan, gasoline
560SEC	126.045	117.968		Coupe, gasoline
560SL	107.048	117.967		Roadster, gasoline

1990:

Model	Years	Chassis Prefix	Engine Prefix	Description
190E 2.6	201.029	103.942		sedan, gasoline
300D 2.5 Turbo	124.128	602.962		sedan, turbo-diesel
300E 2.6	124.026	103.940		sedan, gasoline
300E	124.030	103.983		sedan, gasoline

Model	Years	Chassis Prefix	Engine Prefix	Description
300CE		124.051	104.980	Coupe, gasoline
300TE		124.090	103.983	wagon, gasoline
300E 4Matic		124.230	103.985	sedan, gasoline
300TE 4Matic		124.290	103.985	wagon, gasoline
350SDL				
Turbo		126.135	603.970	sedan, turbo-diesel
300SE		126.024	103.981	sedan, gasoline
300SEL		126.025	103.981	sedan, gasoline
420SEL		126.035	116.965	sedan, gasoline
560SEL		126.039	117.968	sedan, gasoline
560SEC		126.045	117.968	Coupe, gasoline
300SL		129.061	104.981	Roadster, gasoline
500SL		129.066	119.960	Roadster, gasoline
1991:				
190E 2.3		201.028	102.985	sedan, gasoline
190E 2.6		201.029	103.942	sedan, gasoline
300D 2.5				
Turbo		124.128	602.962	sedan, turbo-diesel
300E 2.6		124.026	103.940	sedan, gasoline
300E		124.030	103.983	sedan, gasoline
300CE		124.051	104.980	Coupe, gasoline
300TE		124.090	103.983	wagon, gasoline
300E 4Matic		124.230	103.985	sedan, gasoline
300TE 4Matic		124.290	103.985	wagon, gasoline
350SD Turbo		126.134	603.970	sedan, turbo-diesel
350SDL				
Turbo		126.135	603.970	sedan, turbo-diesel
300SE		126.024	103.981	sedan, gasoline
300SEL		126.025	103.981	sedan, gasoline
420SEL		126.035	116.965	sedan, gasoline
560SEL		126.039	117.968	sedan, gasoline
560SEC		126.045	117.968	Coupe, gasoline
300SL		129.061	104.981	Roadster, gasoline
500SL		129.066	119.960	Roadster, gasoline
1992:				
190E 2.3		201.028	102.985	sedan, gasoline
190E 2.6		201.029	103.942	sedan, gasoline
300D 2.5				
Turbo		124.128	602.962	sedan, turbo-diesel
300E 2.6		124.026	103.940	sedan, gasoline
300E		124.030	103.983	sedan, gasoline
400E		124.034	119.975	sedan, gasoline
500E		124.036	119.974	sedan, gasoline
300CE		124.051	104.980	Coupe, gasoline
300TE		124.090	103.983	wagon, gasoline
300E 4Matic		124.230	103.985	sedan, gasoline
300TE 4Matic		124.290	103.985	wagon, gasoline
300SD Turbo		140.134	603.971	sedan, turbo-diesel
300SE		140.032	104.990	sedan, gasoline
400SE		140.042	119.971	sedan, gasoline
500SEL		140.051	119.970	sedan, gasoline
600SEL		140.057	120.980	sedan, gasoline
300SL		129.061	104.981	Roadster, gasoline
500SL		129.066	119.960	Roadster, gasoline
1993:				
190E 2.3		201.028	102.985	sedan, gasoline
190E 2.6		201.029	103.942	sedan, gasoline
300D 2.5				
Turbo		124.128	602.962	sedan, turbo-diesel
300E 2.8		124.028	104.942	sedan, gasoline
300E		124.032	104.992	sedan, gasoline
300CE		124.052	104.992	Coupe, gasoline
300CE Cabriolet		124.066	104.992	Convertible, gasoline
300TE		124.092	104.992	wagon, gasoline
300E 4Matic		124.230	103.985	sedan, gasoline
300TE 4Matic		124.290	103.985	wagon, gasoline
400E		124.034	119.975	sedan, gasoline
500E		124.036	119.974	sedan, gasoline
300SD		140.134	603.971	sedan, turbo-diesel
300SE		140.032	104.990	sedan, gasoline
400SEL		140.043	119.971	sedan, gasoline
500SEL		140.051	119.970	sedan, gasoline
600SEL		140.057	120.980	sedan, gasoline
500SEC		140.070	119.970	Coupe, gasoline
600SEC		140.076	120.980	Coupe, gasoline
300SL		129.061	104.981	Roadster, gasoline
500SL		129.067	119.960	Roadster, gasoline
600SL		129.076	120.981	Roadster, gasoline
1994:				
C220		202.022	111.961	sedan, gasoline
C280		202.028	104.941	sedan, gasoline
E300 Diesel (1995)		124.131	606.910	sedan, diesel
E320		124.032	104.992	sedan, gasoline
E320 Coupe		124.052	104.992	Coupe, gasoline
E320 Cabriolet		124.066	104.992	Convertible, gasoline
E320 Station Wagon		124.092	104.992	wagon, gasoline
E420		124.034	119.975	sedan, gasoline
E500		124.036	119.974	sedan, gasoline
S350 Turbo-Diesel		140.134	603.971	sedan, turbo-diesel
S320		140.032	104.990	sedan, gasoline
S420		140.043	119.971	sedan, gasoline
S500		140.051	119.970	sedan, gasoline
S600		140.057	120.980	sedan, gasoline
S500 Coupe		140.070	119.970	Coupe, gasoline
S600 Coupe		140.076	120.980	Coupe, gasoline
SL320		129.061	104.981	Roadster, gasoline
SL500		129.067	119.960	Roadster, gasoline
SL600		129.076	120.981	Roadster, gasoline

Index